Ethnicity and Race in the U.S.A.

W9-CLG-268

Ethnicity and Race in the U.S.A.

Toward the Twenty-First Century

Edited by
Richard D. Alba

Routledge

New York   London

Published in 1988 by
Routledge
an imprint of
Routledge, Chapman & Hall, Inc.
29 West 35 Street
New York, NY

Published in Great Britain by
Routledge
11 New Fetter Lane
London EC4P 4EE

These articles were also published as a special issue of
Ethnic and Racial Studies, Volume 8, Number 1

Printed in the USA
© Routledge & Kegan Paul 1985

Library of Congress Cataloging in Publication Data

Main entry under title:

Ethnicity and race in the U.S.A.

  Includes bibliographies and indexes.
  1. Minorities – United States – Addresses, essays,
lectures. 2. Ethnicity – United States – Addresses,
essays, lectures. 3. United States – Ethnic relations –
Addresses, essays, lectures. 4. United States – Race
relations – Addresses, essays, lectures. I. Alba,
Richard D.
E184.A1E884 1985   305.8'00973   85-2044

ISBN 0-415-00772-0

Contents

Preface

The papers assembled here are the fruits of the Conference on Ethnicity and Race in the Last Quarter of the Twentieth Century, held at the State University of New York at Albany on April 6–7, 1984. The focus of the conference was on ethnic and racial developments in the United States since midcentury, with an eye to their trajectory toward the century's end. This set of papers is unusual in its comprehensiveness: the full range of U.S. ethnic and racial experience is represented. In addition, all the papers provide fresh data, and many give us the first results from the 1980 Census.

As a set, the papers testify to the truth of Abner Cohen's aphorism, 'Ethnicity is a variable.' All document the dynamic yet divergent unfoldings of ethnicity and race in the United States. Change is particularly evident at the boundaries between groups, but the changes are far from uniform. In some instances, ethnic boundaries seem less and less consequential, and it appears quite possible that they may recede into a dim background, although perhaps never disappear entirely. In at least one case, that of Jews, the pressure on the boundary has generated new boundary-straddling ethnic forms, but the boundary is still salient. In still other cases, racial and ethnic cleavages remain profound, even in the face of important socioeconomic advances.

As a number of papers point out, no single model, at least of those presently known, seems capable of encompassing this diversity. Nevertheless, the diversity does resonate with some familiar themes. Most important is the polarity between minority and ethnic models, highlighted in the paper by Nelson and Tienda. The minority model corresponds with the experiences of some non-European groups; in different ways, blacks, Native Americans, and Mexican Americans can serve as prototypes. The ethnic model conforms to the experience of most of the European groups.

On the minority side, Reynolds Farley's paper provides a much-needed comprehensive assessment of black advancement. He demonstrates that no simple characterization accurately captures the complex mix of progress and stasis in the indicators for black Americans. While advances did clearly occur in some important respects, the gulf between blacks and the white majority remains wide. Robert Jarvenpa's paper on American Indians describes how the separateness of Native Americans is maintained by continuing social

1

innovations. These innovations, which may be cultural, economic, or political, help to define a dynamic boundary preserving Indian communities.

The papers dealing with the white ethnic groups limn a very different set of developments and suggest that a deep-seated convergence among these groups has been taking place in recent decades. My paper traces this convergence in the case of Italian Americans with socioeconomic and cultural indicators and also through the rapidly rising intermarriage rate. The ultimate proof of this process may lie in the fact that the great majority of young Italian Americans, like the members of many other European-ancestry groups, now has mixed ethnic ancestry. Stanley Lieberson's paper entertains the bold proposal that convergence has moved so far as to usher a new ethnic group on the American scene, whose hallmark is the lack of attachment to any extra-American ancestry. He uses recent survey data to portray the sizeable group who cannot or do not identify their ancestral origins and argues that this group is likely to grow considerably larger in coming decades.

Two other papers set some limits on this process of convergence. William Yancey, Eugene Ericksen and George Leon analyse both European and non-European ethnic groups in Philadelphia. Their analysis, which reveals a deep cleavage along the European – non-European dividing line, indicates that Catholic ethnics have most clearly followed the traditional model of assimilation (although their urban villages remain); however, Jews remain a solidary ethnic group, as well as a very mobile one. Walter Zenner's paper gives insight into the boundary-maintenance processes operating in the Jewish case. An intriguing aspect is the marginal ethnic forms, such as the 'Jews for Jesus,' that surface as a result of the pressures of American individualism.

The remaining two papers examine groups that pose problems for the conventional equations of non-Europeans with colonized minorities and Europeans with ethnic groups. Candace Nelson and Marta Tienda's paper portrays the variation in the experiences of some major Hispanic groups. While that of the Chicanos and Puerto Ricans approximates what would be expected from the minority model, the Cubans appear to be following the same paths as earlier European immigrants, although whether they will arrive at the same destination remains to be seen. Victor Nee and Jimy Sanders analyze the socioeconomic achievements of three Asian-American groups. They find that, despite early handicaps far more severe than those faced by European ethnics, the attainments of Chinese and Japanese Americans are comparable, if not superior, to those of whites. Filipinos, however, lag behind.

Obviously, no schematic overview such as the one above can do justice to a set of papers as comprehensive as the one that follows. What is more difficult to convey in such a short space is the many reverberations among the papers. To take just one tantalizing example, the papers by Yancey *et al.*, Nelson and Tienda, Nee and Sanders, and myself all address in detailed ways how the mode of a group's incorporation into the United States and the opportunities and constraints present in its initial American context have exerted profound effects on group destiny. But I must leave it to readers to find the basic accord on many other significant points among the authors.

I would be terribly ungrateful if I did not acknowledge in closing some of the many benefactors who made possible the conference from which the papers have come. The conference was the fourth in a now annual series hosted by SUNY-Albany's Sociology Department, and I am grateful for the encouragement and advice given me by my predecessors as conference organizers: Richard Hall, Nan Lin, and especially John Logan. Funds were provided by the American Sociological Association, the State University of New York's Conversations in the Disciplines Program, and, at SUNY-Albany, by the Vice President for Research, the College of Social and Behavioural Sciences, the Department of Sociology, and the Center for Social and Demographic Analysis.

Many more participants than are represented on the following pages contributed to the conference's success. I regret that there was not enough space to publish the papers of Edna Bonacich, Frank Bonilla, Howard Taylor, Peggy Thoits, Karen Solomon, and Richard Williams; or the commentary of Christine Bose, Frank Femminella, Barbara Heyns, Jorge Klor de Alva, John Logan, William McCready, and Douglas Massey. Those who were present know how significant their contributions were.

The last words I owe to Gail Gates. Without her tireless efforts to bring under control the myriad and troublesome details of the arrangements, there would have been no conference at all.

Richard D. Alba
Slingerlands, New York

1 Three steps forward and two back? Recent changes in the social and economic status of blacks*

Reynolds Farley
University of Michigan

When he wrote about race relations in the early 1940s, Gunnar Myrdal (1944) described a fundamental dilemma. Americans endorsed the principle that all persons were created equal and endowed with inalienable rights, that the government existed to protect these rights and that, before the law, all persons had the same status. In hundreds of ways, Americans — both black and white — patriotically supported these ideals. The nation's churches and schools taught them to children, politicians pledged to uphold them and, from time to time, wars were fought to extend these American values. However, the ideals of equality and democracy were only abstract principles so far as blacks were concerned. In the South, blacks had almost no civil rights which whites respected. They could not hope to hold public office, to vote or serve on juries. The system of segregated education often provided nothing but deficient grammar school training for southern blacks. In the North, explicit practices and legal agreements designated where blacks could live and set strict limits on their occupational achievements. Blacks who served in the Armed Forces during World War II were usually trained in Jim Crow camps and then assigned to support tasks.

The civil rights revolution

Following Word War II, Americans confronted the basic issue of whether the principles of democracy extended to blacks. We can identify six distinct but overlapping aspects of the civil rights movement of the last several decades. First, the litigation strategy of the National Association for the Advancement of Colored People (NAACP) laid the groundwork for challenging the legitimacy of state-imposed discrimination and came to fruition in the post-World War II era. For decades, NAACP lawyers filed suit if blacks were denied their right to vote, were kept off juries, or provided with unequal schools. During the 1930s and 1940s, they were sometimes victorious in the federal courts. Undoubtedly, the key decision, *Brown* v. *Board of Education* (1954), greatly strengthened the civil rights movement by upholding the principles of equality and by overturning — at least in theory — state-imposed discrimination.

Second, in the period after 1960, there was a massive increase in the number and proportion of blacks actively involved in the struggle for rights. This is symbolized by the bus boycott in Montgomery in 1957 and the Greensboro lunch counter sit-in in 1960. There was certainly nothing new about these protests but it was not until 1960 that sit-ins, peaceful protests and other demonstrations became widespread in the Deep South where racial discrimination was most blatant (Carson, 1981). In 1963, the civil rights organizations were able to assemble upwards of half a million people for the March on Washington, and two years later a series of marches in the Birmingham and Selma areas led to passage of the Voting Rights Bill (Garrow, 1978).

Third, there was a changing involvement of whites in the civil rights movement as a growing number recognized the dilemma which Myrdal described. This is not easy to document but there are several indicators of this change. The proportion of national samples of whites who said they would object if a Negro with an education and income similar to their own moved next door diminished from 62 percent in 1942 to 39 percent in 1963 and then to 15 percent in 1972 (Pettigrew, 1973: Table 1). In 1942, only 44 percent of the whites approved of racially-integrated public transportation, but this rose to 60 percent in 1956 and was so universally approved by whites in the mid-1960s that the question was no longer of any interest for attitude studies (Sheatsley, 1966: Table 1; for a summary of these trends, see Schuman, Steeh and Bobo, forthcoming). A growing number of whites participated in the protest movement in the South by marching hand-in-hand with blacks, organizing freedom schools or by helping blacks register to vote. Andrew Goodman and Michael Schwerner were slain for their civil rights activities in Mississippi in 1964.

Fourth, by the mid-1960s, the elected officials of the federal government gradually came to support effective civil rights laws, laws which overturned the principle of states' rights. The Twenty-Fourth Amendment, passed by Congress in 1962, ended the poll tax requirement for federal elections. The Civil Rights Act of 1964 was the most far-reaching of the new laws since it outlawed racial discrimination in public accommodations, provided assistance for school integration, sought to put the Justice Department on the side of plaintiffs in civil rights litigation, banned discrimination in the use of federal funds and outlawed discrimination in all aspects of employment. The Civil Rights Act of 1965 was uniquely effective in bringing blacks into the electoral process because it called for the appointment of federal registrars (Scher and Button, 1984). Following the killing of Dr. King, Congress passed the Civil Rights Act of 1968 which banned discrimination in the housing market.

Fifth, following 1960, there was a change in the pace and scope of federal court rulings in the area of civil rights. Rather than focusing upon the theoretical legal rights of individual blacks, the courts began to protect the interests of blacks as a class and considered their actual status vis-à-vis that of whites. In several areas, new ground was broken. After fourteen years of delays and inaction, the Court finally insisted upon the actual integration of southern public schools. The *Green* v. *New Kent County* decision (1968) ended reliance upon ineffective freedom-of-choice plans. In a unanimous decision (*Swann* v. *Charlotte-Mecklenburg, 1973*), the court approved the use of racial ratios and busing to integrate schools. The Court gradually came to endorse affirmative action programs designed to increase educational and employment opportunities for blacks. In the 1978 *Bakke* decision (*Regents of the University of California* v. *Bakke*), they ruled that universities might use race as one of a number of criteria when deciding whom to admit. In the 1979 *Steelworkers* v. *Weber* ruling, the Court upheld a quota system which specifically reserved some of the better-paying jobs for blacks.

Sixth, the period since 1960 was marked by a high level of racial violence. In the summers of 1963 and 1964, more than two dozen Alabama and Mississippi black churches were burned or bombed (Franklin, 1967:637; Meier and Rudwick, 1975:222). Civil rights protestors in Birmingham were regularly attacked by Police Chief 'Bull' Connor with his German Shepherd dogs and his fire hoses. The decade of the 1960s was also an era of urban racial violence. In 1967 alone, some 164 incidents of racial disorders were recorded in American cities and eighty-three people died in urban racial riots that summer (U.S. National Advisory Commission on Civil Disorders, 1968:114–16).

What did the civil rights revolution accomplish? There are three summary views. A group of optimists believe that racial progress has been great, that the practice of discrimination has declined or even been eliminated and that a man's skin color now has relatively little to do with his educational attainment or occupational achievements. A group of pessimists portray a very different picture. Many of the changes are viewed as superficial. Indeed, defenders of this viewpoint stress that in such areas as family income, poverty and unemployment, progress during the era following the civil rights movement was minimal. Finally, there are those who argue that blacks are increasingly divided into a successful elite group and a downtrodden underclass. Some highly-trained or skilled blacks took advantage of the opportunities provided by the civil rights changes and they are now prospering much like similar whites. Other blacks, however, are seen as locked into hopeless central city ghettos.

After examining many indicators of the changing status of blacks, we find that it is impossible to state that one of the three views is correct while the other two are wrong. The best way to summarize racial change is to divide indicators into three categories: those which clearly show that racial gaps are declining, those which show no improvement in the status of blacks and those that are mixed.

Indicators showing improvements

Trends in educational attainment

Racial differences in educational attainment are certainly decreasing. On the eve of World War II, blacks averaged about three fewer years of schooling

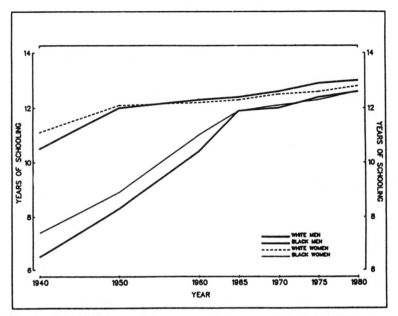

Figure 1. *Median educational attainment for persons at ages 25–29 by race and sex, 1940–80.*

Source: U.S. Bureau of the Census, *Sixteenth Census of the United States, 1940*, Vol. IV, Characteristics by Age, Table 18; *Census of Population: 1960*, Vol. 1, Part I, Table 173; *Census of Population: 1970*, Vol. 1, Part A, Table 199; *Current Population Reports*, Series P-20, Nos. 158, 207, 295 and 390, Table 1. (Data for years through 1965 refer to whites and nonwhites.)

than whites but the racial difference declined to one and one-half years by the early 1980s. Throughout the post-World War II era, the rates of secondary school attendance of blacks and whites converged, and by the mid-1970s racial differences in enrollment through age 17 just about disappeared. In the decade following Sputnik – the 1960s – college enrollment rates increased more rapidly among whites than blacks, but in the 1970s, the college enrollment rates of blacks moved closer to those of whites.

Information about trends in attainment is shown in Figure 1. This indicates the median educational level of people who recently completed their schooling – people at ages 25 to 29 in the years indicated at the base of the figure. The racial convergence in schooling is immediately evident. Among those who finished their education during the Depression, blacks lagged about three to four years behind whites. By the 1980s, this difference was about half a year.

Despite obvious progress, there is still a racial difference. Among those in their early twenties in 1981, about 85 percent of the whites compared to 75 percent of the blacks completed high school. Among those in their late twenties, about one white in four compared to one black in eight reported at least four years of college education (U.S. Bureau of the Census, 1984a: Table 1). This comes about partially because enrollment rates at ages 18 to 24 are still lower for blacks and partially because of grade retardation. Among men 18 and 19 attending school, 77 percent of the whites were in college, while among black men 52 percent were still in high school and only 48 percent went to college (U.S. Bureau of the Census, 1983a: Table 6). Because of retardation, blacks have to spend more years getting to a given attainment level than do whites.

Occupational prestige

Another area of obvious racial progress involves the occupations of those people who are at work. Without doubt, blacks now hold more prestigious and higher-paying jobs than they ever did in the past.[1] Since 1960, there has been only a little upgrading of the occupational distribution among whites and thus the proportion of them with white-collar jobs rose just a bit. Among blacks, the proportion with white-collar positions went up rapidly as they moved into the professional, managerial and craft occupations. In 1960, about 10 percent of all workers were black but they held only 3 percent of the professional and managerial jobs. In 1982, blacks still made up about 10 percent of the work force but they held 8 percent of the managerial and professional jobs (U.S. Bureau of Labor Statistics, 1979: Table 18; 1983: Tables 46 and 48).

Improvements in the occupational position of blacks can be seen in Figure 2. We indicate the proportion of men and women who held jobs at the top of the occupational ladder, that is, they were employed as professionals, managers or as clerical or sales workers. We also report trends in the index of occupational dissimilarity computed from an 11-category distribution. If blacks and whites were identically distributed across these broad occupational classes, this measure would equal zero implying that the black and white distributions were similar. If segregation were so thorough that all job categories were either exclusively white or exclusively black, the index would be at its maximum, 100. Declines over time in this measure imply decreases in the occupational segregation of blacks.

In 1960, about one employed black man in seven worked at a white-collar position. This was far different from the situation among whites, since 40 percent of them held such jobs. Racial differences contracted in the next decades as the proportion white-collar increased more rapidly among blacks. The index of occupational dissimilarity moved lower during both prosperous and lean periods and was cut by at least one-third.

Changes are particularly impressive among black women. Traditionally, black women cleaned the homes of whites, cooked their food and washed their clothes. As recently as 1963, one-third of all employed black women were domestic servants (U.S. Bureau of Labor Statistics, 1979: Table 18). This changed rapidly as black women moved into clerical work and the

Figure 2. *Proportion of employed workers holding white-collar jobs by race and sex and indexes of occupational dissimilarity, 1960–82.*

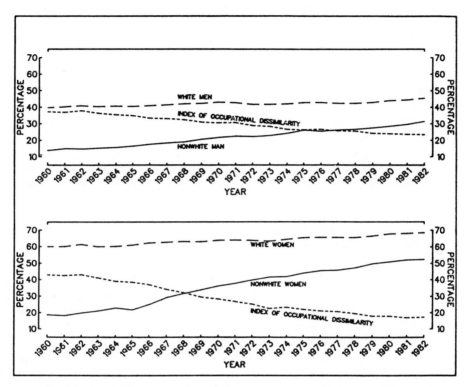

Sources: U.S. Bureau of Labor Statistics, *Handbook of Labor Statistics: 1978* (Bulletin 2000), Table 18; *Handbook of Labor Statistics* (Bulletin 2070), Table 20; *Employment and Earnings*, Vol. 28, No. 1, Table 22; Vol. 29, No. 1, Table 22; Vol. 30, No. 1, Table 22 (Data for all years refer to whites and nonwhites. Indexes of dissimilarity calculated from an eleven-category occupational distribution.)

professions, leading to a sharp drop in the index of occupational dissimilarity. Clearly, racial segregation of occupations is declining.

Despite several decades of impressive improvements, a very large gap still distinguishes the occupational distribution of blacks and whites, especially men. In 1982, about 30 percent of the employed black men who worked held white-collar jobs. This is just about the white-collar proportion among white men on the eve of World War II (U.S. Bureau of Labor Statistics, 1983: Table 22; U.S. Bureau of the Census, 1943: Table 62). Thus, there is a four-decade gap separating the occupational attainments of black men and white men. There is an unambiguous trend toward a racial convergence of the occupational distribution but the substantial racial difference which remains will disappear only if there are several more decades of improvement.

Earnings of employed workers

An important area in which there has been progress concerns the earnings of workers. Racial differences are gradually declining among men and are disappearing much more rapidly among women. As an indication of these trends, Figure 3 shows the median income reported by adults 15 and over for the period from 1959 through 1983.[2] At the start of this interval, black men had median incomes of about $6,800 compared to $14,400 for white men (amounts are shown in constant 1983 dollars to control for inflation). Incomes gradually rose until the recession of 1973–75 but the gains were somewhat greater for blacks. During the most recent decade income levels have declined, especially among men, but the decreases have been somewhat greater for whites. The racial gap in median incomes for men, which was $7,600 in 1959, has decreased by a modest amount since it fell to $6,400 in 1983. Income gains for black women, relative to whites, have been larger since the shift away from farm labor and domestic service led to a doubling of the income of black women between 1960 and the mid-1970s.

The lower panel in Figure 3 shows income trends for those people who worked full-time for fifty or more weeks during a year.[3] Income levels, of course, are much higher for this subset of workers but the trends are similar: a rise in income before the 1974–75 recession and a general decline – especially for men – in the subsequent years. Among year-round, full-time men, there has been a slight contraction in the racial gap in income, while among women the racial difference has been greatly reduced.

About 80 percent of the income reported in the United States comes from earnings while the other one-fifth comes from rents, interest, dividend payments and governmental transfers (U.S. Bureau of the Census, 1984b; Table C–1). Since income trends are influenced by changes in sources other than earnings, we wished to focus on the actual earnings of employed blacks and whites. We used data from the 1960 Census and from the March 1970 and March 1980 Current Population Surveys pertaining to men and women 25 to 64 to see if the racial gap in earnings diminished.

In 1959 white men earned $8.03 per hour, and black men $4.93, meaning that black men received only 61 percent as much as white men or $3.10 less for each hour of work (amounts are shown in constant 1983 dollars). Twenty years later, white men earned $9.88 per hour and blacks $7.30. The racial gap had fallen to $2.58 per hour and black men earned, on an hourly basis, 74 percent as much as white men. An analysis of annual earnings reveals a larger racial differential since black men work fewer hours, but there were also clear improvements in the relative earnings of blacks. In 1959, on an annual basis, black men earned 49 percent as much as white men; in 1979, 55 percent as much.

The racial gap in earnings has all but disappeared among women. In 1959, black women earned only 61 percent as much as white women for each hour of work; in 1978, 98 percent as much. Since black women typically spend more hours on the job than white women, the white advantage in annual

Figure 3. *Trends in personal income by race and sex, 1959–83 (amounts shown in constant 1983 dollars).*

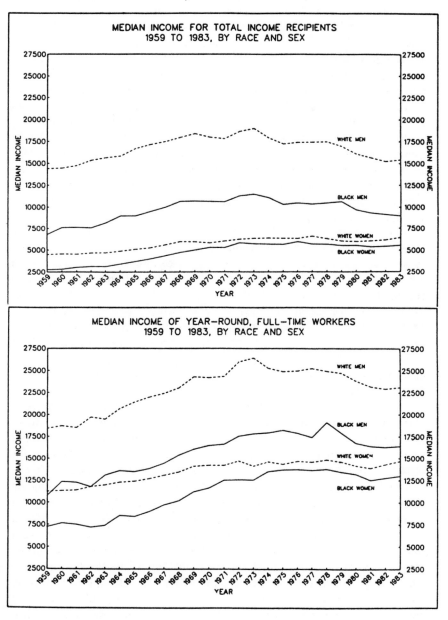

Sources: U.S. Bureau of the Census, *Current Population Reports*, Series P-60, Nos. 37, 39, 41, 43, 47, 51, 53, 60, 66, 75, 80, 85, 90, 97, 101, 105, 114, 118, 123, 129, 132, 137, 142 and 145. (Data for years through 1966 refer to nonwhites and whites.)

earnings disappeared by the later 1970s. The sex difference, on the other hand, did not disappear. By 1980, both black and white women had actual hourly earnings about 55 percent those of white men.

One reason why blacks earn less than whites is that they complete fewer years of school, and a second is that they are more likely to live in the South where wages have traditionally been low. If black and white workers had the same characteristics, would they earn similar hourly wages? If the evidence shows that similar blacks and whites earn vastly different amounts, we may have indications of racial discrimination. Of course, there is a need for caution in this type of analysis since not all factors which influence earnings can be precisely measured. As a result, this type of evidence about racial discrimination is more qualified than the evidence which led to the 1973 A.T. & T. consent decree, an agreement which eventually awarded upwards of eighty million dollars to women and minorities (Wallace, 1976). In the present investigation, a worker's hourly wage rate is seen as depending upon his or her educational attainment, years of potential labor force experience and region of residence.

Table 1 presents results from this analysis. The upper panel reports actual hourly wage rates of men and women of each race. Since the wages of white men exceed those of the other groups, the wage rates of blacks and women are compared to those of white men. We show the difference in wage rates and the hourly wages of a group as a proportion of those of white men. For example, the average hourly wage for black women in 1959 was $3.07 or $4.96 less than the hourly earnings of white men (constant 1983 dollars). In relative terms, the wages of black women were 38 percent as great as those of white men. Twenty years later, the gap in hourly wages between white men and black women decreased to $4.40, and their hourly earnings were 55 percent those of white men.

The bottom panel of Table 1 shows the hypothetical hourly earnings of blacks and women. Suppose that black men had the educational attainment, years of labor market experience and regional distribution of white men but were paid for these labor market characteristics at the rates observed for black — not for white — men. How much would black men earn? We can calculate a hypothetical wage rate which results from statistically equating black and white men with regard to their characteristics but allows for racial differences in rates of return. Similarly, we can statistically equate women with white men and calculate hypothetical wage rates. If the hypothetical wages for a group equal those of white men, we can be quite certain that the groups have rates of return which are equivalent to those of white men, implying the absence of discrimination. In such a case, the difference in actual wages would come about because the group differed from white men in labor market characteristics. If the hypothetical wage rate is much lower than the actual wages of white men, we have an indication that a group is paid less than white men for ostensibly similar characteristics, perhaps reflecting discrimination in the labor market.

In 1959, if a black man had the labor market characteristics — that is, education, years of experience and region of residence — of the typical white

Table 1. *Actual hourly earnings of black and white male and female workers, 25–64, in 1959, 1969 and 1979, and hypothetical hourly earnings of women and blacks assuming they had the labor market character-istics of white men but their own rates of return (amounts shown in constant 1983 dollars).*

	1959	1969	1979
White men			
Actual hourly earnings	$8.03	$10.21	$9.88
— Actual hourly earnings —			
Black men			
Hourly earnings	$4.93	$6.96	$7.30
Difference from white men	−3.10	−3.25	−2.58
Percentage of white men	61%	68%	74%
Black women			
Hourly earnings	$3.07	$4.21	$5.48
Difference from white men	−4.96	−6.00	−4.40
Percentage of white men	38%	41%	55%
White women			
Hourly earnings	$5.06	$5.63	$5.57
Difference from white men	−2.97	−4.58	−3.31
Percentage of white men	63%	55%	56%
— Hypothetical hourly earnings —			
Black men			
Hourly earnings	$6.49	$8.39	$8.66
Difference from white men	−1.54	−1.82	−1.22
Percentage of white men	81%	82%	88%
Black women			
Hourly earnings	$4.24	$5.43	$6.27
Difference from white men	−3.79	−4.78	−3.61
Percentage of white men	53%	53%	63%
White women			
Hourly earnings	$5.02	$5.76	$5.69
Difference from white men	−3.01	−4.45	−4.19
Percentage of white men	63%	56%	58%

Source: U.S. Bureau of the Census, *Census of Population and Housing, 1960; Current Population Survey*, March, 1970 and March, 1980. Public Use Sample Files for each source.

man but was paid for those characteristics at the rates actually observed among black men, he would have earned $6.49 per hour. If a white man had the same characteristics but was paid for them at the rates actually observed among white men, he would earn $8.03 per hour. The difference comes about because similar black and white men were paid differently. The racial gap — $1.54 per hour — has been called the 'cost of being a Negro' (Siegel, 1965; Duncan, 1969) and is one estimate of the dollar cost of apparent racial discrimination. In 1979, a black man with the characteristics of the typical white would have earned $8.66 per hour, and a white man $9.88, or a racial difference of $1.22 per hour. In 1959, the hypothetical hourly earnings of blacks — calculated in this fashion — were 81 percent as much as those of whites; in 1979, 88 percent as much. This reveals that the 'cost of being black' or the apparent cost of racial discrimination decreased substantially but has not yet been eliminated.

In this analysis, we wished to distinguish sexual differences in earnings from racial differences. Black women in the labour market once suffered from the dual burdens of being both black and female but this is no longer the case. In 1959, if an employed black woman had the characteristics of the typical white woman but was paid for those characteristics at the rates observed for black women, she would have earned 84 percent as much as a white woman on an hourly basis (data not shown in Figure 1). In 1979, she would have earned about 8 percent more than the white woman. With regard to women, there is no evidence of racial discrimination in earnings. Black women who are as well-qualified as white women will earn at least as much as white women.

Black women, however, have made only modest progress in 'catching up' with those who have the greatest earnings: white men. In 1959, if a black woman had the labor market characteristics of the typical white man but was paid for them at the rates observed among black women, she would have earned 53 percent as much as the white man. In 1979, this improved to 63 percent as much. The position of white women vis-à-vis white men is even more bleak. In 1959, the hypothetical hourly earnings of white women were 63 percent those of white men; in 1979, just 58 percent as much.

We investigated whether gains in the earnings of blacks were restricted to certain favored groups such as the highly-educated, the young or those employed by the government. We found that the improvements were not limited in this fashion. For almost all segments of the population, the actual earnings of blacks rose faster than those of whites and the apparent cost of labor market discrimination declined. This was true in the 1960s when the per capita Gross National Product increased at a high rate — 2.6 percent annually — but it was also true in the following decade when the economy expanded more modestly — a rise of 2.1 percent per year. In all regions, for different occupational groups, for different attainment categories and for those employed in core industries, in the peripheral sector of the economy and by the government, the earnings of black workers moved closer to those of whites.

Indicators showing no improvements

Employment

Not all indicators of racial change show progress. At least one reveals that blacks were as far behind whites in the 1980s as in the 1960s. This is employment itself. The unemployment rate among black men reached a level twice that of white men in the mid-1950s and the ratio has changed little since then (Killingsworth, 1968:20).

The upper panel in Figure 4 shows the proportion of adult men who were in the labor force but could not locate jobs, that is, it shows unemployment rates for 1959 through 1983.[4] We would expect improvements in the employment situation for black men in the last few decades since the educational attainment of blacks has risen more rapidly than that of whites and because federal laws now ban discrimination in hiring. The situation has not improved. Unemployment rates have fluctuated sharply with the changing economic conditions, but at all dates a black man in the labor force has been twice as likely as a white man to be unemployed.

There is a related trend which indicates an actual deterioration in employment opportunities for black men. We presume that most adult men are either at work or are looking for jobs. A growing proportion of adult men, however, are neither working nor seeking a position. They are just not participating in the labor force. This trend is evident for both races but the changes have been much greater among blacks.

One succinct way to summarize trends in both labor force participation and unemployment is to look at the proportion of adults who are employed. These trends are shown in the bottom panel of Figure 4. To eliminate the changes which might be attributable to earlier retirement or prolonged enrollment in school, these data pertain to the population ages 25 to 54. In 1959, the racial difference in the proportion of adult men holding jobs was about 8 percentage points since 94 percent of the white men and 86 percent of the black held jobs. By the early 1980s, the racial difference increased to 11 points. This occurs, in large part, because a declining share of adult black men are in the labor force. In the two decades following 1960, the percentage of black men aged 25 to 54 who were neither working nor looking for employment rose from 5 to 12; for white men, from 3 to 5. Among younger black men, there has been an even more dramatic increase in the proportion who were out of the labor force (for an analysis of these trends, see: Sullivan, 1978: Chapter 8; Mare and Winship, 1979, 1984; Clogg, 1982). Black men who are employed are clearly moving closer to their white peers in terms of occupational prestige and earnings. However, a decreasing proportion of black men are at work.

There have been few investigations of how these men support themselves or spend their time. Do many men frequently drift into and out of the labor force or are they non-participants for long intervals? Ethnographic accounts based on observations in the ghettos of Philadelphia (Anderson, 1980) and Washington (Liebow, 1967) imply that men with limited skills

Figure 4. *Trends of employment among men by race and proportion of total population 25–54 employed by race and sex, 1959–83.*

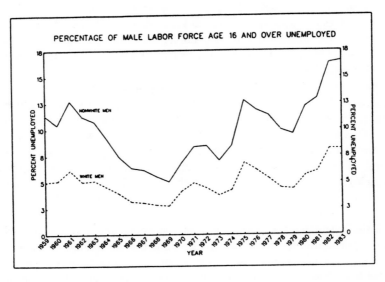

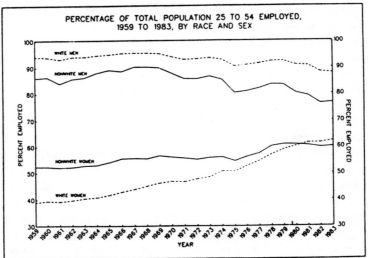

Source: U.S. Bureau of Labor Statistics, *Labor Force Statistics Derived from the Current Population Survey: A Databook*, Vol. 1 (Bulletin 2096), Tables A–2, A–3, A–10 and A–20. (Data for all years refer to whites and nonwhites.)

work sporadically, implying that there is not a large group who have withdrawn from the labor force for good. These men may mix periods of work with others in which they depend on welfare, engage in illegal activities or are supported by their friends and relatives.

Among women, the unemployment rate for blacks has persistently been about twice that of whites. Trends in the unemployment rate of women are not shown in Figure 4 but they parallel those for men. However, the major change involves employment itself. Traditionally, the proportion of women holding jobs was greater for black women than for white. Since 1960, the proportion at work has gone up for both groups but the rise was greater among whites. By the early 1980s, a greater proportion of white than black women were employed.

Mixed indicators

Racial residential segregation

This is a mixed indicator since neighbourhood segregation has declined in some locations but not in others. There is a great deal of convincing evidence showing that blacks and whites seldom share the same urban neighbourhoods, that black-white residential segregation is unlike the residential segregation of white ethnic groups including Hispanics, and that economic factors account for little of the observed residential segregation of blacks from whites (Lieberson, 1963: Chapter 4, 1980: Chapter 9; Taeuber and Taeuber, 1965; Hermalin and Farley, 1973; Kain and Quigley, 1975; Massey, 1979). Racial segregation is seemingly not a consequence of the desires of blacks, since they prefer to live in racially-mixed areas rather than all-black areas (Pettigrew, 1973: Table 5; Farley *et al.*, 1978). Additionally, numerous studies report that black and white clients are treated differently in the housing market, implying that discriminatory practices help to keep blacks and whites isolated (Saltman, 1975; Pearce, 1979; Wienk *et al.*, 1979; Lake, 1981: Chapters 7 and 9).

In large cities of all regions, racial residential segregation decreased little between 1940 and 1970 (Taeuber and Taeuber, 1965: Table 4; Sørenson, Taeuber and Hollingsworth, 1975: Table 1; Van Valey, Roof and Wilcox, 1974: Table 1), but perhaps the real test of changing segregation came during the 1970s. The Civil Rights Act of 1968, which banned discrimination in the housing market, was in effect for the entire decade and the incomes of black families rose more rapidly than those of similar white families. These changes, along with the continued liberalization of white attitudes, may have made it easier for blacks to enter formerly white neighbourhoods (Lamb, 1984).

The thorough analysis of residential segregation trends during the 1970s has not yet been completed. One investigation looked at changes in those central cities which have the largest black populations (Taeuber, 1983). The measure of residential segregation is the index of dissimilarity. If there were a situation of total apartheid such that all city blocks were exclusively black or exclusively white, the index would take on its maximum value of 100. If blacks and whites were randomly distributed across neighborhoods in the city, the index would approach its minimum value of zero. The indexes of segregation for the 25 cities with the largest black population in 1980 were based upon city block data. They are shown in Table 2.

There has been a mixed pattern of change in residential segregation. In Houston, Dallas, Jacksonville and Richmond, segregation declined by a dozen or more points on this scale, and in Detroit and Los Angeles there were decreases of nine points. Perhaps there have been fundamental changes in these locations since the declines in the 1970s seem large compared to the changes of the three previous decades (Taeuber and Taeuber, 1965: Table 4; Sørenson, Taeuber and Hollingsworth, 1975: Table 1). However, a trend toward the integration of neighborhoods was far from universal since the scores did not change in three cities, while in Philadelphia and Cleveland residential segregation apparently became more thorough during the 1970s. Despite decades of racial change and numerous civil rights acts, the segregation scores for Chicago, St. Louis and Cleveland in 1980 were not far from the maximum value which would occur only when every block in the city was exclusively black or exclusively white.

If the findings from a more extensive array of cities and metropolitan areas parallel these, we will have confirmed a mixed indicator of racial progress: declines in black-white residential segregation in some locations but no change in other places (Taeuber *et al.*, 1984; Logan and Schneider, 1984).

The racial integration of public schools

Another mixed indicator involves the racial integration of public education. In most rural areas of the South, in many small and medium-sized cities in all regions, and in those southern metropolises where schools are organized on a county-wide basis, e.g., Charlotte, Jacksonville, Nashville, St. Petersburg and Tampa, the promise of the *Brown* decision has largely been achieved and black and white children now attend the same schools. In addition, the majority of black college students, instead of attending the traditionally black institutions, now go to predominantly white colleges and universities. Significant progress has been made in dismantling the nation's system of dual schools (Bullock, 1984; Ayres, 1984).

On the other hand, little progress has been made in integrating public schools in the nation's largest metropolises. In many central cities, there has been no more than a modest integration program and white enrollments have fallen sharply because of declining birth rates and the continuing migration of whites to the suburbs or to rural areas. In Baltimore, Chicago, Detroit, Houston, Los Angeles, Philadelphia, New York, Washington and most other large metropolises, entire public school districts are now very clearly coded by color. The central city district has a predominantly black or Spanish enrollment, most suburban districts have largely white enrollments, while a few suburban

Table 2. *Racial residential segregation scores for twenty-five central cities with the largest black populations in 1980; 1970, and 1980.*[a]

	1970	1980	Change, 1970–80
New York	77	75	−2
Chicago	93	92	−1
Detroit	82	73	−9
Philadelphia	84	88	+4
Los Angeles	90	81	−9
Washington	79	79	0
Houston	93	81	−12
Baltimore	89	86	−3
New Orleans	84	76	−8
Memphis	92	85	−7
Atlanta	92	86	−6
Dallas	96	83	−13
Cleveland	90	91	+1
St. Louis	90	90	0
Newark	76	76	0
Oakland	70	59	−11
Birmingham	92	85	−7
Indianapolis	90	83	−7
Milwaukee	88	80	−8
Jacksonville	94	82	−12
Cincinnati	84	79	−5
Boston	84	80	−4
Columbus	86	75	−11
Kansas City	90	86	−4
Richmond	91	79	−12
Average for 25 central cities	84	78	−6
Average for 10 southern cities	90	80	−10
Average for 15 northern and western cities	80	75	−5

Note: Cities are ranked by their black population in 1980.

Source: K. Taeuber, 'Racial Residential Segregation, 25 Cities, 1970–1980,' CDE Working Paper 87–12 (Madison: University of Wisconsin, Center for Demography and Ecology).

    a Indexes compare the black and nonblack populations.

enclaves are almost all-black. A high proportion of the nation's black students attend school in these metropolises where persistent segregation effectively negates the *Brown* ruling. In most of the nation's population centers, black and white students go to separate schools now just as they did when *Plessey* v. *Ferguson* (1896) was the constitutional principle.

The income of black and white families

Another area of mixed trends concerns family welfare and poverty. With regard to family income, there was much progress for blacks in the 1960s but little change in the 1970s. Figure 5 shows the median income of black families as a percentage of that of white families. Back in 1959, black families had incomes about 52 percent as great as those of whites. During the prosperous 1960s this improved, and by 1970 black families had incomes 64 percent as large as whites. A different trend characterizes the more recent period, and in 1983 the incomes of black families were only 56 percent those of whites

Figure 5. *Median income of black families as a percentage of that of white families and percentage of blacks and whites below poverty line, 1959–83.*

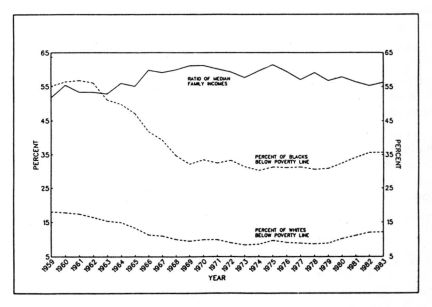

Source: U.S. Bureau of the Census, *Census of Population: 1960*, PC(2)–4B; *Current Population Reports*, Series P-20, Nos. 155, 168 and 175; Series P-60, Nos. 59, 66, 75, 80, 85, 90, 97, 101, 105, 114, 118, 120, 125, 132, 137, 142 and 145. (Data for all years refer to blacks and whites. Poverty rates for 1960 through 1965 for blacks and for 1960 and 1961 for whites are estimates.)

(U.S. Bureau of the Census, 1984c: Table 15; 1984b: Table 3). At first glance, it appears that the gains of the 1960s were thoroughly eliminated after 1970. However, the ratio of black-to-white median family income is hardly an adequate measure of changes in the economic status of blacks. It is confounded by racial differences in the types of families. When we examine better measures of family welfare, we find a mixed picture.

The two most common types of families are those which include a married couple and those headed by a woman who lives apart from her spouse, frequently a woman who has been separated or divorced from her husband but has responsibility for raising children.[5] Income levels, of course, are much lower in families headed by women than in husband-wife families (Bianchi, 1981: Chapter 6). When income statistics are examined for these different kinds of families, we find that blacks continued to 'catch up' with similar white families in the 1970s just as they did in the 1960s.

Figure 6 shows trends in per capita income by type of family and reveals why this is a mixed indicator of racial progress. In 1959, black husband-wife families had a per capita income of $3,200; whites, $6,500. Incomes generally increased until the recession which began in 1979, when they stagnated or fell. In the early 1980s, per capita income in black husband-wife families was $6,300 or just about at the level similar white families attained in the late

Figure 6. *Per capita income for families by type and race, 1959–83 (amounts in constant 1983 dollars).*

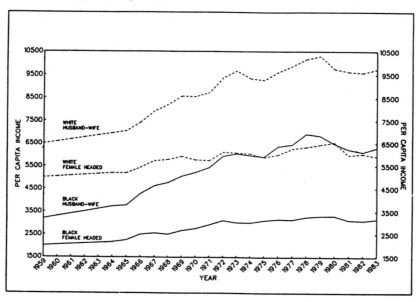

Source: See Figure 5. Also, U.S. Bureau of the Census, *Current Population Reports*, Series P-20, Nos. 106, 116, 125, 139, 153, 164, 173, 191, 200, 218, 233, 246, 248, 276, 291, 311, 326, 340, 352, 366, 371, 381 and 388. (Data for all years refer to blacks and whites.)

1950s. In white husband-wife families, per capita income was about $9,700 in 1983.

There is clear evidence of a gain for blacks, since their incomes – as a percentage of those of whites – went up from 49 to 65 percent. Stated differently, during this quarter-century the per capita income of black husband-wife families went from one-half to two-thirds that of whites. However, when we look at the actual racial difference in purchasing power – that is, the dollar difference in per capita income – we see no substantial change. Indeed, the white advantage in per capita purchasing power was greater at the start of the 1980s than in 1960. In relative terms, black husband-wife families have gained on whites; in absolute terms, they have not.

Turning to trends for families headed by women, we see a similar pattern. The period through the 1970s was one of rising incomes but the rates of gain were greater for families headed by black women. As a result, per capita income levels in these families headed by blacks went from 40 percent of those of similar white families to 54 percent. However, the absolute racial gap in per capita income remained just about constant. Once again, we find relative but not absolute progress for blacks.[6]

Turning back to Figure 5, we see that the overall ratio of black-to-white median family income improved very little after 1970, but the trends shown in Figure 6 imply that, at least in relative terms, black families were doing a little better compared to whites. We would expect this to produce a higher ratio of black-to-white family income. The apparent discrepancy can be explained by changes in family living arrangements. A declining share of families are married couples and an increasing proportion are families headed by a woman.

There has been a sharp change in family structure, especially among blacks, as women head their own families instead of living as wives. Between 1960 and 1983, the proportion of total black families which were headed by a woman, rather than a married couple, rose from 20 to 42 percent. An identical trend involving more separation, more divorce and more childbearing before or outside marriage occurred among whites although the pace was slower. The proportion of white families headed by a woman rose from 8 to 12 percent in this period (U.S. Bureau of the Census, 1963: Table 187; 1984c: Table 2; Ross and Sawhill, 1975). These changes had a great impact on the overall ratio of black-to-white family income.

Poverty

Since 1959, the Census Bureau has defined a poverty line and determined the proportion of blacks and whites who fell below that minimum. In 1983, a family of four was impoverished if its cash income was under $10,200 (U.S. Bureau of the Census, 1984b: Table A–1). Trends in poverty are also shown in Figure 5.

The recent period may be divided into three distinct intervals with regard to poverty. Between 1959 and the recession which began in late 1973, poverty was reduced. Particularly dramatic gains improved the welfare of blacks, since the proportion below the poverty line fell from 55 percent to 30 percent. Poverty was reduced by almost one-half in fifteen years. The interval between the 1973–75 recession and that which began in 1979 involved little change in poverty rates. About one black in three and one white in eleven lived in an impoverished family or household. The interval since 1979 is also different, since, for the first time since poverty has been measured by a federal agency, it has increased for four consecutive years. Among both races, poverty rates in 1983 were equivalent to those of the later years of the 1960s. Because of population growth, as well as the higher incidence of poverty, the actual number of black poor, which had fallen to 7.1 million at the start of the 1970s, rose to 9.9 million in 1983. Among whites, the number of poor people had been as low as 17 million and increased by about 40 percent to 24 million in 1983 (U.S. Bureau of the Census, 1984b: Table 15).

These are disturbing statistics, since they suggest that little progress was made in reducing poverty since the mid-1970s. However, caution is needed when interpreting these recent trends. On the one hand, changes in family structure helped to keep the poverty rate high, since female-headed families are much more likely to be impoverished than are husband-wife families. This is not to suggest that a statistical adjustment eliminates poverty. Obviously there are an increasing number of black women and children who have few financial resources. Nevertheless, shifts in family living arrangements help explain much of the persistence of high rates of poverty among blacks in the 1970s.

On the other hand, the 1970s saw the expansion of federally-sponsored non-cash transfer programs such as food stamps, school lunches, subsidized housing and Medicare. None of these benefits are included when poverty estimates are developed by the Census Bureau, but their surveys show that the majority of low-income households obtain such benefits. In 1982, for example, 61 percent of the white and 36 percent of the black impoverished households received food stamps (U.S. Bureau of the Census, 1984e: Tables 1 and 5). There are numerous problems in determining who actually gets benefits and what is the appropriate way to estimate their cash value. Without doubt, a poverty rate which includes non-cash benefits will be lower than the 'official' poverty rate which is based on cash income alone. In 1979, the 'official' poverty rate for blacks was 30 percent. Including non-cash benefits reduces that rate to between 21 and 25 percent, depending upon how you estimate the value of benefits (Smeeding, 1982: Table 17).

In the 1960s, poverty declined among blacks because of higher wages, the shifting regional distribution and some cash benefit programs. In the 1970s, there were more modest reductions in poverty and they came about largely because of non-cash programs. Without doubt, the poor in the 1980s were, in some sense, better off than the poor were two decades earlier since they often had access to food stamps, their children received school lunches and, if sick or injured, the Federal Government paid their medical expenses.

Conclusion

At the outset, we contrasted three views of racial change; first, that progress has been widespread and that discrimination is rapidly fading; second, that racial progress has been superficial and that the status of blacks, relative to that of whites, has hardly changed; and third, that one segment of the black population took advantage of new opportunities but that a much larger share remains no better off than they were before the civil rights revolution of the 1960s.

In describing blacks in this nation, we are dealing with a large and diverse group, since their number exceeds the total population of such major countries as Argentina, Canada or South Africa. No simple generalization will adequately describe racial trends. Each of the views contains some accuracy but also fails to describe the changes which have occurred.

There is good reason to be particularly critical of the view that black gains are superficial. In many important areas — education, occupations and earnings — racial differences declined substantially. This is not tokenism. Throughout the entire economy and in all regions, racial differences on the most important indicators are smaller now than before.

There are also good reasons to doubt the view that the black community is increasingly polarized into a black elite and a black underclass. There are some aspects of this perspective which are accurate. There has always been a prosperous segment of the black community and a large group of impoverished blacks. Perhaps the most widely-cited book about blacks in the 1950s was Franklin Frazier's (1957) statement of polarization: *Black Bourgeoisie.* In recent decades, the black elite has grown larger and more visible although we do not know if they are as financially secure as middle-class whites. The black poor have moved to cities where they are also more visible and threatening than in the rural South. There has been an improvement in their welfare because of the expansion of government services and transfer payments.

There is one type of economic polarization which is certainly occurring, but it is quite different from the social class polarization which is described most frequently. That is, the income gap which distinguishes individuals in husband-wife families from those in families headed by a woman has grown larger for both races (see Figure 6).

This leaves us with the view that black gains are widespread. This is accurate. Although blacks will not soon attain parity with whites, a prolonged continuation of the trends of the 1960s and 1970s will eventually lead to a convergence in educational attainment, occupational prestige and earnings. In the area of employment itself, it seems less likely that this will happen, since black men have not improved their position in comparison to white men. With regard to family income and poverty, progress will also occur slowly, if at all, because of the shift away from husband-wife families. We will be able to explain much more about the improvements which have been made and the gaps which remain when we understand why the proportion of men holding jobs is declining more rapidly among blacks than among whites and why changes in family structure have been so great in the black community.

Notes

*This paper was presented at the conference on Ethnicity and Race in the Last Quarter of the Twentieth Century held at the State University of New York at Albany on April 6, 1984. It summarizes data and findings which are contained in the book *Blacks and Whites: Narrowing the Gap?* (Cambridge, Massachusetts: Harvard University Press, 1984). Support for this research was provided, in part, by the Russell Sage and Cornerhouse Foundations and by a grant from the National Science Foundation's Program in Measurement Methods and Data Resources to the Social Science Research Council's Committee on Social Indicators. The author thanks Lisa J. Neidert and Judy Mullin for their assistance.

1. Data concerning occupational and employment trends pertain to nonwhites and whites rather than blacks and whites. In 1983, 81 percent of the adult nonwhites in the Bureau of Labor Statistics data were blacks (U.S. Bureau of Labor Statistics, 1984: Table 3). The term 'black' will be used in the text.

2. In most figures, data are presented for the interval beginning in 1959 and ending with the most recent year for which data are available. We start with 1959 because the earnings and income questions in the Census of 1960 pertain to that year.

3. There are large racial and sexual differences in the proportion of all income recipients who are year-round, full-time workers. White men are much more likely than blacks or women to be full-time, year-round workers. Data for 1983 are shown below.

	Men		Women	
	Black	White	Black	White
	%	%	%	%
Full-time, year-round	43.9	52.7	33.1	29.5
Part-time or part-year	56.1	47.3	66.9	70.5

Source: U.S. Bureau of the Census, 1984b: Table 8.

4. Unemployment rates vary by age, since young people are more likely to be unemployed than are middle-aged people. To eliminate the confounding effects of changes in age composition, data in Figure 4 have been standardized for age.

5. According to Census Bureau definitions, a family consists of two or more persons who are related by blood, marriage or adoption and share a housing unit. Families are commonly divided into three types: husband-wife families, those headed by a woman who does not live with a husband, and those headed by a man who does not live with a wife. The distribution of families by type is shown below.

	Nonwhite or black		White	
	1960	1983	1960	1983
	%	%	%	%
Husband-wife families	74.8	53.4	89.2	84.7
Female-headed families	20.9	41.9	8.1	12.2
Other male-headed	4.3	4.7	2.7	3.1

Source: U.S. Bureau of the Census, 1963: Table 187; 1984d: Table 1.

6. Per capita family income has increased for several reasons, including increases in earnings and higher employment rates for women. A very important reason has been the decline in fertility, which led to smaller-sized families. Shown below are the average number of people in families in 1960 and 1983. The decrease in family size has been greater among blacks, leading to higher per capita incomes.

	Nonwhite or black families			White families		
	1960	1983	% Change	1960	1983	% Change
Husband-wife families	4.4	3.8	−14%	3.7	3.3	−10%
Female-headed families	4.0	3.5	−13%	2.9	2.8	−3%

Source: U.S. Bureau of the Census, 1963: Table 187; 1984d: Table 1.

References

ANDERSON, ELIJAH 1979 'Some Observations of Black Youth Employment,' in Bernard E. Anderson and Isabel V. Sawhill (eds.), *Youth Employment and Public Policy*. Englewood Cliffs, New Jersey: Prentice-Hall.

AYRES, Q. WHITFIELD 1984 'Racial Desegregation in Higher Education,' in Charles S. Bullock, III, and Charles M. Lamb (eds.), *Implementation of Civil Rights Policy*. Monterey, California: Brooks/Cole.

BIANCHI, SUZANNE M. 1981 *Household Composition and Racial Inequality*. New Brunswick, New Jersey: Rutgers University Press.

BROWN v. BOARD OF EDUCATION OF TOPEKA 1954 347 U.S. 483.

BULLOCK, CHARLES S., III 1984 'Equal Education Opportunity,' in Charles S. Bullock, III, and Charles M. Lamb (eds.), *Implementation of Civil Rights Policy*. Monterey, California: Brooks/Cole.

CARSON, CLAYBORNE 1981 *In Struggle: SNCC and the Black Awakening of the 1960s*. Cambridge, Massachusetts: Harvard University Press.

CLOGG, CLIFFORD 1982 *Measuring Underemployment: Demographic Indicators for the United States*. New York: Academic Press.

DUNCAN, OTIS DUDLEY 1969 'Inheritance of Poverty or Inheritance of Race?' in Daniel P. Moynihan (ed.) *On Understanding Poverty: Perspectives from the Social Sciences*. New York: Basic Books.

FARLEY, REYNOLDS, HOWARD SCHUMAN, SUZANNE BIANCHI, DIANE COLASANTO and SHIRLEY HATCHETT 1978 'Chocolate City, Vanilla Suburbs: Will the Trend Toward Racially Separate Communities Continue?' *Social Science Research* 7 (December): 319–44.

FRANKLIN, JOHN HOPE 1967 *From Slavery to Freedom*, New York: Knopf.

FRAZIER, E. FRANKLIN 1957 *Black Bourgeoisie: The Rise of a New Middle Class in the United States*, New York: The Free Press.

GARROW, DAVID J. 1978 *Protest at Selma*, New Haven: Yale University Press.

GREEN v. NEW KENT COUNTY SCHOOL BOARD 1968 391 U.S. 430.

HERMALIN, ALBERT I., and REYNOLDS FARLEY 1973 'The Potential for Residential Integration in Cities and Suburbs: Implications for the Busing Controversy,' *American Sociological Review* 38, No. 5 (October): 595–610.

KAIN, JOHN F., and JOHN M. QUIGLEY 1975 *Housing Markets and Racial Discrimination*, New York: National Bureau of Economic Research.

KILLINGSWORTH, CHARLES C. 1968 *Jobs and Income for Negroes*, Ann Arbor: Institute of Labor and Industrial Relations, University of Michigan.

LAKE, ROBERT M. 1981 *The New Suburbanites: Race and Housing in the Suburbs*, New Brunswick, New Jersey: Center for Urban Policy Research, Rutgers University.

LAMB, CHARLES M. 1984 'Equal Housing Opportunity,' in Charles S. Bullock, III, and Charles M. Lamb (eds.), *Implementation of Civil Rights Policy*, Monterey, California: Brooks/Cole.

LIEBERSON, STANLEY 1963 *Ethnic Patterns in American Cities*, New York: The Free Press.

LIEBERSON, STANLEY 1980 *A Piece of the Pie: Blacks and White Immigrants since 1880*, Berkeley: University of California Press.

LIEBOW, ELLIOT 1967 *Talley's Corner*. Boston: Little, Brown.

LOGAN, JOHN R., and MARK SCHNEIDER 1984 'Racial Segregation and Racial Change in American Suburbs, 1970–1980,' *American Journal of Sociology* 89, No. 4 (January): 874–89.

MARE, ROBERT D., and CHRISTOPHER WINSHIP 1979 'Changes in Race Differentials in Youth Labor Force Status,' in *Fifth Annual Report to the President and the Congress of the National Commission for Employment Policy, Expanding Employment Opportunities for Disadvantaged Youth: Sponsored Research*. Washington: National Commission for Employment Policy.

MARE, ROBERT D., and CHRISTOPHER WINSHIP 1984 'Racial Inequality and Joblessness,' *American Sociological Review* 49, No. 1 (February): 39–55.

MASSEY, DOUGLAS S. 1979 'Residential Segregation of Spanish Americans in U.S. Urbanized Areas,' *Demography* 16, No. 4 (November): 533–64.

MEIER, AUGUST, and ELLIOTT RUDWICK 1975 *CORE: A Study on the Civil Rights Movement, 1942–1968*. Urbana: University of Illinois Press.

MYRDAL, GUNNAR 1944 *An American Dilemma: The Negro Problem and Modern Democracy*, New York: Harper & Row.

PEARCE, DIANA 1979 'Gatekeepers and Homeseekers: Institutionalized Patterns in Racial Steering,' *Social Problems* 26 (February): 325–42.

PETTIGREW, THOMAS F. 1973 'Attitudes on Race and Housing: A Social-Psychological View,' in Amos H. Hawley and Vincent P. Rock (eds.), *Segregation in Residential Areas*, 21–84. Washington: National Academy of Science.

PLESSEY v. FERGUSON 1896 163 U.S. 537.

REGENTS OF THE UNIVERSITY OF CALIFORNIA v. BAKKE 1978 438 U.S. 265.

ROSS, HEATHER L., and ISABEL V. SAWHILL 1975 *Time of Transition: The Growth of Families Headed by Women*. Washington: The Urban Institute.

SALTMAN' JULIET 1975 'Implementing Open Housing Laws Through Social Action,' *Journal of Applied Behavioral Science* 11, No. 1: 39–61.

SCHER, RICHARD, and JAMES BUTTON 1983 'Voting Rights Act: Implementation and Impact,' in Charles S. Bullock, III, and Charles M. Lamb (eds.), *Implementation of Civil Rights Policy*. Monterey, California: Brooks/Cole.

SCHUMAN, HOWARD, CHARLOTTE STEEH and LAWRENCE BOBO 1985 *Racial Attitudes in America: Trends and Interpretations*. Cambridge, Massachusetts: Harvard University Press.

SHEATSLEY, PAUL B. 1966 'White Attitudes Toward the Negro,' *Daedalus* 95, No. 1 (Winter): 217–38.

SIEGEL, PAUL M. 1965 'On the Cost of Being a Negro,' *Sociological Inquiry* 35 (Winter): 41–57.

SMEEDING, TIMOTHY M. 1982 *Alternative Methods for Valuing Selected In-Kind Transfer Benefits and Measuring Their Effect on Poverty*. U.S. Bureau of the Census, Technical Paper 50.

SØRENSON, ANNEMETTE, KARL E. TAEUBER and LESLIE J. HOLLINGSWORTH, JR. 1975 'Indexes of Racial Residential Segregation for 109 Cities in the United States, 1940 to 1970,' *Sociological Focus* 8, No. 2 (April): 125–42.

STEELWORKERS v. WEBER 1979 99 S. Ct. 2278.

SULLIVAN, THERESA A. 1978 *Marginal Workers, Marginal Jobs: Underutilization in the United States Work Force*. Austin: University of Texas Press.

SWANN v. CHARLOTTE-MECKLENBURG 1971 402 U.S. 1.

TAEUBER, KARL E. 1983 'Racial Residential Segregation, 28 Cities, 1970–1980,' CDE Working Paper 83–12. Madison: Center for Demography and Ecology, University of Wisconsin.

TAEUBER, KARL E., and ALMA F. TAEUBER 1965 *Negroes in Cities*. Chicago: Aldine.

TAEUBER, KARL E., ARTHUR SAKAMOTO, JR., FRANKLIN W. MONFORT, and

PERRY A. MASSEY 1984 'The Trend in Metropolitan Racial Residential Segregation,' paper presented at the 1984 meetings of the Population Association of America, Minneapolis, May 5.

U.S. BUREAU OF THE CENSUS 1943 *Sixteenth Census of the United States: 1940, Population,* Vol. III, Part 1.

U.S. BUREAU OF THE CENSUS 1963 *Census of Population: 1960,* PC(1)–1D.

U.S. BUREAU OF THE CENSUS 1983 *Current Population Reports,* Series P–20, No. 373.

U.S. BUREAU OF THE CENSUS 1984a *Current Population Reports,* Series P–20, No. 390.

U.S. BUREAU OF THE CENSUS 1984b *Current Population Reports,* Series P–60, No. 145.

U.S. BUREAU OF THE CENSUS 1984c *Current Population Reports,* Series P–60, No. 142.

U.S. BUREAU OF THE CENSUS 1984d *Current Population Reports,* Series P–20, No. 388.

U.S. BUREAU OF THE CENSUS 1984e *Current Population Reports,* Series P–60, No. 143.

U.S. BUREAU OF LABOR STATISTICS 1979 *Handbook of Labor Statistics, 1978,* Bulletin 2000.

U.S. BUREAU OF LABOR STATISTICS 1983 *Employment and Earnings* 30, No. 1 (January).

U.S. NATIONAL ADVISORY COMMISSION ON CIVIL DISORDERS 1968 *Report of the National Advisory Commission on Civil Disorders.* New York: Bantam Books.

VAN VALEY, THOMAS L., WADE CLARK ROOF, and JEROME E. WILCOX 1977 'Trends in Residential Segregation: 1960–1970,' *American Journal of Sociology* 82, No. 4 (January): 826–44.

WALLACE, PHYLLIS A. (ed.) 1976 *Equal Employment Opportunity and the A.T.&T. Case.* Cambridge, Massachusetts: MIT Press.

WIENK, RONALD E., CLIFFORD E. REID, JOHN C. SIMONSON, and FREDERICK J. EGGERS 1979 *Measuring Racial Discrimination in American Housing Markets: The Housing Market Practices Survey.* Washington: Department of Housing and Urban Development, Office of Policy Development and Research.

2 The political economy and political ethnicity of American Indian adaptations and identities*

Robert Jarvenpa
State University of New York at Albany

Introduction

The purpose of this essay is threefold: (1) to provide a brief synthetic overview of contemporary economic, social and political adaptations of North American Indians, (2) to relate such adaptations to changes in cultural identity and emerging accculturative, assimilative and separatist postures vis-à-vis the larger society, and (3) to offer a theoretical rationale for such behavior which combines the frameworks of political ethnicity, political economy of underdevelopment, and cultural evolution.

While the focus of discussion will be the Indian population of the United States, parallel developments in neighboring Canada cannot be ignored. The U.S. and British Canadian cultures have provided broadly similar environments for Indian people. Although their systems of government are quite different, both countries developed land cession arrangements (or 'treaties') for displacing natives from valuable lands, and the subsequent development of reservations and reserves has perpetuated racial segregation, administrative paternalism and lower-class status for Indian people. Moreover, the Indian policies created by the two countries have exhibited many parallels, with Canada often lagging behind the U.S. by two decades or more in dealing with such issues as citizenship, land claims, per capita grants in education, lifting of alcohol prohibitions, and even the termination of federal responsibility (McNickle, 1973; Price, 1982: 49–51).

Historical perspective

By the time of the first European migrations to America in the late fifteenth century, Native American populations had adaptively radiated into all of the major geographic environments on the continent (Jennings, 1983; Kroeber, 1939; Oswalt, 1973). With a population of 2,200,000 to 4,400,000 north of Mexico (Denevan, 1976: 291; Ubelaker, 1976), the cultural diversity of Indian people in North America probably surpassed that of Renaissance Europe. It is something of a paradox, therefore, that early European settlers so often and so dispassionately ignored the unique developments and contributions of the many Indian societies. Rather, the posture of the European through history has been an ethnocentric lumping of the many into the pejorative category of 'Indian.' Jennings (1975) and Kehoe (1981a, 1981b) have eloquently demonstrated how overt racial propaganda and subtle deep-seated mythical charters about cultural superiority served the needs of colonial conquest and expansion and continue to distort Euro-american attitudes toward and dealings with Indians.

It is important to note that the European philosophy of Indians as childlike subordinates still confounds the relationship of Indians to national governments and the larger society. Despite major historical shifts in U.S. government policy from removal, treaty-making and allotment in the nineteenth century to the culturally sensitive Indian Reorganization Act of 1934 (McNickle, 1973), the basic model remains that Indians are subordinate within the nation and require special regulation by a federal bureaucracy. Washburn (1984) argues that the New Deal exuberance of John Collier's 1930s reforms both promised and provided economic development and political self-determination, but critics view the reforms as a new kind of paternalism which merely permitted autonomy for adopting general American cultural practices (Kehoe, 1981a: 535–7). Since the late 1960s activists in the pan-Indian political movement have voiced their rejection of assimilationist philosophy and policy, and by seeking ties with other 'Fourth World' minorities and 'internal colonies' on other continents have advocated a renewed attention to their own cultural traditions (*Saskatchewan Indian*, 1982). Yet the basic structural dilemma remains for federally recognized or enrolled Indians in both the U.S. and Canada. That is, their special federal status makes them politically subservient to the state in a way which does not affect the general population or any other racial-cultural minority.

Native American populations declined to a collective low ebb of 250,000 to 500,000 people at the end of the nineteenth century (Driver, 1968, 1972: 63–5). Yet by the mid-1970s there were 900,000 U.S. citizens claiming native Indian or Inuit ancestry, and about 600,000 of these were enrolled tribal members recognized by the federal government. In the late 1970s Canada had 700,000 citizens of native ancestry, of which 310,299 maintained federal status as band-registered Indians (Price, 1982: 44). The rate of population increase for Native Americans approached 100 percent in the period between 1950 and 1970, suggesting that in the decade of the 1980s the American Indian and Inuit population will be reaching or surpassing its level at the time of early European contact (Spicer, 1980: 59).

Yet demographic changes reveal little about the complex sociocultural adaptations of Indians. Provinse (1954) and his colleagues predicted that many Indian communities would continue to persist as 'cultural islands' in the American social landscape while growing numbers of individual Indians would seek personal adjustments in the mainstream society. Although the connotations of 'cultural island' are unappealingly static, the idea of tension or interplay between community and individual adjustments is relevant for our discussion. Equally pertinent is the notion of a dialectic between the traditional forces of 'tribalism' (or group-specific social life and identity) and the historically emerging impact of 'pan-Indianism' as a collective Indian identity and unified response to the pressures of acculturation and assimilation.

It often comes as a surprise to the uninitiated that pan-Indian movements developed rather late in American history, and that the externally imposed category of 'Indian' itself has often been a tenuous and distant concern for many Native Americans. The earliest responses to European encroachment invariably were phrased in tribal terms, since local groups and communities were involved with traders and missionaries, engaged in frontier warfare, endured dispossession and removal, and negotiated treaties. Although a number of inter-tribal political-military confederations had coalesced earlier in history to oppose European encroachment (Hertzberg, 1971: 6–8), it was the common experience of the reservation system, beginning in 1870 in the U.S., which crystallized a feeling of shared oppression and fate among the diverse tribes who were being uniformly administered as 'Indians.' Intense pressure for assimilation, spearheaded by the Dawes Severalty Act of 1887 (or General Allotment Act) (Washburn, 1975), ultimately spawned a pan-Indian religious movement, the Ghost Dance, which swept the plains area in the 1890s (Mooney, 1896). The Peyote movement followed a similar path of diffusion through the plains later in time, and it is still a vibrant religion (La Barre, 1938). It is noteworthy that both movements were facilitated by the institution of the boarding school, part of the enforced assimilation program of the early reservation system.

One of the ironies of pan-Indianism in recent history is that certain traits and institutions from historical Plains culture, such as the pow wow complex, have become symbolic of a general 'Indian' identity for many Native American groups on the one hand, while increased interaction and communication between groups have contributed to the decline of local indigenous languages and a secularization of life on the other hand. Thomas (1968) interprets pan-Indianism as a defensive response to the stresses of rapid incorporation and assimilation by a bureaucratic nation-state. The pan-Indian identity, by this view, is a compromise to complete assimilation, since it permits partial incorporation while maintaining the solidarity of a new social collectivity. A somewhat different view is given by Bernard (1974), who challenges what he terms the new 'myth of the non-melting pot' in America. For him pan-Indianism is more instructive of processes of acculturation and ethnic emergence than of cultural persistence. However, Lurie (1971: 443–8) has identified a set of core values and behaviors which transcend local tribal differences and appear to be too widespread to be the product of common experiences with whites. The multiplicity of meanings and definitions applied to pan-Indianism attests to the complex dynamics involved. We will return to these issues later in the discussion.

Rural and reservation contexts

Despite a dramatic increase in rural–urban migration since World War II, nearly half of the Indian population still resides on federal or state administered reservations or in rural off-reservation settings. In the U.S. most of these communities are west of the Mississippi River, reflecting the process of Indian removal from eastern regions historically desirable for white settlement and exploitation. Canada's Indian and Inuit population is somewhat more evenly distributed across its provinces and territories.

Sheer physical location, however, is not a sensitive indicator of degree of integration into regional and national economies or of acculturative orientation. Relative isolation of groups like the Chipewyan in the sub-Arctic frontier has facilitated the retention of their native language, nomadic band social organization and subsistence behavior associated with a historical fur trading economy (Jarvenpa, 1977, 1980). On the other hand, the Navajo, with the largest population and reservation of any North American Indian group, have retained a high degree of cultural distinctiveness and have remained apart from the mainstream of involvement in pan-Indian affairs (Keyes, 1981). This has occurred even though large numbers of Navajo migrate to and return-migrate from major cities in the southwest, plains and California (Hodge, 1971; Price, 1968; Weppner, 1971). The Navajo, in Spicer's (1971) theoretical frame of reference, represent an 'enclavement' or 'persistent cultural system,' a people whose unique historical experience has been translated into a powerful identity which opposes incorporation into the state. The enclavement model applies to the Yaquis, Cherokees, and many other Native American groups who may interact intensely with non-natives but maintain separateness through an oppositional process.

A striking commonality in adaptation among many other rural and reservation communities in recent years has been the forging of new general identities as a means of coping with limited resources and economic stresses upon social organization. White (1974), for example, interprets the contemporary 'tribalistic movement' among Sioux in the Rapid City–Pine Ridge Reservation area of South Dakota as an attempt to halt assimilation policy, with its concomitant deterioration of the local economic base, and to gain more autonomy in accordance with traditional tribal values. In essence, this involves creating a contemporary Sioux culture that replaces normlessness and hopelessness with guides to effective action, a strengthening of personal social ties and sense of commitment among members of the Sioux community, and attainment of a feeling of control and influence over the environment in terms of their own perception of their problems.

Perhaps a limited example of this philosophy in operation is the nearby Yankton Sioux Reservation in South Dakota, where an electronics plant was established in a way which did not seriously compromise either Western industrial or local native values. Its scheduling flexibility and piece-work incentives apparently revived both community and factory reputations

(Bigart, 1972). The experience is consistent with recommendations offered by Tax and Stanley (1969) that economic development programs will best proceed where group or tribal identities are nourished, rather than individual identification as 'Indian.'

New forms of boundary maintenance and identity management may accompany relatively prosperous economic conditions, although even under these circumstances there may be an appeal to a general tribal identity. Over the past several decades the northern Ute reservation in Utah has materially prospered from land claims settlements, mineral royalties and federally sponsored economic development programs. In turn, dramatically changing economic opportunities since 1970 have fostered greater social heterogeneity resulting in an incipient class structure of elites, laborers and underemployed. Nonetheless, Collins (1975) notes that there is consensus among all segments of the community to 'keep things Indian.' This is expressed in an increasingly outward symbolization of their Ute Indianness in terms of speech, dress and ceremonial activity. Such symbolic displays do not vary by occupation or economic status, suggesting a need to define the ethnic self in the context of an 'outside' group. Fearing future erosion or termination of federal support and services, which have reinforced their economic security, the Utes 'are determined to maintain their ethnicity as a device for their continuing defense of their reservation and their desired life-style' (Collins, 1975: 72).

The Choctaw (or Chata) present an interesting contrast to rural adaptations in the western U.S.. Resisting the government removal policy in the early nineteenth century, a small percentage of the Choctaw population remained in its indigenous Mississippi lands as squatters and sharecroppers. While they adopted some features of rural culture common to whites and blacks, they steadfastly maintained a separate identity in the midst of the rigidly bounded Southern social system. A central element in maintaining separateness has been retention of the Choctaw language (Thompson and Peterson, 1975: 179–81). New employment opportunities in cities distant from the traditional Choctaw communities make assimilation possible for some individuals, but many prefer to combine access to community services, employment and residential cohesiveness as a means of maintaining cultural separation (Peterson, 1972). Thompson and Peterson (1975) argue that the future economic well-being and autonomy of the various Chata peoples will depend on their success in forging both a strong Choctaw symbolic identity and a common identity as American Indians with non-Choctaw tribes and communities. Thus far, their identification with a larger universe of Indian peoples is only embryonic.

The Hupa Indians of California are instructive of general changes in behavior and identity which separate many Indian groups from other racial-ethnic minorities. Bushnell (1968) characterizes their accommodation to reservation life between the 1860s and World War II as uniquely 'American Indian,' while post–World War II modernization involved an adaptation to the larger society as 'Indian Americans.' The latter term signifies that the Hupa now parallel other U.S. minority groups in retaining a unique sense of ethnic identity while possessing a culture that is predominantly American in content. Perhaps a significant difference in this regard is that many immigrant minorities symbolize their ethnic distinctiveness through references to a foreign 'motherland' or 'fatherland.' Of course, Indians may emphasize their special indigenous attachment to the land, but they also express their separateness through religious and magico-medicinal tradition.

Thus, the Hupa experience and project their Indianness in the context of prayers, relations with spirits, good and bad 'medicine,' the notion of retribution following the violation of sacred proscriptions, and the performance of the Deerskin Dance as a world renewal ceremony. To a large extent religion and ceremonialism serve the same functions in identity maintenance for the Hupa which the Chata language assumes for the Choctaw. Nonetheless, I concur with Bushnell's (1968: 1115) assertion that the Hupa situation reflects a widespread process:

> This persisting substratum of belief in the continuing sanctity and
> efficacy of Indian paraphernalia, religious ritual, and ceremonial sites
> can be seen as one of the more significant forces serving to perpetuate
> an enduring core of Indian identity in the midst of a twentieth-century
> America.

As the foregoing discussion illustrates, the situational or contextual nature of identity is important in understanding contemporary Indians in America. Such a view challenges the traditional acculturation paradigm which often interpreted change as a linear process of cultural loss and replacement.

The responses of individuals to Euroamerican institutions, however, have never been homogeneous within Indian groups (McFee, 1968). The history of Indian–white relations is laden with references to conflict between Indian 'Progressives' and 'Conservatives,' 'Reformers' and 'Traditionalists,' 'Angry Nationalists' and 'Uncle Tomahawks' (Warrior, 1964; Wax 1971: 174–98). Many reservation communities harbor an assortment of unresolved conflicts and factional disputes which occasionally erupt in incidents attracting media attention (*Akwesasne Notes*, 1976: 8–11). Endemic factionalism may be one of the most striking products of stress produced in culture contact situations (Jarvenpa and Zenner, 1979; Savishinsky, 1972).

Deep-seated factional disputes among the Prairie Potawatomi of Kansas involve efforts by conservative and assimilationist contingents to control access to tribal government and B.I.A. officials and to restrict or expand definitions of tribal membership as ways of competing for claims case revenues and other resources. Clifton (1968) demonstrates the value of rigorous historical analysis in tracing the roots of Potawatomi factionalism to ideological ancestors in the early nineteenth century. The Potawatomi case is important in showing the relationship between cultural ambiguity, as expressed in uncertain criteria about community or tribal membership, and the rise of factionalism. Historically the primary foci of identity for many Indians were the family, the kindred or descent group, and the locality of their birth, and more encompassing allegiances were less meaningful. The imposed category of 'tribe,' as a bureaucratic artifice of the state, therefore, is a source of confusion and tension. Although the factionalism which arises from such situations often remains unresolved or unregulated, Clifton (1968: 127–30) notes that it is not necessarily reflective of normlessness and social disorganization. The Potawatomi, at least, are confronted with multiple and competing norms for defining their political identity, and the conflict is compartmentalized within the society by factions which appear to relish scheming and maneuvering. There is little doubt, however, that factionalism in other Indian communities can be pervasive and demoralizing.

The profound problems of Indian poverty, disease, inadequate shelter and low attainment in formal education have been systematically observed by the U.S. government from the time of Lewis Meriam's (1928) report on their economic and social conditions in the late 1920s. In a relative sense, these conditions have changed very little in the past fifty years despite a massive growth in federally administered programs for Indians. About three-quarters of all Indians in the U.S., and over half of all Canadian Indians, have incomes below official poverty levels. Half of all U.S. and Canadian Indians tallied in the labor force are unemployed, Indian infant mortality rates are 50 to 100 percent higher than national rates, and Indian life expectancy is considerably lower than national averages (Kehoe, 1981b: 540).

Given these harsh realities, it is not surprising that many researchers have interpreted the prevalence of social pathologies, such as homicide, suicide and alcoholism, as a direct product of economic deprivation and exploitation (Graves, 1970; Jorgensen, 1971) or as an inability to generate institutions for controlling deviance introduced in the acculturation process (Leighton and Kluckhohn, 1947). This view has been challenged recently by Levy and Kunitz (1971), who note that much scholarship on Indian culture change is handicapped by a Western romantic tradition contrasting deviance-free 'Gemeinschaft' societies with anomic urban industrial society. They do not dispute the fact of Indian material poverty, but rather the idea of social systems without pathologies. Their historical analysis of homicide, suicide and alcoholism data for the Navajo and Hopi suggests a patterning and prevalence in these behaviors that are consistent with persisting features of aboriginal culture.

Indians in urban environments

Until very recently in history North American Indians were rural dwellers. In the U.S., modest migrations to towns and cities occurred in the early years of this century as a landless class of Indians struggled in the wake of the disruptive General Allotment Act. However, a larger surge of migration began with the return of thousands of World War II Indian servicemen who were induced to move into cities by the B.I.A.'s Employment Assistance Program. In the 1950s and 1960s there was a large migration of Indians to the industrial centers of the western U.S. in particular. By 1970 about 43 percent of the U.S. Indian population was located in towns and cities, and the current figure may be over 50 percent (Spicer, 1980: 109–11). Large-scale migrations of Indians to Canadian cities began somewhat more recently, in the early 1960s, as they became aware of economic possibilities beyond their small reserves and as their rapidly expanding population put enormous pressure on local resources (Dosman, 1972: 7–12).

Despite their relatively recent movement into urban environments, Indians have spread rather quickly into all levels of the socioeconomic hierarchy. Individuals near the upper end of the socioeconomic scale may have some Indian ancestry, but their lives are not structured by ties to rural Indian communities or by involvement in Indian associations. Indeed, they may not identify themselves as Indians, except under advantageous circumstances, while expressing contempt for and distancing themselves from less affluent Indians in ghettos and on reservations. On the other hand, recent immigrants to the city may be difficult to enumerate because of their residential instability. This is particularly the case for urban areas in close proximity to reservation communities where concentrations of transient, unemployed Indians experiencing adjustment and health problems become targets for discrimination by the general population (Wax, 1971: 157–9).

Somewhere in between these extremes is a relatively stable urban Indian working class. Generally, these are people who have adapted to cities over the course of a generation or longer and who maintain active involvement in Indian institutions such as pow wow associations, social and welfare centers, native churches and sports leagues. Like the Gowanus Mohawk of Brooklyn, New York and many Chippewa in Minneapolis–St. Paul, Minnesota, such Indians maintain strong ties and seasonal visiting patterns with family and kin in reservation and rural communities (Freilich, 1970). Indeed, the prevalence of such vibrant Indian communities belies a common assumption that the eventual result of Indian urbanization will be acculturation or assimilation into mainstream society.

Steele's (1975) research on urban Indians in Kansas refutes simplistic notions of a rural–urban continuum in Indian adaptations and the idea that acculturation is a prerequisite to successful urban adjustments. In 'Prairie City' (pseudonym), Kansas Indian identity is a matter of 'badges' or credentials which people adopt because they are imposed or required by external majority groups. In this situation, Indian ethnicity becomes a mechanism or device which the Potawatomi, Kickapoo and others employ to create a community of solidarity to act as a unit against exploitation. A pow wow club, a singing and dancing group, sports associations, an Indian Protestant Church, and an Indian Center provide an organizational focus and leverage for bargaining purposes by an Indian group proclaiming a right to resources by its badges.

In many medium-sized cities the cultural background of the Indian population is rather homogeneous, reflecting migration from limited hinterlands. Large cities may harbor Indians from tribes and reservation communities throughout the country. Los Angeles and San Francisco, for example, have Indian residents from at least 101 and 100 different tribal groups respectively (Price, 1968; Spicer, 1980: 112). While the majority of these people derive from the southwest and plains areas, small numbers from distant groups like Inuit, northern Athapaskans, Tlingit and Cree also occur.

Los Angeles, with nearly 50,000 Indian residents by 1970, is the largest such concentration in North America and, therefore, instructive of the more complex forms of urbanization. Navajo are presently the largest group in the city, reflecting their numerical dominance nationally, but there are large contingents of Sioux, Pueblo peoples, Apache and Cheyenne as well as non-reservation Cherokee, Creek, Choctaw and Seminole deriving from Oklahoma. Price (1968) arranged some of these groups along a scale of 'urban adaptation' ranging from weak to strong. The Navajo adaptation to the city is placed on the weak end of the continuum reflecting their greater connectivity to reservation life, their persisting use of the Navajo language, and their heavy social involvement with other Navajo. The Sioux adaptation is viewed as moderate, while the Oklahoman groups are seen as strongly adapted to urban life. The latter interact with other Indian groups in athletic leagues, use their native language infrequently, and on the whole view their Indianness as only one component in an identity fashioned by occupation, religious and political affiliations, and residential situation.

While Price's (1968) survey is a valuable description of certain behavioral changes, the scale or continuum model inappropriately equates 'successful adaptation' with assimilation. The troublesome assumption here is that assimilation into white urban society is somehow inevitable or necessary for survival in the city. Thus, only Indians themselves are seen as accountable for their poverty and unassimilated condition, regardless of the economic and political institutions oppressing them. Some anthropologists like Lurie (1966, 1971) assert that the option to assimilate is more open for Indians than most minorities, and indeed, this appears to be supported by some of Price's Los Angeles data. For example, discrimination in housing may be less pronounced for Indians than for blacks and Mexican Americans.

A similar flexibility is suggested by rates of intermarriage with other tribes and with non-Indians, rates which appear to increase with successive generations. Measures of outbreeding and intermarriage have been widely used as gauges of assimilation into Euroamerican society (Walker, 1972), but this interpretation should be applied cautiously. For example, Steele's (1975: 169–70) fine-grained study of eighteen Indian/non-Indian marriages indicates that in many instances the non-Indian partner experiences a resocialization into an Indian subsociety with a concomitant 'internalization of new (Indian) norms and meanings.'

The case of Los Angeles is also instructive in distinguishing acculturation from 'adjustment,' the latter referring to relative social and psychological

health in the Western clinical sense. Price (1968) notes that the two processes
are not always positively correlated. Navajo men exhibit higher levels of
acculturation than Navajo women, since their activities bring them into
the public sphere of interaction. Yet, Navajo women appear to be better
adjusted than their men, showing lower rates of mental illness and criminality
(Martin, 1964).

An emerging body of research approaches the question of Indian
urbanization more as a matter of *process* than of place. The Moenkopi
Hopi and Navajo and their relationships with Tuba City and Flagstaff,
Arizona, are part of an 'urbanism' of reservation lands. Nagata (1971)
analyzes the impact of growth in tribal governments and the federal
government in generating localized economic programs and social services
which, in turn, have spawned an underdeveloped sector of administrative
'agency towns' and associated reservation villages:

> All these communities are the sites of federal, state, and tribal agencies
> and include an assortment of Christian missionaries and private enterprises.
> Their industry is service-oriented [administrative, medical and educational],
> from which a majority of residents derive their primary income. The
> resident population is heterogeneous in race, ethnicity, and occupation,
> and a considerable portion of it is transient. In spite of the heterogeneity
> of the population and the decentralization of administrative power in
> these communities, the division between the client population of Indians
> and the professional population of mainly non-Indians permeates many
> aspects of community life. [Nagata, 1971: 149]

Agency towns of this kind have appeared in otherwise disparate settings
across North America where government and commercial enterprises
coalesce in the servicing of a native clientele (Fried, 1964; Jarvenpa, 1982:
286–8).

Structurally, the agency communities occupy an intermediate position
that connects the reservation to Washington, D.C., or to Ottawa, and the
larger society. They also provide a transitional step in rural–urban migration.
Indeed, some Indian migrants to large off-reservation cities return to the
agency towns as a means of combining better material lifestyles with a more
familiar cultural setting. Yet the net effect of this process often is the
creation of a new class of deprived Indians. Reservation residents frequently
are displaced to the position of wage laborers in an unstable employment
environment while having little power in a patchwork political system
composed of externally controlled agencies and industries (Nagata, 1971:
153–7).

In a similar vein, Jorgensen (1971) develops a hypothesis termed the
'metropolis-satellite political economy' for explaining the underdeveloped
socioeconomic conditions in most American Indian communities. Simply
expressed, the 'metropolis' represents a process involving concentration of
economic and political power and political influence by exploiting labor in

'satellite' areas, thereby generating a downward spiral in population displacements, impoverishment and dependency for both rural and urban minorities. This framework is convincingly applied to the Utes of northeastern Utah between 1850 and the present. After 100 years of frontier warfare, disease, starvation, relocation to agriculturally marginal lands, and alienation of most of their reservation property through allotment, the Utes have become largely consumers in the local economy rather than active wage earners. Since 1951 they have been heavily dependent on unearned income, but royalties from mineral leases and government welfare payments have only underwritten a low standard of living while insulating Utes from any direct control over local resources (Jorgensen, 1971: 99–109).

Jorgensen's (1971) 'metropolis-satellite' model may be the most severe and cogent critique of the acculturation paradigm. From this perspective Indian economic *underdevelopment* has been caused by the development of the white-controlled national economy. Moreover, the socioeconomic conditions of Indians are not improving or progressing along a linear path toward full acculturation, according to this interpretation, because Indian communities have been fully integrated into the national political economy for over a century.

The 'marginal' tri-racial and bi-racial groups

The identity of most American Indian people is firmly anchored in a combination of distinctive cultural traditions, racial characteristics and social structural relationships, including membership in legally defined tribal groups. Yet there are hundreds of thousands of other U.S. and Canadian citizens who have some Indian biological ancestry and a sense of cultural separateness as Indians but who have no federal recognition and whose projected identity is regarded with ambivalence or hostility by whites and many Indians of legal status.

Such groups have been termed 'tri-racial isolates,' 'little races' and 'marginal peoples' by social scientists, mostly in reference to eastern U.S. communities which, since colonial times, have derived from real or alleged admixture of Indian, black and white populations (Beale, 1972; Berry, 1963; Pollitzer, 1972; Thompson, 1972). These include some relatively large, publicly visible groups with quasi-official federal status and a wealth of pride-giving history and legend, like the Lumbees of North Carolina (Blu, 1980), as well as dozens of small rural enclaves such as the Wesorts (or Brandywines) of Maryland, the Issues of Virginia, the Haliwa and Sampson County Indians of North Carolina (Dane and Griessman, 1972), and the Brass Ankles and Turks of South Carolina. The process of ethnic emergence and identity management currently unfolding among these people may well mark an important new chapter in Indian–Euroamerican relations.

As Thompson (1972) notes, these people became aware of themselves as 'marginal groups' as they became objects of derogatory epithets applied to them by the larger society. The American 'ideology of race' is based on a rigid bi-polar model of white and non-white categories (Daniels and Kitano, 1970), so that any degree of admixture is perceived as non-white, and any degree of black admixture is perceived as black. The admixed Indian groups generally have been treated as blacks by outsiders, so that their history can be viewed as a quest for a dignified image emphasizing descent from esteemed Indian ancestors replete with justifying origin myths.

The dynamics involved are well illustrated by the 'Monhegan Indians,' a pseudonym used by Hicks and Kertzer (1972) for a group in southern New England. Since their defeat by colonists in the late seventeenth century these people have intermarried with whites and blacks. Since the 1870s they have had no reservation, and without any distinctive language, dress or occupations to bound them from the larger society, they have been perceived and treated as blacks. In the modern setting Monhegan identity, therefore, has a contingent quality as each individual strives to assert his or her Indianness and to have it validated. The most important validation derives from local whites who witness 'Indian' performances and activities, such as pow wows, and from other Monhegans who can reinforce genealogical claims to Indian ancestry.

Identity maintenance in this situation involves an attempt to restructure the bi-polar racial model to include the third category of 'Indian,' on the one hand, and to have certain individuals accepted into or rejected from the new category, on the other hand (Hicks and Kertzer, 1972: 21; Hicks, 1975: 88). It is noteworthy that neither cultural nor structural continuity adequately explains such behavior. The efforts of the Monhegan and other tri-racial groups to be accepted as distinctive Native American peoples may be more properly viewed, as Hicks and Kertzer (1972) suggest, as forms of 'political ethnicity.' Thus, ties of *interest*, as well as ties of kinship and friendship, may integrate an ethnic group, and this implies a tactical or strategical underpinning (Glazer and Moynihan, 1965). Cohen (1974: xvi–xviii) has argued that political ethnicity comes into being particularly in situations where interest groups have difficulty organizing themselves formally and, therefore, 'tend to make use, though largely unconsciously, of whatever cultural mechanisms are available to articulate the organization of their grouping.'

Whether or not the admixed groups should be interpreted as interest groups, revitalizing aboriginal societies, or some other social process, may be clarified in the next few decades as more of these communities present claims for legal recognition before the federal government. Of course, 'recognition' itself has to be placed in the political economy of the times, and undoubtedly there will be enormous pressures to resurrect cherished stereotypes and to view non-status Indians as masquerading blacks. During periods of conservative spending on social programs, any revenues distributed to newly created tribes will be seen as a strain on the federal budget and money taken from the pockets of already established tribes.

The position of the Metis in Canada offers intriguing parallels and differences with the admixed groups of the eastern U.S.. As offspring of Indian–European unions (especially Algonkian–French) in the subarctic frontier during the eighteenth and nineteenth centuries, the Metis became a rather cohesive rudimentary working class in the fur trade industry and, thereby, served as a linkage between Indian hunting bands and the European managerial class (Brown, 1976; Jarvenpa and Brumbach, 1982; Slobodin, 1964, 1981). The Metis developed a distinctive hybrid culture and separate identity, a non-conformist blend of Indian 'reticence' and Gallic *joie de vivre* (Douaud, 1983: 72). Under the impact of white agricultural settlement in the mid to late nineteenth century, the Metis of the plains coalesced into a nationalistic movement that culminated with the leadership of Louis Riel (Patterson, 1972: 130–5). This contrasts sharply with the various Indian groups which did not develop strong inter-tribal ties and a sense of pan-Indian identity until well into the twentieth century.

It is somewhat ironic that after Riel's defeat by the Canadian government in 1885 many Metis found themselves without land or status, and their subsequent dispersal initiated a long period of destitution and hopelessness (Douaud, 1983: 74–5). At the same time, many of their Indian relatives were receiving reserve lands, annuities and other federal benefits, however limited, through treaty negotiations, permitting some retention of social solidarity and identity (Harper, 1972). Along with non-Treaty Indians, the Metis today comprise anywhere from 400,000 to one million people in Canada (Douaud, 1983: 72; Price, 1982: 44). Douaud (1983) argues that these are a 'forgotten people' in a society which has difficulty comprehending social or ideological overlaps. The familiar American bi-polar racial formula of white/non-white = 'black' is closely paralleled by the Canadian ideology of white/non-white = 'Indian.' The Metis do not easily fit either category in the latter model. They are viewed as Euro-peanized Indians by some, as Indianized whites by others, and thus rebuffed by both.

However, since the early 1960s Metis leaders have been attempting to forge a new sense of unity and pan-Metis political power, and they are drawing upon the symbols of their frontier culture and their historical experience as a 'nation.' The Native Council of Canada's recent 'Metis Declaration of Rights' is a charter and political philosophy justifying a claim to true nationalism on the basis of a unique indigenous hybrid status. That is, the Metis see themselves as the 'true natives' of Canada while Indians and whites are immigrants differing in their time of arrival (Daniels, 1979). Thus far, it is unclear if the Metis movement primarily seeks tolerance for a 'Fourth World' status or more tangible benefits from the government. If the latter path is pursued very strong resistance can be expected. An attempt at 'termination' of Indian 'special status' was made by the Trudeau government in 1969, and renewed attacks on Canadian Treaty pro-visions have been instigated in recent years (*Saskatchewan Indian*, 1981, 1982).

Pan-Indian identity and ethnic emergence

The emergence of the tri-racial and bi-racial groups raises questions about the nature of pan-Indian political movements and the dialectics of ethnic change among Native Americans generally. Some observers believe that the heightened political activity within and among Indian tribes since World War II represents a rather special social process in American society, distinguishing it from the black civil rights movement and its emphasis upon social and cultural acceptance, and from revitalization movements seeking internal reforms. Lurie (1971) uses the expression 'articulatory movement' to refer to a system of widely shared goals and patterned action in the absence of identifiable leadership and spokesmen. From this perspective, the movement is an attempt to escape the unappetizing alternatives of economic marginality or complete assimilation by redefining their relationship with the larger socioeconomic system. A formal contractual basis of interaction with the larger society is adopted, and Indians share and refine models of such interaction which will assure successful material adaptations while maintaining Indian identity and satisfactory community life.

Pan-Indian political activity can also be interpreted as the transformation of diverse tribal societies into an *ethnic group* by mobilizing a shared history. Trosper (1981) develops the concept 'charter' to refer to an historical event, or a series of events, which aids in ethnic mobilization by imbuing the past with a 'primordial' quality (Geertz, 1963; Keyes, 1981), by defining the boundaries of a group, and by providing a guide to action. Thus, Indian nationalism is based upon a charter of common bio-cultural ancestry and descent from people experiencing treaty negotiations and subsequent breaking of treaty agreements. Despite considerable diversity in actual historical experiences of individuals and groups, the notion of a shared past of intense suffering and broken agreements becomes a quasi-mythic structure that defines important cultural elements in pan-Indian identity. In turn, such ideas suggest concerted action in justifying claims to the right of self-government (or self-determination) and compensation for lands unfairly taken. Trottier (1981) builds a similar argument, but places special emphasis upon the symbolism of 'land' and its relationship to treaty breaking in formulating a charter of pan-Indian identity.

Another framework for viewing Indian nationalism incorporates some of the foregoing perspectives by integrating both a *cultural interpretation* of ethnicity as a primordial characteristic of identity and the *social manipulation* of ethnicity in the pursuit of objective interests. Keyes' (1981) model of ethnic change, for example, involves a dialectical process, beginning when people experience a radical shift in their social circumstance, as in the case of migration, displacement or political subjugation. As people develop new social adaptations in response to stressful circumstances, they begin to reassess the cultural foundation of their ethnic identity. Ultimately, as new cultural meanings are applied to their identity, they generate social patterns consistent with the precepts of that identity. For American Indians in recent years this process has involved the use of pre-existing ethnic identities in new ways to realize objective goals in their dealings with the bureaucratic machinery of the state. By claiming common interests Indian activists have attempted to fashion a pan-Indian ethnic identity through a symbolic reinterpretation of the history of Indian—white relations for the entire country. Therefore, assertion of new interests, and assertion of a new ethnic identity, are intimately linked (Keyes, 1981: 25–7).

The efforts to formulate a pan-Indian identity occasionally involve dramatic symbolic actions that capture public attention and fill Indian participants with an emotional commitment and intensity reminiscent of emotionally charged Indian—white confrontations in history. This was the case for the occupation and forcible removal of Indian leaders from Alcatraz Island between 1969 and 1971 (Indians of All Tribes, 1972). Equally evocative was the 1973 armed siege of Wounded Knee on the Pine Ridge Reservation by American Indian Movement leaders and local Oglala Sioux supporters (*Akwesasne Notes*, 1974).

Conclusions

Undoubtedly, there will be renewed attempts in the future to foster Indian unity through dramatic symbolic displays. Pan-Indianism is still a segmented, decentralized political movement, and some tribes have remained relatively autonomous as ethnic enclaves removed from the mainstream of pan-Indian political ideology. Moreover, the common interests of the reservation and non-reservation Indian, or the status and non-status Indian, are often obscure. These realities are a challenge to the maintenance of a common identity, and they may explain, in part, the recent forging of international ties and identification with oppressed indigenous peoples in other nations (*Akwesasne Notes*, 1975, 1976). Public symbolic dramas may be shifting from the confrontational displays evoking memories of past tragedy and suffering to international festivals of native fellowship and harmony. The World Assembly of First Nations was hosted by the Federation of Saskatchewan Indians in 1982 drawing 35,000 people and representatives from more than thirty countries. From the perspective of the local Indian hosts the assembly was

> something so big, that the world would have to take notice that Indigenous people exist, that Indians are alive and knocking at the doors of power, not as observers or lobbyists but as powers in our own right. . . . It opened a doorway to the world for thousands of us. Hopefully, we will see the sober reality of other indigenous peoples and know that we're not alone. [*Saskatchewan Indian*, 1982: 8–9]

It is likely that the future position of Indians in American and Canadian society will best be understood in a framework that combines the political economy of underdevelopment, as explicated by Jorgensen (1971), with dynamic views of ethnicity as presented by Hicks (1975), Keyes (1981) and others. On the one hand, such a synthesis would further clarify the history of material deprivation and exploitation which Indians have endured through their integration into the Euroamerican capitalist economy. On the other hand, the synthesis would illumine the creative and complex changes in social forms and identity among Indians as a system of response to adverse socioeconomic environments.

Of course, the system of response has never been and probably never will be uniform among tribes and communities. Despite recent cautions about the ethnocentric bias permeating evolutionary models in anthropology (Kehoe, 1981b), the traditional sociopolitical complexity of particular Indian groups may account for their relative well-being and the nature of their relations with the state. Price (1982) has observed that Indians with band and tribal level backgrounds in French Canada, and those from complex farming chiefdoms in the U.S., are among the most vibrant Indian people today. They successfully manage communal businesses, adjust well to urban living, and often are intellectually involved with their own heritage through historical research and museum liaisons. By contrast, Indian people who derive from band and tribal level hunting societies in the U.S. and in British Canada experience considerable difficulty with alcoholism, violence and fragmented family life among other problems. It is clear from Price's survey that much greater attention should be given to specific structural-historical contexts in understanding current Indian—white relations.

For the past three decades innovations in pan-Indian culture, religion, art and education have developed among Indians in Oklahoma, New Mexico and Arizona, areas where the Pueblos and other settled horticultural societies have flourished. Future centers of inspiration, perhaps, will rise among the last Native Americans to receive the full impact of Western economic development. The egalitarian hunting bands of the distant Arctic and sub-Arctic regions are only beginning to build political alliances. The formation of the Dene Nation by farflung Athapaskan Indian groups in the 1970s to declare an aboriginal right to self-determination and to block the Mackenzie Valley pipeline project is a preview of the creative forces gestating in the far north (Watkins, 1977).

The general goal of political autonomy, or self-determination, with its emphasis upon group rights, stands in opposition to the concept of individual rights embedded in Western law and institutions (Trosper, 1981). This fundamental distinction will continue to define the separateness of Indians in North American society legally, socially and ideologically. These group rights are seen by most Indians as an integral part of their traditions, along with other cultural assets that are either absent or lost among the technologically acquisitive urban peoples of European tradition.

Note

*Richard Alba and Walter Zenner kindly encouraged me to write this paper. I am grateful for many years of wise counsel and inspiration from Indian friends in the U.S. and Canada, and I extend special gratitude to the Chipewyan people of Patuanak, Saskatchewan.

References

AKWESASNE NOTES 1974 *Voices from Wounded Knee, 1973*, ed. R. Anderson, J. Brown, J. Lerner, and B. L. Shafer. Rooseveltown, New York.

AKWESASNE NOTES 1975 'Death at Oglala.' Vol. 7, No. 3, pp. 4—13. Rooseveltown, New York.

AKWESASNE NOTES 1976 'Native People in Guatemala Need Our Help.' Vol. 8, No. 1, pp. 3—5. Rooseveltown, New York.

AKWESASNE NOTES 1979 'Pine Ridge — 1976.' Vol. 8, No. 1, pp. 8—11. Rooseveltown, New York.

BEALE, CALVIN L. 1972 'An Overview of the Phenomenon of Mixed Racial Isolates in the United States.' *American Anthropologist* 74: 704—10.

BERNARD, JAMES J. 1974 'Reply to Tim Roufs' "Myth in Method: More on Ojibwa Culture."' *Current Anthropology* 15: 309—10.

BERRY, BREWTON 1963 *Almost White*. New York: Macmillan.

BIGART, ROBERT JAMES 1972 'Indian Culture and Industrialization.' *American Anthropologist* 74: 1180—8.

BLU, KAREN I. 1980 *The Lumbee Problem: The Making of an American Indian People*. Cambridge: Cambridge University Press.

BROWN, JENNIFER 1976 'A Demographic Transition in the Fur Trade Country: Family Sizes and Fertility of Company Officers and Country Wives, ca. 1759—1850. *Western Canadian Journal of Anthropology* 6: 61—71.

BUSHNELL, JOHN H. 1968 'From American Indian to Indian American: The Changing Identity of the Hupa.' *American Anthropologist* 70: 1108—16.

CLIFTON, JAMES A. 1968 'Factional Conflict and the Indian Community: The Prairie Potawatomi Case,' in S. Levine, N. O. Lurie (eds.), *The American Indian Today*. Deland, Florida: Everett Edwards.

COHEN, ABNER 1974 'Introduction: The Lesson of Ethnicity,' in A. Cohen (ed.), *Urban Ethnicity*. A.S.A. Monograph No. 12. London: Tavistock.

COHEN, ABNER 1981 'Variables in Ethnicity,' in C. F. Keyes (ed.), *Ethnic Change*. Seattle: University of Washington Press.

COLLINS, THOMAS W. 1975 'Behavioral Change and Ethnic Maintenance Among the Northern Ute: Some Political Considerations,' in J. W. Bennett (ed.), *The New Ethnicity: Perspectives from Ethnology*. St. Paul: West Publishing.

DANE, J. K., and B. EUGENE GRIESSMAN 1972 'The Collective Identity of Marginal Peoples: The North Carolina Experience.' *American Anthropologist* 74: 694—704.

DANIELS, H. W. (ed.) 1979 *A Declaration of Metis and Indian Rights*. Ottawa: Native Council of Canada.

DANIELS, ROGER, and HARRY H. L. KITANO 1970 *American Racism: Exploration of the Nature of Prejudice*. Englewood Cliffs, N.J.: Prentice-Hall.

DENEVAN, WILLIAM M. (ed.) 1976 *The Native Population of the Americas in 1492*. Madison: University of Wisconsin Press.

DOSMAN, EDGAR J. 1972 *Indians: The Urban Dilemma*. Toronto: McClelland & Stewart.

DOUAUD, PATRICK C. 1983 'Canadian Metis Identity: A Pattern of Evolution.' *Anthropos* 78: 71—88.

DRIVER, HAROLD E. 1968 'On the Population Nadir of Indians in the United States.' *Current Anthropology* 9: 330.

DRIVER, HAROLD E. 1972 *Indians of North America*. Chicago: University of Chicago Press.

FREILICH, MORRIS 1970 'Mohawk Heroes in Structural Steel,' in M. Freilich (ed.), *Marginal Natives: Anthropologists at Work*. New York: Harper & Row.

FRIED, JACOB 1964 'Urbanization and Ecology in the Canadian Northwest Territories.' *Arctic Anthropology* 2: 56–60.

GEERTZ, CLIFFORD 1963 'The Integrative Revolution: Primordial Sentiments and Civil Politics in the New States,' in C. Geertz (ed.), *Old Societies and New States: The Quest for Modernity in Asia and Africa*. New York: Free Press.

GLAZER, NATHAN, and DANIEL P. MOYNIHAN 1965 *Beyond the Melting Pot: The Negroes, Puerto Ricans, Jews, Italians and Irish of New York City*. Cambridge, Mass.: M. I.T. Press.

GRAVES, THEODORE D. 1970 'The Personal Adjustment of Navajo Indian Migrants to Denver, Colorado.' *American Anthropologist* 72: 35–54.

HARPER, ALLEN G. 1972 'Canada's Indian Administration: The Treaty System,' in D. E. Walker (ed.), *The Emergent Native Americans: A Reader in Culture Contact*. Boston: Little, Brown.

HERTZBERG, HAZEL W. 1971 *The Search for an American Indian Identity: Modern Pan-Indian Movements*. Syracuse: Syracuse University Press.

HICKS, GEORGE L. 1975 'The Same North and South: Ethnicity and Change in Two American Indian Groups,' in J. W. Bennett (ed.), *The New Ethnicity: Perspectives from Ethnology*. St. Paul: West Publishing.

HICKS, GEORGE L., and DAVID I. KERTZER 1972 'Making a Middle Way: Problems of Monhegan Identity.' *Southwestern Journal of Anthropology* 28: 1–24.

HODGE, WILLIAM H. 1971 'Navajo Urban Migration: An Analysis from the Perspective of the Family,' in J. O. Waddell, O. M. Watson (eds.), *The American Indian in Urban Society*. Boston: Little, Brown.

INDIANS OF ALL TRIBES 1972 *Alcatraz Is Not An Island*, ed. P. Bluecloud. Berkeley: Wingbow Press.

JARVENPA, ROBERT 1977 'Subarctic Indian Trappers and Band Society: The Economics of Male Mobility.' *Human Ecology* 5: 223–59.

JARVENPA, ROBERT 1980 *The Trappers of Patuanak: Toward a Spatial Ecology of Modern Hunters*. National Museum of Man Mercury Series, Canadian Ethnology Service Pub. No. 67. Ottawa: National Museums of Canada.

JARVENPA, ROBERT 1982 'Intergroup Behavior and Imagery: The Case of Chipewyan and Cree.' *Ethnology* 11: 283–99.

JARVENPA, ROBERT, and HETTY JO BRUMBACH 1982 'Occupational Status, Ethnicity and Ecology: Metis Cree Adaptations in a Canadian Trading Frontier.' Paper presented at the 81st Annual Meeting of the American Anthropological Association.

JARVENPA, ROBERT, and WALTER P. ZENNER 1979 'Scot Trader/Indian Worker Relations and Ethnic Segregation: A Subarctic Example.' *Ethnos* 1–2: 58–77.

JENNINGS, FRANCIS 1975 *The Invasion of America*. Chapel Hill: University of North Carolina Press.

JENNINGS, JESSE D. 1983 *Ancient North Americans*. San Francisco: W.H. Freeman.

JORGENSEN, JOSEPH G. 1971 'Indians and the Metropolis,' in J. O. Waddell, O. M. Watson (eds.), *The American Indian in Urban Society*. Boston: Little, Brown.

KEHOE, ALICE B. 1981a *North American Indians: A Comprehensive Account*. Englewood Cliffs, N.J.: Prentice-Hall.

KEHOE, ALICE B. 1981b 'Revisionist Anthropology: Aboriginal North America.' *Current Anthropology* 22: 503–17.

KEYES, CHARLES F. 1981 'The Dialectics of Ethnic Change,' in C. F. Keyes (ed.), *Ethnic Change*. Seattle: University of Washington Press.

KROEBER, ALFRED L. 1939 *Cultural and Natural Areas of Native North America*. University of California Publications in American Archaeology and Ethnology, Vol. 38.

LA BARRE, WESTON 1938 *The Peyote Cult*. New Haven: Yale University Press.

LEIGHTON, DOROTHEA C., and CLYDE KLUCKHOHN 1947 *Children of the People*. Cambridge, Mass.: Harvard University Press.

LEVY, JERROLD E., and STEPHEN J. KUNITZ 1971 'Indian Reservations, Anomie, and Social Pathologies.' *Southwestern Journal of Anthropology* 27: 97–128.

LURIE, NANCY O. 1966 'The Enduring Indian.' *Natural History* 75: 10–22.

LURIE, NANCY O. 1968 'An American Indian Renascence?' in S. Levine and N. O. Lurie (eds.), *The American Indian Today*. Deland, Florida: Everett Edwards.

LURIE, NANCY O. 1971 'The Contemporary American Indian Scene,' in E. B. Leacock and N. O. Lurie (eds.), *North American Indians in Historical Perspective*. New York: Random House.

McFEE, MALCOLM 1968 'The 150% Man, a Product of Blackfeet Acculturation.' *American Anthropologist* 70: 1096–1107.

McNICKLE, D'ARCY 1973 *Native American Tribalism: Indian Survivals and Renewals*. London: Oxford University Press.

MARTIN, HARRY W. 1964 'Correlates of Adjustment Among American Indians in an Urban Environment.' *Human Organization* 23: 290–5.

MERIAM, LEWIS, *et al.* 1928 *The Problem of Indian Administration*. Washington, D.C.: Brookings Institution.

MOONEY, JAMES 1896 *The Ghost Dance Religion and the Sioux Outbreak of 1890*. 14th Annual Report, Bureau of American Ethnology.

NAGATA, SHUICHI 1971 'The Reservation Community and the Urban Community: Hopi Indians of Moenkopi,' in J. O. Waddell and O. M. Watson (eds.), *The American Indian in Urban Society*. Boston: Little, Brown.

OSWALT, WENDELL H. 1973 *This Land Was Theirs*. New York: Wiley.

PATTERSON, E. PALMER 1972 *The Canadian Indian: A History Since 1500*. Don Mills, Ontario: Collier-Macmillan Canada.

PETERSON, JOHN H. 1972 'Assimilation, Separation, and Out-Migration in an American Indian Group.' *American Anthropologist* 74: 1286–95.

POLLITZER, WILLIAM S. 1972 'The Physical Anthropology and Genetics of Marginal People of the Southeastern United States.' *American Anthropologist* 74: 719–34.

PRICE, JOHN A. 1968 'The Migration and Adaptation of American Indians to Los Angeles.' *Human Organization* 27: 168–75.

PRICE, JOHN A. 1982 'Historical Theory and Applied Anthropology of U.S. and Canadian Indians.' *Human Organization* 41: 43–53.

PROVINSE, JOHN, *et al.* 1954 'The American Indian in Transition.' *American Anthropologist* 56: 387–94.

SASKATCHEWAN INDIAN 1981 'The Constitution: Existing Rights Recognized But . . .' Vol. 11, No. 11: pp. 2–4. Saskatchewan: Federation of Saskatchewan Indians.

SASKATCHEWAN INDIAN 1982 'Constitution Commission Meets in Emergency Session.' Vol. 12, No. 1: pp. 3–35. Saskatchewan: Federation of Saskatchewan Indians.

SASKATCHEWAN INDIAN 1982 'The WAFN Gamble.' Vol. 12, No. 6: pp. 6–9. Saskatchewan: Federation of Saskatchewan Indians.

SAVISHINSKY, JOEL S. 1972 'Coping with Feuding: The Missionary, the Fur Trader and the Ethnographer.' *Human Organization* 31: 281–90.

SLOBODIN, RICHARD 1964 'The Subarctic Metis as Products and Agents of Culture Contact.' *Arctic Anthropology* 2: 50–5.

SLOBODIN, RICHARD 1981 'Subarctic Metis,' in J. Helm (ed.), *Handbook of North American Indians, Volume 6, Subarctic*. Washington, D.C.: Smithsonian Institution.

SPICER, EDWARD H. 1971 'Persistent Cultural Systems.' *Science* 174: 795–800.

SPICER, EDWARD H. 1980 'American Indians,' in S. Thernstrom, A. Orlov, O. Handlin (eds.), *Harvard Encyclopedia of American Ethnic Groups*. Cambridge, Mass.: Harvard University Press.

STEELE, C. HOY 1975 'Urban Indian Identity in Kansas: Some Implications for Research,' in J. W. Bennett (ed.), *The New Ethnicity: Perspectives from Ethnology*. St. Paul: West Publishing.

TAX, SOL, and SAM STANLEY 1969 'Indian Identity and Economic Development,' in *Toward Economic Development for Native American Communities: A Compendium of Papers Submitted to the Subcommittee on Economy in Government of the Joint Economic Committee, Congress of the United States*. Washington, D.C.: U.S. Government Printing Office.

THOMAS, ROBERT K. 1968 'Pan-Indianism,' in S. Levine and N. O. Lurie (eds.), *The American Indian Today*. Deland, Florida: Everett Edwards.

THOMPSON, EDGAR T. 1972 'The Little Races.' *American Anthropologist* 74: 1295–1306.

THOMPSON, BOBBY, and JOHN H. PETERSON 1975 'Mississippi Choctaw Identity: Genesis and Change,' in J. W. Bennett (ed.), *The New Ethnicity: Perspectives from Ethnology*. St. Paul: West Publishing.

TROSPER, RONALD L. 1981 'American Indian Nationalism and Frontier Expansion,' in C. F. Keyes (ed.), *Ethnic Change*. Seattle: University of Washington Press.

TROTTIER, RICHARD W. 1981 'Charters of Panethnic Identity: Indigenous American Indians and Immigrant Asian Americans,' in C. F. Keyes (ed.), *Ethnic Change*. Seattle: University of Washington Press.

UBELAKER, DOUGLAS H. 1976 'The Sources and Methodology for Mooney's Estimates of North American Indian Populations,' in W. M. Denevan (ed.), *The Native Population of the Americas in 1492*. Madison: University of Wisconsin Press.

WALKER, DEWARD E. 1972 'Measures of Nez Perce Outbreeding and the Analysis of Cultural Change,' in D. E. Walker (ed.), *The Emergent Native Americans: A Reader in Culture Contact*. Boston: Little Brown.

WARRIOR, CLYDE 1964 'Five Types of Young Indians.' *Americans Before Columbus* II, 4.

WASHBURN, WILCOMB E. 1975 *The Assault on Indian Tribalism: The General Allotment Law [Dawes Act] of 1887*. Philadelphia: J. B. Lippincott.

WASHBURN, WILCOMB E. 1984 'A Fifty-Year Perspective on the Indian Reorganization Act.' *American Anthropologist* 86: 279–89.

WATKINS, MEL 1977 *Dene Nation: The Colony Within*. Toronto: University of Toronto Press.

WAX, MURRAY L. 1971 *Indian Americans: Unity and Diversity*. Englewood Cliffs, N.J.: Prentice-Hall.

WEPPNER, ROBERT S. 1971 'Urban Economic Opportunities: The Example of Denver,' in J. O. Waddell and O. M. Watson (eds.), *The American Indian in Urban Society*. Boston: Little, Brown.

WHITE, ROBERT A. 1974 'Value Themes of the Native American Tribalistic Movement among the South Dakota Sioux.' *Current Anthropology* 15: 284–303.

3 The structuring of Hispanic ethnicity: historical and contemporary perspectives *

Candace Nelson and Marta Tienda
Department of Rural Sociology, University of Wisconsin-Madison

A dominant myth about the social and economic experiences of U.S. immigrants is that most groups confronted similar opportunity structures and reception factors in the host society. Without regard for differences in the historical context of the migration, reception factors in the new society, or the migration process itself, ethnic groups are evaluated by how they fare in becoming American. Those who do not succeed socially or economically — the unmeltable ethnics — contribute towards the demise of the American 'melting pot' as the dominant metaphor guiding our understanding of ethnic relations. Despite the plethora of alternative interpretations that have surfaced to explain the social significance of ethnicity and the persistence of racial and ethnic stratification in contemporary U.S. society, the melting pot metaphor has yet to be replaced.

One perspective of the persistence of racial and ethnic stratification maintains that ethnic bonds are promulgated as the natural extension of primordial ties. This view nurtures the idea that the disadvantaged, marginal position of certain ethnic and racial groups results from their cultural deficiencies which disappear as individuals assimilate into the dominant culture. At the opposite end of the spectrum, ethnic divisions are seen as mere reflections of class divisions. There exist several variants of the class interpretation of persisting ethnic differentiation, but the unifying theme is their focus on economic and social rather than cultural factors as determinants of ethnic inequality, and their emphasis on structural instead of individual explanatory factors.

The great diversity in the ethnic experience in the United States challenges both of these explanations and most that fall between them. Reducing ethnic stratification to a class phenomenon is reasonable only under the assumption that all members of an ethnic group are in the same class. Similarly, because ethnic identity and solidarity shift across groups and historical eras, it is equally inappropriate to deny the importance of social factors in molding ethnicity over time and place. By challenging widely held assumptions that high socioeconomic standing goes hand in hand with assimilation to the dominant culture, examples of ethnic groups who combine high levels of economic success with strong expressions of ethnic identity present a trouble spot for theories of race and class (Hirschman, 1982).

The complexities involved in interpreting ethnicity are aptly demonstrated by the case of the U.S. Hispanic population. While their presence in the United States predates the emergence of the American nation, their numerical strength and national visibility resulting from high fertility coupled with continuing inflows of new immigrants presents a challenge for students of ethnic stratification. 'Hispanic' as a label combines colonized natives and their offspring, foreigners and political refugees under one ethnic umbrella, but the coherence of this label is questionable on theoretical and historical grounds. Unlike the European immigrants of the nineteenth and early twentieth centuries, the majority of Hispanics have not become structurally integrated into the broader society. And, in contrast to other white immigrants, use of Spanish has not disappeared among the second or third generations reared in the United States. Today Hispanic enclaves and the Spanish language thrive in diverse regions of the country, although there is evidence of linguistic acculturation among all Spanish-speaking national origin groups who have lived in the United States over a generation.

While common ancestral ties to Spain manifested in language, religion and various traditions suggest an underlying cultural commonality, the diverse incorporation experiences of Mexicans, Puerto Ricans and Cubans have contributed to significant social and economic differences that have remained intact over time. It is this persistence of socioeconomic differentiation among national origin groups that challenges the conception of 'Hispanic' as a coherent ethnic category, and requires further specification of the underlying commonalities and divergencies.

In an attempt to clarify the meaning of 'Hispanicity' in contemporary U.S. society, this paper explores the roots of Hispanic ethnicity as it has emerged and evolved with the entry and social integration of each of the three major Hispanic national origin groups. It is a task that initially requires separating conceptually the structural elements of ethnicity from its cultural manifestations. In so doing, we emphasize historical comparisons between Mexicans, Puerto Ricans and Cuban origin populations, calling attention to the factors affecting their migration to this country and their incorporation into the labor market. Our ultimate goal is to critically evaluate the coherence of 'Hispanicity' as an ethnic category as well as a social and political force in shaping the contemporary pattern of ethnic stratification.

To guide our interpretation of the historical circumstances that have shaped the integration of the Hispanic population into the U.S. society and economy, we first set forth the theoretical framework which outlines the processes underlying the emergence, consolidation and reformulation of Hispanic ethnicity. Following a brief historical vignette of the integration experience of the three major Hispanic origin populations, we summarize the contemporary socioeconomic position of each group through a descriptive analysis of selected social indicators derived from recent census data. These data are intended to illustrate empirically the extensive social and economic diversity among the national origin groups, and to highlight the direction of change among successive cohorts of Hispanic immigrants. We conclude with a reflection about the unifying and divisive elements inherent in the notion of 'Hispanicity,' and emphasize the distinction between symbolic identity and minority status.

On the social construction of ethnicity: theoretical considerations

We choose to view ethnicity as a social construct rather than simply as a collection of ascriptive traits. While their importance as rallying points drawing people of similar cultural backgrounds together cannot be denied, the explanatory power of primordial ties for ethnic group solidarity conflicts with what is essentially a social phenomenon. This is demonstrated by the fact that ethnic group boundaries are not only defined by socially produced descent rules, but can be changed by group members themselves. One becomes an ethnic by virtue of leaving the homeland and by subsequent status vis-à-vis the dominant majority in the receiving society. Often it is only after immigration that a common sense of nationality emerges (Bonacich, 1980; Yancey *et al.*, 1976).

Starting with the idea that ethnicity is a variable, William Yancey and his associates (1976) identified several factors that contribute to the emergence of ethnicity among immigrant groups, including: conditions affecting immigration; availability of wage labor; urban ecology; technology and the changing structure of industry. The impact that these structural variables have had on U.S. immigrants can explain their residential and occupational concentration better than the traditional notion of cultural disposition or preference to certain types of work. These two factors — residential and occupational concentration — are especially crucial to the formation of ethnic group solidarity in that they produce common class interests, lifestyles and friendships. When the ethnic experience includes rejection, discrimination and oppression, the elaboration of ethnic ties provides a ready system of support for groups distinguishable by race, national origin or language. As Yancey and his colleagues conclude, 'Ethnicity may have relatively little to do with Europe, Asia or Africa, but much more to do with the requirements of survival and the structure of opportunity in this country' (Yancey *et al.*, 1976).

Yancey applied his notion of emergent ethnicity to European immigrants who settled in the eastern coastal cities. In order to distinguish between this early group of immigrants and later Hispanic waves, one must draw attention to the additional factors of timing of immigration, and modes of entry and integration of specific national origin groups. Like Yancey and his associates, we argue that these are more relevant to the understanding of Hispanic ethnicity than are the vestiges of Latin American or Spanish culture. Time of immigration is crucial because of temporal changes in employment opportunities and changing demand for various skills mixes. Europeans settled in large Eastern and Western cities during a period of industrial expansion. In contrast the Hispanic influx — at least the early Mexican immigration —

began as a rural phenomenon (Tienda, 1981). As a predominantly urban population after the 1950s, Hispanics faced an economic system characterized by periods of restricted growth coupled with dramatic changes in the structure of production (Singelmann and Tienda, 1984). Race and racial discrimination must also be considered as a force shaping incorporation experiences even though a racial classification of Hispanics is complicated by the fact that they are brown, black and white. What is clear, however, is that predominantly white Europeans gave birth to the melting pot metaphor while the very different experience of Hispanics continues to destroy it. That most Hispanics have not assimilated and occupy the lower ranks of the stratification hierarchy brings into focus the issue of the convergence of ethnicity and low socio-economic position – an issue that needs to be explored in both theoretical and empirical terms.

Following the predictions of evolutionary theories of social change, Park (1950), an early prominent theorist on ethnic relations, maintained that the importance of ascriptive ties would eventually disappear under modern capitalism as industrial organizations recruited individuals based on unversalistic criteria, such as skill and efficiency rather than ethnic origin. Using the same frame of reference – social changes resulting from the expansion of modern industrial capitalism – structural analysts and neo-Marxist theorists have reached diametrically opposed conclusions about the impact of capitalist expansion on race and ethnic relations. Bonacich (1972, 1980) and others (Portes and Bach, 1982) argued that ethnic stratification is the result of a split or segmented labor market that generates ethnic oppression from both capital and labor. By rooting ethnic segregation in labor competition that generates hostility from white workers while maintaining rates of profit for the employer, Bonacich provides a valuable insight into how ethnicity can override class consciousness. She also challenges the basic tenets of assimilationist ideology that faults individuals for their failures resulting from their lack of education, skills, and motivation and the persistence of culturally distinct values.

What both evolutionary and structural perspectives of ethnic inequality have left unexplained, however, is why certain ethnic groups are singled out for segregation in the least desirable low-skill, low-paying jobs, while others are not. A related and perhaps more central question for understanding the persistence of ethnic stratification is why some groups manage to experience mobility from low to high status jobs while others do not. Racism is an important element in this explanation, but it is a mistake to view the situation of European immigrants and racial minorities as polar opposites (Blauner, 1975). At the time of initial entry, European immigrants served many of the same functions that racial and ethnic minority workers currently do, and also were segregated residentially and occupationally by national origin. The key issue is why Europeans experienced social mobility from low status positions to the higher status, better-paying jobs while many blacks and Hispanics are seemingly unable to make this transition. These contrasting outcomes bring into focus a critical distinction between ethnic groups and minority groups.

Although minority groups and ethnic groups are not coterminous, some ethnic groups become minorities. For example, Cubans are seldom identified as a minority group, but Mexicans and Puerto Ricans usually are. The reason, we maintain, has to do with their very different modes of incorporation and socioeconomic integration experiences.

Vincent (1974) has elaborated at some length the distinction between minorities and ethnics, and this is helpful for interpreting the Hispanic experience in the United States. A minority, according to Vincent, is a group whose members are subjected to unequal treatment through prejudice and discrimination by a dominant group. Ethnic groups, on the other hand, are a collectivity sharing common cultural norms, values, identities and behaviors, and who both recognize themselves, and are recognized by others as being ethnic. The extent to which ethnicity is a matter of individual choice depends on the group's access (or lack thereof) to the reward system of a dominant society. For the lower socioeconomic strata, choices to elaborate or conceal national origin are considerably more limited, if they exist at all. The convergence of ethnic origin and economic disadvantage requires an investigation of the circumstances that structures ethnicity into a disadvantaged minority position for some, and a symbolic identity for others (Gans, 1979). Such a pursuit might fruitfully uncover the areas of convergence and divergence among Hispanic origin groups, and help clarify the origins of the differential access to resources and social rewards that structure Hispanic ethnicity in different ways for Mexicans, Puerto Ricans, and Cubans.

The emergence and consolidation of 'Hispanicity'

Figure 1 maps the major historical and social processes describing the emergence, transformation and reformulation of ethnicity which we elaborate to interpret the diverse experiences of Hispanics. These processes are by nature interactive and the ways in which the social and historical dimensions intersect are central to understanding the relegation of Hispanics to a minority group status, or their eventual adoption of a more symbolic ethnicity, one less intertwined with economic and social standing.

The Hispanic population emerged as an ethnic group historically through international migration and conquest. The reasons for their entry to the United States, combined with the historical moment of that entry, determined both the composition of the ethnic population and its ultimate geographical configuration and socioeconomic position. Patterns of inter-ethnic contact, once established, were determined by occupational and residential segregation, and the changing climate of prejudice and xenophobic sentiment. Integration processes also changed in accordance with shifting economic conditions, the passing of generations, and legal prescriptions governing both immigration flows and labor practices.

Once consolidated, ethnic groups can reformulate their position vis-à-vis the dominant society in response to any number of circumstances. Gordon (1964) has provided useful insights as to the diverse forms that any experience

Figure 1. *Structuring of Hispanic ethnicity: a conceptual framework.*

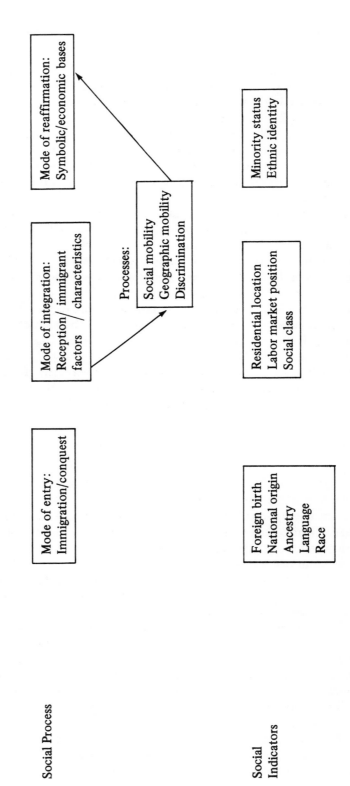

Social Process

Mode of entry:
Immigration/conquest

Mode of integration:
Reception / immigrant
factors / characteristics

Processes:

Social mobility
Geographic mobility
Discrimination

Mode of reaffirmation:
Symbolic/economic bases

Social
Indicators

Foreign birth
National origin
Ancestry
Language
Race

Residential location
Labor market position
Social class

Minority status
Ethnic identity

may assume, ranging from limited acculturation to structural and identificational assimilation. Which outcomes eventually emerge along this spectrum depends heavily on the preceding experiences of a group.

Hispanics having more 'successful' integration experiences are more likely to maintain a symbolic connection to their ethnic heritage, as manifested by the continued observance of holidays, the revival of ethnic foods, the practice of cultural rituals, etc., while in the areas of occupation, education, language and residence they increasingly model Anglos. The elaboration of these ethnic traits acquires a symbolic character which constitutes the cultural pluralism dimension of the melting pot metaphor. Alternatively, for Hispanics who have not gained access to new opportunities, and for whom isolation within minority occupational and residential enclaves and systematic discrimination have remained the rule, their ethnicity has become coterminous with minority status. For ethnic minorities, the significance of ethnicity extends beyond the symbolic manifestations of cultural heritage. It also is more than a simple reflection of economic relationships. The survival of distinct ethnic cultures, while structurally determined, attests to the reflexive nature of ethnicity as it offers refuge to its adherents against the very system that produces stratification and oppression.

Theoretical constructs such as those abstractly presented thus far need to be translated into social experience with the stories of real people. It is to these that the focus now shifts. In discussing the very different experiences of Mexicans, Puerto Ricans and Cubans in the United States, the elements that translated Hispanic origin to a symbolic ethnicity for some and a minority status for others will become apparent.

Mexicans

The structure of opportunity for Chicanos (encompassing both native- and foreign-born people of Mexican origin) is rooted in the history of the westward expansion, the geographical proximity and poverty of Mexico that facilitate continued immigration, and the historical labor functions of Mexican workers in the U.S. economy. Capitalist penetration of the Southwest dispossessed Chicanos of their land, created a cheap labor force and brought about the eventual destruction or transformation of the indigenous social systems governing the lives of the Mexican residents.

Immigration is the main vehicle by which the Mexican population grew and consolidated its regional and residential segregation in the Southwest; its significance cannot be understated. Most Mexican origin workers were channeled into the rural economy as a mobile, seasonal labor force subject to a colonial labor system whereby Mexican wages were paid for Mexican tasks in areas of agriculture, mining and railroad construction (Barrera, 1979; Alvarez, 1973; Tienda, 1981). Immigrant workers, however, were politically and socially vulnerable in that they could be deported. The history of Mexican immigration in the twentieth century is cyclical with the doors open in times of labor shortage, followed by massive deportations during periods of economic recession (Acuña, 1971; Samora, 1971; Barrera, 1979).

Immigrant vulnerability made them cheap workers and placed them in the position of a reserve labor force, exerting downward pressure on wages and undermining union organizing. The resulting hostility from Anglo workers combined with opposition from small farmers who were unable to compete with large enterprises employing cheap labor isolated Chicanos from class bases of support and further cut them off from potential avenues of integration into the social and economic mainstream. Racism was used by employers to pursue economic interests which resulted in a set of conditions that both structured the lives of Chicanos and gave racial and ethnic prejudice in the Southwest a life of its own. The continued entry of new immigrants maintains and renews this process.

The dimensions of immigration from Mexico to the United States in the twentieth century are so staggering that some have argued that the process has become self-sustaining via kinship ties and ethnic barrios which provide contacts and resources for incoming workers (Barrera, 1979; Tienda, 1980). This helps explain its 'irrational' continuation despite stricter immigration policy and the shrinking job market of the 1970s and 1980s. The relationship between family networks and ongoing migration has several implications for Chicano ethnicity. Reliance of these workers on assistance from their families is a form of subsidy to employers in that their wages do not have to cover all of their maintenance costs (Burowoy, 1976; Tienda, 1980). Secondly, the influx of recent arrivals to the Mexican community reinforces and juxtaposes the values of Mexican culture against the corrosive forces of Anglo hegemony transmitted through the schools, mass media, industrial discipline, etc. (Saragoza, 1983).

Today, although the historical legacy remains, dramatic changes have occurred in the residence patterns and the structure of opportunity open to Chicanos. Mexicans as a group are principally an urban-based population, but one clear vestige of their rural origins is their disproportionate representation in agriculture − not as farmers, but as seasonal and permanent laborers. Unionization and legal sanctions against discriminatory practices have waged war on the colonial labor system while urban residence has provided access to a wider range of employment opportunities. Cultural manifestations of these changes include the trend toward a language shift away from Spanish (Gaarder, 1977; Arce, 1981), the declining isolation of the barrio (Moore, 1970) and indicators pointing to a greater degree of assimilation into Anglo society (Massey, 1981). Mario Barrera (1979) concedes that the segmentation line separating them from the majority culture across all classes has been weakening since World War II. This indicates that class divisions could become more salient than ethnicity as Chicanos become more integrated into the non-subordinate part of the labor force, but the prospects of this occurring also depend on the process of immigration and the vitality of the economy.

Puerto Ricans

The colonized position of Puerto Ricans on both the mainland and the island is more glaringly evident than that of Mexicans, but their labor experience is a similar one of ongoing deployment and circulation of both workers and capital across national borders (although fuzzy ones in the case of Puerto Rico). The island's Commonwealth status has obliterated economic boundaries and protective mechanisms that Third World nations are beginning to develop in order to defend local interests. United States hegemony on the island makes it difficult to define that society culturally or ethnically, for that which is Puerto Rican is partly North American as well. A dramatic illustration of this duality is the massive migration that has shifted one-third of the island's population to the U.S. mainland since World War II.

These intense demographic and economic changes are largely the result of a decision to transform and develop Puerto Rico's plantation economy through a program of rapid industrialization. The apparent success of the infamous Operation Bootstrap (in operation from 1948 to 1965) hinged on several key factors including unrestricted migration between the mainland and the island. Even with the help of the burgeoning Commonwealth bureaucracy (employing three out of ten workers by 1976), the new industrial order could not absorb the available workers, whose numbers rose steadily, owing to population growth and a severe decline in the plantation sector. The resulting movement of young urban dwellers toward blue-collar jobs in the northeastern cities of the United States gained momentum in the 1950s; migration flows from Puerto Rico to New York rose from an annual average of 18,700 in the 1940s to 41,200 between 1950 and 1960 (Centro de Estudios Puertoriqueños, 1979).

One would expect that the easy access of Puerto Ricans to the United States would, in comparison to other immigrants, carry over to their transition to mainland resident. In fact, the opposite occurred. Puerto Ricans were relegated to the lowest levels of the socioeconomic ladder, and often fared much worse economically than blacks who migrated to the North. Two features distinguish their mainland experience and strongly influence their class and ethnic identity. The first is a disproportionate representation in the secondary labor market. Three labor categories – clerical and sales, unskilled and semiskilled blue-collar workers and service workers – account for 70 percent of employed Puerto Rican men and 82 percent of employed women (Tienda, 1984). In addition, they are employed in industries with seasonal fluctuations and in the declining manufacturing sector of the city. The suburbanization of industry, coupled with inadequate mass transit, has further restricted opportunities for those tied to their central city neighborhoods, a situation which seems to have worsened during the 1970s, as the flight of industry from the Frostbelt to the lower-wage Sunbelt progressed. Their marginal position in the labor market is reflected in other indicators of social well-being: of the three Hispanic groups considered, they have the lowest labor force participation rates, the highest unemployment levels, the highest incidence of poverty, and the lowest levels of education (Tienda, 1984).

The second feature in the ethnic structuring process for Puerto Ricans is the pattern of circular migration that emerged during the 1960s. In 1969–70 alone, 129,000 persons returned to Puerto Rico (Commission on Civil Rights 1976); by 1972, 14 percent of the island's population consisted of return migrants (Lopez, 1974). The circular migration means that island population and mainland community are two parts of one whole, a situation which distinguishes Puerto Ricans from all former immigrants. It means that elements of both cultures thrive in both places, which requires a dual functional ability: children must be able to switch school systems, and must cope with competing value systems. It has resulted, as Frank Bonilla states, in 'an unprecedented job of psychological and cultural reconstitution and construction that must rest on a very special political and economic infrastructure' (Bonilla, 1974: 444).

The image of a single monolithic Puerto Rican community spanning the two locations is not entirely accurate, however. Members of the second generation raised in New York City have been dubbed 'Nuyoricans,' indicating their simultaneous separateness from Puerto Rico and their connection to it. Being caught between two value systems, especially with respect to race and ethnicity, is not only a feature of life on the mainland but also, given the U.S. hegemony over the island, plays an important role there as well, producing ideological divisions that transcend those of class hierarchy.

Thus Puerto Rican ethnicity can be interpreted as structurally determined by their colonial status, a pattern of migration that places Puerto Ricans between two worlds, and extreme occupational segregation, all of which contribute to their marginality vis-à-vis the rest of society. Their reaction is found in the maintenance of strong ethnic communities, low intermarriage rates (Fitzpatrick and Gurak, 1979) and the rejection of a quick transfer of cultural identity. Although in part a response to and protection against oppression, the persistence of ethnic distinctiveness, despite massive pressure towards homogeneous consumer culture, can also be interpreted as a form of protest. The settings for most Puerto Ricans – the schools, the streets, the military, the prisons and the sweatshops – are radicalizing contexts. That Puerto Rican ethnicity is reaffirmed here is 'a sign of remarkable survival in the face of radical ambiguity' (Bonilla, 1974).

Cubans

Three factors clearly distinguish the incorporation experience of Cubans from that of Mexicans and Puerto Ricans. They are primarily political refugees rather than economic migrants. Their reception in this country was not the tacit acceptance by employers hungry for cheap labor, but rather a public welcome by the Federal government eager to harbor the heroic victims of a communist dictatorship. And finally, among the exiles, those from professional, white-collar urban and more highly educated sectors were greatly overrepresented, at least during the early phase of the exodus (Bach, 1980).

Until the Cuban refugees arrived, no other refugee group in this hemisphere had been so advantaged in terms of socioeconomic background and host country reception. In that sense the Cubans' 'success' would not be surprising were it not for the serious obstacles they did face initially. Not the least of these were their widespread downward occupational mobility vis-á-vis the positions held in Cuba. Also, many believed that their stay in the United States would be temporary. A comparison of early occupational positions in the United States with the last occupations in Cuba showed that in Miami the percentage of unskilled laborers had doubled. Cubans who had been employed as professionals, managers and technicians dropped from 48 percent in Cuba to 13 percent in the United States (Casal and Hernandez, 1975).

In many ways, during the sixties Cubans found themselves in a situation similar to that of many other immigrants: residentially segregated; concentrated in blue-collar 'ethnic' jobs; lacking English language skills; and tied to their ethnic communities. However, Cubans were never restricted to a position of second-class workers in an ethnically split labor market, nor was their success precedented by the assimilationist patterns of earlier European immigrants. In addition to the warm welcome and massive aid received under the auspices of the Cuban Refugee Program, two factors help explain their very different integration experience: these are class background and the emergence of an ethnic enclave economy in Miami.

Unlike Puerto Ricans and Mexicans, Cubans did not enter the United States as colonized or subordinate workers. They were fleeing the real and perceived persecution and harrassment of a new regime. The same individualism that led upper- and middle-class Cubans to reject Castro provided both a cultural link to the socioeconomic orientation of the United States and the basis for effective competition. Therefore, the initial loss of occupational position was often compensated for by strong individualism and an orientation toward the future. Rogg and Cooney (1980) found that middle-class Cubans aggressively sought to learn English and new skills necessary for the socioeconomic rewards that would eventually signal their real integration. Furthermore, while occupational position in Cuba was unrelated to the first job acquired in this country, it was found to be a principal variable affecting subsequent upward mobility, along with education and age upon arrival. Clearly then, the current advantaged position of Cubans relative to other Hispanics is partly the result of the differential attitudes and resources derived from their class background.

The emergence of the Cuban enclave economy (also class related) is the other key factor in understanding the Cuban experience in the United States. Close to one-third of all businesses in Miami are Cuban-owned, while 75 percent of the workforce in construction is Cuban (Bach, 1980), and 40 percent of the industry is Cuban owned. Twenty percent of the banks are controlled by Cubans (Wilson and Portes, 1980) who account for sixteen out of sixty-two bank presidents and 250 vice presidents. Other ethnic strongholds in the enclave economy include textiles, food, cigars and trade with Latin America.

In Miami, one can proceed from birth to death Cuban style (Bach, 1980). For the refugee with fewer marketable skills, the enclave not only provides a home, but also can shelter workers from the harsh realities of the open competitive market. Its success depends on low wages paid to Cuban workers, ethnic preference in hiring *and* the reciprocal obligation to help fellow ethnic members in their own financial ventures. The other crucial components are, of course, sufficient operating capital and entrepreneurial skills to initiate a successful enterprise, as well as an economic climate conducive to the flourishing of small-scale, private enterprises. The early Cuban exodus, with its upper-class bias and access to financial credit, was able to provide both elements. Later arrivals, however, became the working class for the 'golden exiles' of the 1960s. As Bach concludes, 'Thus there has been a total trans- plantation of the pre-revolutionary Cuban social structure to Miami, with all the implications of unequal wealth, power and prestige' (Bach, 1980: 45).

Reaffirmation of 'Hispanicity': economic and symbolic bases

Our previous discussion not only emphasized the importance of economic factors in structuring the meaning of Hispanic origin as a coherent ethnic label, but also called attention to the distinction between symbolic ethnicity and minority status. In accordance with the predictions of evolutionary per- spectives of ethnic integration, the cultural content of 'Hispanicity' acquires a largely symbolic character as the different national origin groups move up the social hierarchy. While the continuing migration streams from Mexico and Puerto Rico will undoubtedly reinforce the cultural manifestations of the Hispanic presence in the United States for some time to come, the historical background of their integration experiences suggests that the ethnic fate of Cubans will differ notably from that of Mexicans and Puerto Ricans. This will occur not only because Cuban immigration is constrained by legal and political barriers, but also because their class background and differing reception factors provided them more favorable opportunities compared to Mexicans and Puerto Ricans. In contrast to Cubans, the substantially different incorporation experiences of Mexicans and Puerto Ricans resulted in the consolidation of their ethnicity with a disadvantaged economic position.

A recent snapshot of the three major Hispanic origin groups sharply illustrates the extent of socioeconomic diversity among the groups according to national origin and birthplace. Cubans have higher levels of formal schooling than either Mexicans or Puerto Ricans, but the differentials between the native- and foreign-born are themselves quite sharp. For Cubans, the edu- cational differential according to nativity is just over one year, but for Mexicans and Puerto Ricans the difference is roughly three years.

A disaggregation of the educational composition of the foreign-born shows the more recent Cuban and Mexican immigrants to be of lower educational origins than their counterparts who arrived during the 1950s and 1960s. Nevertheless, for all cohort comparisons, Cuban immigrants exhibit notably higher educational levels than Mexican immigrants. The sharpest contrast

Table 1. *Selected sociodemographic characteristics of the Hispanic civilian population age 16 and over by national origin and immigration cohort, 1980.*

Selected Characteristics	Natives	Foreign-Born[a]	Immigration cohort					
			Before 1950	1950–59	1960–64	1965–69	1970–74	1975–80
Mexicans								
Education[b]	10.0	6.9	6.0	8.0	7.5	7.2	6.8	6.6
Male LFPR[c]	77.6	82.3	46.8	84.9	85.5	86.8	88.9	86.2
Female LFPR[c]	51.6	43.2	22.1	46.8	49.0	48.7	48.0	42.6
Male unemployment rate	8.6	8.7	9.5	8.8	8.5	8.8	7.0	7.3
Female unemployment rate	8.7	12.6	8.9	10.1	13.2	12.8	13.6	13.7
Mean household income ('000)	19.0	16.8	15.0	19.7	18.2	17.6	16.7	15.5
Mean household size	4.2	4.6	3.3	4.5	4.9	5.0	5.1	4.8
% female headed household	13.2	9.2	12.2	9.7	9.7	9.6	8.3	8.1
% below poverty	17.8	24.0	21.2	17.0	20.7	21.6	23.1	31.3
% black	2.5	0.3	0.6	0.5	0.3	0.2	0.3	0.3
% speak English well	92.6	45.4	60.4	63.3	60.6	52.5	41.9	25.3
(N)	(177,149)	(93,422)	(11,438)	(11,253)	(9,916)	(12,856)	(21,724)	(26,235)

Table 1. Continued

Table 1. Selected sociodemographic characteristics of the Hispanic civilian population age 16 and over by national origin and immigration cohort, 1980.

Selected Characteristics	Natives	Foreign-Born[a]	Immigration cohort					
			Before 1950	1950–59	1960–64	1965–69	1970–74	1975–80
Puerto Ricans								
Education[b]	12.0	9.1						
Male LFPR[c]	64.6	72.7						
Female LFPR[c]	46.9	36.6						
Male unemployment rate	13.9	9.9						
Female unemployment rate	12.6	12.7						
Mean household income ('000)	16.6	14.2						
Mean household size	3.8	3.8						
% female headed household	24.3	23.4						
% below poverty	25.5	31.2						
% black	4.9	2.7						
% speak English well	96.1	69.5						
(N)	(19,078)	(43,677)						

			Cubans					
Education[b]	12.2	10.9	10.5	11.3	12.4	10.2	9.5	9.8
Male LFPR[c]	67.4	79.3	57.4	87.0	85.9	77.5	76.0	62.9
Female LFPR[c]	55.7	55.1	37.3	57.4	59.6	55.0	55.3	36.5
Male unemployment rate	7.8	4.5	4.2	3.9	3.4	4.5	4.5	13.8
Female unemployment rate	5.9	7.1	3.3	6.0	4.8	7.8	8.0	21.2
Mean household income ('000)	21.8	21.6	19.6	22.5	25.3	20.6	19.7	14.3
Mean household size	3.4	3.5	2.8	3.3	3.4	3.6	3.7	3.8
% female headed household	14.1	9.7	10.1	8.2	8.4	11.2	9.8	9.6
% below poverty	11.4	12.4	12.4	8.6	8.6	12.1	13.8	37.0
% black	10.6	1.9	4.5	3.1	1.0	1.5	2.3	2.9
% speak English well	94.3	58.0	79.0	71.6	72.4	52.2	43.5	29.3
(N)	(3,503)	(29,888)	(938)	(2,875)	(8,975)	(9,768)	(5,699)	(1,639)

Source: 1980 Census of Population, 5% PUMS, Sample A.

a   Puerto Ricans born on the island are considered native-born citizens, therefore the immigration cohort data are unavailable for them. For purposes of these comparisons, Puerto Ricans born on the U.S. mainland are classified as native-born and all others are foreign-born.

b   Refers to all individuals 25 years and over. Other characteristics are for all civilians 16 years and over.

c   Labor force participation rate.

occurred during the 1960–64 period, denoted the 'golden exile' of Cuban emigration (Portes, 1969). During the seventies, the educational differentials between Mexican and Cuban immigrants have converged, stabilizing at about three years.

How these differences in educational attainment are economically significant is illustrated by the income and employment data. Despite the higher rates of labor force participation by Mexican origin men, particularly the foreign-born, average Mexican household income lags far behind that of Cuban households. While there was a negligible household income differential between units headed by native and immigrant Cubans, 1980 household income disparities between native and foreign Mexican and Puerto Rican adults were substantial. Puerto Ricans had the lowest household income levels, averaging between $16,600 and $14,200, respectively, for the U.S. mainland- and island-born heads. The highest rates of poverty, female headship and unemployment also correspond to Puerto Ricans, with the island-born population faring notably worse than the mainland-born population. In a socioeconomic profile Cubans emerge as the most advantaged, Puerto Ricans most disadvantaged, with Mexicans falling in between.

The only indicator of acculturation available in the 1980 Census is a measure of English proficiency. Although not a particularly precise measure of acculturation, when evaluated against indicators of socioeconomic status, this variable is nonetheless quite revealing. Puerto Ricans combine the highest levels of English proficiency with the lowest levels of socioeconomic achievement. Cuban immigrants, in contrast, are the least linguistically proficient, yet they are more successful in the labor market than either of the two 'older' immigrant groups. A comparison of the changes in English proficiency between Mexican and Cuban immigrant cohorts suggests that the Cuban linguistic assimilation process may be more rapid, but it also may be tied to the educational background of the groups entering at different periods, as well as to their locational and associational patterns after their arrival to the United States.

That the mode of entry and integration of the Hispanic population has been of major consequence for the contemporary social and economic standing of the three major national origin groups is undeniable. As the data in Table 2 show, the advantaged class population of Cubans vis-à-vis Mexicans and Puerto Ricans has remained intact to the present time. The foreign-born Cuban population has consolidated its white-collar position while the foreign-born Mexican and Puerto Ricans continue to dominate in blue-collar jobs. Note that while recent Cuban immigrants – those who arrived during the 1970s – were largely blue-collar workers, members of this cohort were almost three times more likely to hold white-collar jobs in 1980 than Mexican immigrants who arrived at the same time. Thus, the significance of the differing class composition of Cuban compared to Mexican and Puerto Rican immigrants is that it is reproduced among the native-born generations. Although the data in Table 2 show that the disproportionate representation of native-born Mexicans and Puerto Ricans in blue-collar occupations had diminished

Table 2. *Distribution of the Hispanic civilian labor force by white and blue collar occupations, national origin and immigration cohort, 1980.*

Immigration Cohort	Mexicans		Puerto Ricans[a]		Cubans	
	Blue collar	White collar	Blue collar	White collar	Blue collar	White collar
Native born	70.9	29.1	63.4	36.6	55.2	44.8
Foreign-born	87.4	12.6	79.4	20.6	62.7	37.3
before 1950	88.7	11.3			39.6	60.4
1950–59	78.8	21.2			39.6	60.4
1960–64	81.3	18.7			48.2	51.8
1965–69	85.7	14.3			67.6	32.4
1970–74	89.8	10.2			72.5	27.5
1975–80	91.8	8.2			78.0	22.0
Total	76.6	23.4	74.6	25.4	61.9	38.1
(N)	(207,259)	(63,312)	(46,785)	(15,970)	(20,676)	(12,715)

Source: 1980 Census Population, 5% PUMS, Sample A.

a Puerto Ricans born on the island are considered native-born citizens, therefore the immigration cohort data are unavailable for them. For purposes of these comparisons, Puerto Ricans born on the U.S. mainland are classified as native-born and all others are foreign-born.

relative to the foreign born generations, this may be more a reflection of the changing structure of industry than of a major improvement in their relative standing in the occupational structure (see Snipp and Tienda, 1982, 1984).

The higher representation of Cubans in managerial and professional jobs coincides also with their participation in an enclave economy consisting of Cuban owned and operated enterprises. As indicated in the historical discussion and affirmed by the data in Table 3, the emergence of the enclave is a direct consequence of the class composition of the early Cuban exiles. Two features of the data in Table 3 are noteworthy. First, the proportion of self-employed workers is substantially higher among the foreign-born Cubans as compared to Mexicans and Puerto Ricans who, for reasons elaborated above, were unable to reinforce their residential concentration in ethnic *barrios* with a viable economic base. The differential self-employment rate between native- and foreign-born Cubans arises largely because of the disproportionately higher share of self-employed workers among those who arrived prior to 1965. Subsequent cohorts continued to be more highly represented among the self-employed in 1980 than Mexicans who arrived during comparable periods, but the differentials were subsequently reduced.

A second noteworthy feature is that the prevalence of self-employment among the native-born was quite similar among Cubans and Mexicans, but not Puerto Ricans. This finding calls into question the long-term viability of the Cuban enclave sector, and supports claims about the deteriorating economic status of Puerto Ricans. It is conceivable that the relative underrepresentation of native-born Cubans among the self-employed simply reflects the lack of sufficient time to witness the inter-generational transfer of Cuban owned and operated enterprises from the immigrant generation to the second generation. However, it is also possible that the native-born generation may achieve its structural integration through employment in the private and public sector, especially if the existence of the enclave sector serves as a stepping-stone for more lucrative employment opportunities. It is too early to predict the fate of the Cuban economic enclave, but its viability may also hinge on the extent of cultural assimilation among the native-born, and its visibility as an ethnic enterprise may depend on the extent to which Cubans chose to elaborate the symbolic bases of their Hispanic ancestry.

Not only has the advantaged class position of Cubans vis-à-vis Mexicans and Puerto Ricans remained intact to the present time, but as a consequence of their greater socioeconomic success and middle-class orientations, the Cuban population may have experienced more extensive cultural assimilation than either Mexicans and Puerto Ricans, despite the fact that they have resided in the United States for a shorter period of time. Census data are not particularly suited to addressing questions about cultural reaffirmation and ethnic identity, but the data presented in Tables 4 and 5, albeit more suggestive than conclusive, provide some insights.

Consistent with the evolutionary perspective of ethnic assimilation, the pattern of Spanish language maintenance among Hispanics is lower among the native-born generations than among the foreign-born. What is striking, however,

Table 3. *Class of worker distribution of the Hispanic civilian labor force by national origin and immigration cohort.*

	Mexicans				Puerto Ricans[a]				Cubans			
	Wage private sector	Wage public sector	Self-employed	Unpaid workers	Wage private sector	Wage public sector	Self-employed	Unpaid workers	Wage private sector	Wage public sector	Self-employed	Unpaid workers
Native born	59.3	14.5	3.1	23.1	54.1	13.6	1.4	30.9	60.7	11.5	4.1	23.8
Foreign-born	65.2	5.2	2.7	26.8	50.3	10.4	2.0	37.2	61.6	7.1	6.8	24.5
1975–80	70.1	3.0	1.4	25.4					46.3	6.1	3.4	44.3
1970–74	73.4	3.8	2.0	20.8					62.0	5.2	5.3	27.5
1965–69	70.2	5.6	2.9	21.3					63.2	6.0	5.4	25.4
1960–64	67.2	7.6	3.3	21.8					64.1	9.4	8.6	17.9
1950–59	62.2	9.3	4.5	24.0					62.0	8.2	10.1	19.6
Before 1950	34.1	6.5	4.4	55.0					42.6	7.0	8.4	41.9
(N)	(166,003)	(30,566)	(8,050)	(65,952)	(32,305)	(7,147)	(1,160)	(22,143)	(20,527)	(2,523)	(2,173)	(8,160)

Source: 1980 Census of Population, 5% PUMS, Sample A.

a Puerto Ricans born on the island are considered native-born citizens, therefore the immigration cohort data are unavailable for them. For purposes of these comparisons, Puerto Ricans born on the U.S. mainland are classified as native-born and all others are foreign-born.

is that the retention of Spanish among U.S.-born Cubans — who, unlike Mexicans and Puerto Ricans, are essentially a second generation — is considerably lower than among Mexicans and Puerto Ricans. That the use of Spanish in the home should be lower among Puerto Ricans who were born on the island compared to foreign-born Mexicans is not surprising, because English is taught regularly in the island schools. However, the more rapid linguistic assimilation among Cubans is striking for it suggests that the socio-economic success of this group is creating class orientations that outweigh ethnic ones. Apparently the native-born generation is choosing *not* to elaborate the symbolic bases of its Hispanic ancestry.

Because of the predominance of immigrants among the Cuban population, it is not surprising that there is little variation in the extent of Spanish language use among those employed in various occupational categories. Nevertheless, Cubans employed as professionals and semi-professionals are less likely to use Spanish in the home than those employed in lower white-collar or blue-collar jobs. Although Mexicans and Puerto Ricans have lower rates of Spanish language retention overall than do Cubans, the aggregate statistic largely captures the higher prevalence of native-born individuals in the population. However, despite the higher rates of Spanish language retention among native-born Mexicans and Puerto Ricans, the corrosive forces of the Anglo environment are manifested in the lower levels of Spanish retention among the more successful members of the community — those whose incomes are well above the poverty levels, and who hold white-collar jobs.

Another indicator of the coherence of 'Hispanicity' among the Mexican, Puerto Rican and Cuban origin populations is found in the extent to which they identify consistently as members of an ancestry group. For the tabulations reported in Table 5 we computed the proportion of individuals whose response to the ancestry question matched their response to the full-enumeration Spanish origin item. In other words, of the individuals who self-identified themselves as being of Spanish origin (specified by nationality), the figures reported indicate the proportions who also reported that their ancestry was either Mexican, Puerto Rican or Cuban. Although this measure is crude, it serves to illustrate the diversity in the extent of uniform ethnic identification among the groups.

Overall, the data indicate greater ethnic consistency among the two most disadvantaged groups, the Mexicans and Puerto Ricans, while the Cubans exhibit greater diversity in the extent to which they identify as ethnics. For Mexicans and Puerto Ricans, the use of Spanish in the home is the major factor differentiating those who are consistent in reporting their Hispanic ancestry, although poverty status and immigration status also contributes to the diversity in their Hispanic identity. Cubans present a different picture. Not only are the native-born notably less likely than their foreign-born counterparts to report an ancestry consistent with their self-reported Spanish origin, but they are also substantially less likely than individuals of either Mexican or Puerto Rican origin to identify consistently as Cubans. In part, this may reflect the homogenizing assimilation processes that often accompany rapid socioeconomic success, but it is noteworthy that this pattern has not been replicated by the native-born Mexicans or Puerto Ricans.

In the case of Hispanics, the overriding explanation for the pronounced differences in the cultural manifestations of ethnicity can only be class-

Table 4. *Percentage of the Hispanic civilian labor force who reported speaking Spanish at home in 1980 by selected socio-demographic characteristics and national origin.*

Characteristic	Mexicans	Puerto Ricans[a]	Cubans
Immigration cohort			
Native-born	72.6	73.0	61.5
Foreign-born	96.8	94.8	96.8
1975–80	98.1		96.7
1970–74	98.0		98.4
1965–69	97.6		98.1
1960–64	96.2		96.4
1950–59	95.0		94.2
Before 1950	93.2		84.4
Occupation			
Professional	74.8	81.4	88.2
Semiprofessional	71.8	82.3	89.6
Farmer	81.3	83.8	81.5
Manager	75.9	81.8	91.0
Clerical	73.4	85.5	93.1
Sales	72.2	79.3	91.5
Craft	80.9	86.3	93.7
Operative	84.7	91.5	95.8
Service worker	79.7	85.3	91.8
Laborer	82.0	86.0	92.6
Farm laborer	93.8	87.2	94.6
Poverty status			
Non-poor	78.5	85.0	93.0
Near poor	86.4	91.5	94.1
Poor	84.9	92.6	92.6
Overall percentage	80.9	88.2	93.1
(N)	(270,571)	(62,755)	(33,391)

Source: 1980 Census of Population, 5% PUMS, Sample A.

a Puerto Ricans born on the island are considered native-born citizens, therefore the immigration cohort data are unavailable for them. For purposes of these comparisons, Puerto Ricans born on the U.S. mainland are classified as native-born and all others are foreign-born.

Table 5. *Proportion of Hispanic civilian labor force who reported consistent ancestry and origin responses in 1980 by selected socio-demographic characteristics and national origin.*

Selected characteristics	Mexicans		Puerto Ricans[a]		Cubans	
	Native	Foreign	Native	Foreign	Native	Foreign
Occupation						
Professional	.87	.90	.81	.88	.70	.91
Semiprofessional	.88	.89	.78	.90	.76	.91
Farmer	.77	.91	.44	.86	.40	.86
Manager	.87	.91	.84	.88	.69	.90
Clerical	.88	.91	.84	.89	.74	.92
Sales	.86	.92	.78	.85	.74	.90
Craft	.87	.94	.80	.89	.68	.91
Operative	.86	.94	.81	.88	.69	.92
Service worker	.84	.93	.78	.87	.70	.90
Laborer	.86	.94	.80	.87	.78	.90
Farm laborer	.85	.93	.69	.88	.36	.76
Spanish spoken[b]						
No	.68	.68	.63	.70	.51	.69
Yes	.92	.94	.88	.89	.85	.91
Poverty status						
Non-poor	.81	.93	.80	.88	.73	.91
Near poor	.85	.94	.83	.89	.72	.91
Poor	.81	.93	.81	.88	.60	.90
Overall proportion	.86	.93	.81	.88	.72	.91
(N)	(177,149)	(93,422)	(19,078)	(43,677)	(3,503)	(29,888)

Source: 1980 Census of Population, 5% PUMS, Sample A.
a Puerto Ricans born on the island are considered native-born citizens, therefore the immigration cohort data are unavailable for them. For purposes of these comparisons, Puerto Ricans born on the U.S. mainland are classified as native-born and others are foreign-born.
b Spanish spoken at home.

based, or in Vincent's (1974) terms, grounded in the coincidence of ethnic origin with minority status. And, while the option of elaborating the symbolic bases of Cuban origin are certainly more open to the Cuban population by virtue of its relatively more advantaged position vis-à-vis Mexicans and Puerto Ricans, members of the native-born generation apparently are not choosing to elaborate their Hispanic ethnicity along cultural lines or nationality. Mexicans and Puerto Ricans, on the other hand, persist in their greater adherence to the cultural and nationality expressions of their ethnicity. In their experience, however, it is not only symbolism that maintains the cultural expressions intact, but also their disadvantaged minority position and the continued revitalization of ethnic symbols through the process of labor migration.

Conclusion

Mexicans, Puerto Ricans and Cubans each hold a distinct place within the range of experiences shaping their economic and cultural integration into American society. The Puerto Rican case provides the strongest support for the link between intense ethnic identity and lower class positioning. That Cubans have not remained segregated in a secondary labor market, have been the most successful of the three groups, and are demonstrating tendencies towards integration with Anglos lends positive support from the other direction. Their distinct status at entry and class resources are the most significant factors distinguishing Cuban refugees from Mexican and Puerto Rican immigrants. That the Mexican-American experience is more ambiguous and diverse can be explained by their numerical size and their longer history in the United States.

The indicators pointing to increasing assimilation of Chicanos must be weighed against the isolation, extreme poverty and lack of control over life as it exists in the *barrios*. In contrast to Barrera's claim to class integration, can the small rising Chicano middle class play the role of native elite within a formerly colonized group? (Almaguer 1974). How is one to interpret the ongoing ethnic contact as it exists between classes (as Chicano businesses, for example, rely on Chicano clientele) or as it is affected by immigration? For Chicanos it is difficult to envision a future when ethnic distinctions within social class divisions will fade away. The cloudiness of what Barrera has labeled 'the current period of confusion and redefinition' is maintained by the continuing influx of new immigrants during a period of economic instability as well as imprecise data to evaluate truly longitudinal comparisons of successive immigrant cohorts and generational transitions.

For Mexicans and Puerto Ricans, isolation in ethnic communities and other manifestations of ethnicity are structurally produced by their concentrations in minority labor markets and by the continued influx of immigrants who help to renew cultural traditions and subsequently elaborate them as a basis for social solidarity. In turn ethnically based solidarity serves as a protection and source of resistance against oppression. For Cubans, the cohesiveness of their ethnic community has been a key factor facilitating initial adjustment and success. Whether that success will ensure the survival of the ethnically enclosed community or lead to its decline remains to be seen. Initial evidence based on the most recent census suggests a decline as the first generation of native-born Cubans demonstrate an unusual ability to assimilate.

Our conceptual framework implies that ethnicity is structured by the relationship of a given national origin group to the system of production. Immigration history, reception factors in the United States and race shape this relationship over time. The elaboration of ethnicity as historically emergent further points to the intersecting nature of class and ethnicity as demonstrated by the diverse outcomes of the three Hispanic national origin groups. The labor market experience of Hispanics has been chosen as a key factor in the structuring of ethnicity because it strongly influences subsequent exposure to and interactions with other races, social classes and cultural forces.

On balance, the market experience of Hispanics has been chosen as a key factor in the structuring of ethnicity because it strongly influences subsequent exposure to and interactions with other races, social classes and cultural forces. Yet obviously, ethnicity is not simply a function of occupational and economic rewards. Ethnic identity as manifested by language, religion, race and national origin is only one part of a much broader, multidimensional social identity (Arce, 1981). For this reason, the process of integration cannot be unidirectional, proceeding from an unassimilated beginning to an assimilated end, from marginality to middle class. The complexities of the interaction between social and ethnic identities are ·beyond the scope of this paper which only provides a starting point for further exploration − an exploration urgently needed if a clearer conception of Hispanic ethnicity is to emerge from the distortions of the past.

Note

*This research was supported by a grant from the Social Science Research Council and Russell Sage Foundation and by funds from the Graduate School Research Committee of the University of Wisconsin-Madison. Computational support is from a grant to the Center for Demography and Ecology from the Center for Population of NICHD (HD–05876). We acknowledge institutional support from the College of Agricultural and Life Sciences of the University of Wisconsin, and computational assistance from Ding-Tzann Lii.

References

ACUÑA, RUDOLFO 1971 *Occupied America: The Chicano Struggle Toward Liberation.* San Francisco: Canfield Press.
ALMAGUER, TOMAS 1974 'Historical Notes on Chicano Oppression: The Dialectics of Race and Class Domination in North America.' *Aztlan* 5 (1): 27–56.
ALVAREZ, RODOLFO 1973 'The Psycho-Historical and Socioeconomic Development of the Chicano Community in the United States.' *Social Science Quarterly* 53 (4): 902–44.

ARCE, CARLOS 1981 'A Reconsideration of Chicano Culture and Identity.' *Daedalus* 110 (Spring): 177–92.

BACH, ROBERT 1980 'The New Cuban Immigrants: Their Background and Prospects.' *Monthly Labor Review* 103 (October): 39–46.

BARRERA, MARIO 1979 *Race and Class in the Southwest*. Notre Dame, Ind.: University of Notre Dame Press.

BLAUNER, ROBERT 1975 'Colonized and Immigrant Minorities,' in *Majority and Minority*, ed. Norman Yetman and C.H. Steele. Boston: Allyn & Bacon.

BONACICH, EDNA 1972 'A Theory of Ethnic Antagonism: The Split Labor Market.' *American Sociological Review* 37 (October): 547–59.

BONACICH, EDNA 1980 'Class Approaches to Ethnicity and Race.' *The Insurgent Sociologist* 10 (1): 9–23.

BONILLA, FRANK 1974 'Por que seguiremos siendo puertorriqueños' in *Puerto Rico and Puerto Ricans*, eds Alberto Lopez and James Petras. Cambridge, Mass.: Schenkman Publishing Co.

BUROWOY, MICHAEL 1976 'The Functions and Reproduction of Migrant Labor: Comparative Material from Southern African and the United States.' *American Journal of Sociology* 81 (5): 1050–87.

CASAL, LOURDES, and HERNANDEZ, ANDRES 1975 'Cubans in the U.S.: A Survey of the Literature.' *Cuban Studies* 5 (2): 25–51.

CENTRO DE ESTUDIOS PUERTORRIQUENOS 1979 *Labor Migration Under Capitalism*. New York: Monthly Review Press.

FITZPATRICK, JOSEPH P., and GURAK, DOUGLAS M. 1979 *Hispanic Intermarriage in New York City*. New York: Hispanic Research Center Monograph, Fordham University.

GAARDER, BRUCE 1977 *Bilingual Schooling and the Survival of Spanish in the United States*. Rawley, Mass.: Newbury House.

GANS, HERBERT J. 1979 'Symbolic Ethnicity: The Future of Ethnic Groups and Cultures in America.' *Ethnic and Racial Studies* 2 (1): 1–19.

GORDON, MILTON 1964 *Assimilation in American Life: The Role of Race, Religion and National Origins*. New York: Oxford University Press.

HIRSCHMAN, CHARLES 1982 'America's Melting Pot Reconsidered.' *American Review of Sociology* 9: 397–423.

LOPEZ, ALBERTO 1974 'The Puerto Rican Diaspora,' in *Puerto Rico and Puerto Ricans*, ed. Alberto Lopez and James Petras. Cambridge, Mass.: Schenkman Publishing Co.

MASSEY, DOUGLAS 1981 'Dimensions of the New Immigration to the U.S. and the Prospects for Assimilation.' *Annual Review of Sociology* 7: 57–83.

MOORE, JOAN 1970 'Colonialism: The Case of the Mexican Americans.' *Social Problems* 17 (4): 463–72.

PARK, R.E. 1950 *Race and Culture*. Glencoe, Ill.: Free Press.

PORTES, ALEJANDRO 1969 'Dilemmas of a Golden Exile: Integration of Refugee Families in Milwaukee.' *American Sociological Review* 34 (4): 505–19.

PORTES, ALEJANDRO, and BACH, ROBERT L. 1980 'Immigrant Earnings: Cuban and Mexican Immigrants in the U.S.' *International Migration Review* 14 (3): 315–37.

ROGG, ELEANOR, and COONEY, ROSEMARY 1980 *Adaptation and Adjustment of Cubans: West New York, N.J.* New York: Hispanic Reserach Center Monograph, Fordham University.

SAMORA, JULIAN 1971 *Loss Mojados: The Wetback Story*. Notre Dame, Ind.: University of Notre Dame Press.

SARAGOZA, ALEX 1983 'The Conceptualization of the History of the Chicano Family,' in Albert Camarillo Valdez and Tomas Almaguer (eds.), *The State of Chicano Research in Family, Labor and Migration Studies*. Stanford, Calif. Stanford Center for Chicano Research.

SINGELMANN, JOACHIM, and TIENDA, MARTA 1984 'The Process of Occupational

74   *Candace Nelson and Marta Tienda*

Change in a Service Economy: The Case of the United States, 1960–1980,' in Ruth Finnegan, Duncan Gallie, and Bryan Roberts (eds.) *Labour Markets*. Manchester, England: University of Manchester Press.

SNIPP, C. MATTHEW, and TIENDA, MARTA 1982 'New Perspectives on Chicano Intergenerational Mobility'. *Social Science Journal* 19 (2): 37–49.

TIENDA, MARTA 1980 'Familism and Structural Assimilation of Mexican Immigrants in the United States' *International Migration Review* 14: (3): 383–408.

TIENDA, MARTA 1981 'The Mexican American Population,' pp. 502–48 in Amos Hawly and Sara Mills Mazie (eds.), *Nonmetropolitan America in Transition*. Chapel Hill: University of North Carolina Press.

TIENDA, MARTA 1984 'The Puerto Rican Worker: Current Labor Market Status and Future Prospects,' in *Puerto Ricans in the Mid-Eighties: An American Challenge*. Washington, D.C.: National Puerto Rican Coalition.

U.S. COMMISSION ON CIVIL RIGHTS 1976 *Puerto Ricans in the Continental United States: An Uncertain Future* Washington, D.C.: U.S. Government Printing Office.

VINCENT, JOAN 1974 'The Structuring of Ethnicity.' *Human Organization* 33 (4): 375–9.

WILSON, KENNETH, and PORTES, ALEJANDRO 1980 'Immigrant Enclaves: An Analysis of the Labor Market Experiences of Cubans in Miami.' *American Journal of Sociology* 86:2.

YANCEY, WILLIAM, ERIKSON, EUGENE, and JULIANI, RICHARD 1976 'Emergent Ethnicity: A Review and Reformulation.' *American Sociological Review* 41(3): 391–403.

4 The road to parity: determinants of the socioeconomic achievements of Asian Americans*

Victor Nee and Jimy Sanders
University of California Santa Barbara

In recent decades Asian Americans have made significant socioeconomic gains, which have resulted in changing societal perceptions of Asian Americans. The pre-World War II pattern of ethnic isolation and discrimination has given way to a trend more similar to the assimilation processes of white ethnic groups, particularly those that have pursued higher education as a means of getting ahead. It is now widely recognized that Asian Americans are an exception among non-white minority groups in that they have made great strides in closing the socioeconomic gap between themselves and whites. Though researchers point to areas of continuing inequality, they emphasize the progress made in achieving parity, especially in the case of Japanese Americans (Hirschman & Wong, 1981; Sowell, 1981). Indexes of assimilation, such as occupational distribution, educational attainment, residence, and intermarriage are cited as evidence of the trend towards full assimilation (Montero, 1977, 1981; Kuo and Lin, 1977; Lee, 1960).

By 1969, Chinese and Japanese Americans nationwide appeared to have pulled roughly even with whites in average earnings (Chiswick, 1980). Immigrant Chinese and Japanese Americans reported earning somewhat less than white immigrants, but on the average, native-born Chinese and Japanese Americans reported having higher incomes than native-born whites. On the other hand, the earnings of native-born and immigrant Filipino Americans were substantially lower than those reported by Chinese, Japanese, and white Americans. These studies have raised serious questions about Blauner's (1972) thesis which maintains that America is divided by a caste system in which nonwhites are locked into positions of subordination. Moreover, the progress made by Asian Americans and Hispanics has stimulated new interest in the viability of America as a society in which ethnic groups eventually assimilate over a long historical process into the mainstream society (Hirschman, 1983; Shibutani and Kwan, 1965; Warner and Srole, 1945). Though the literature provides considerable evidence that Asian Americans have improved their economic lot, there remains uncertainty about the relative economic advances of different Asian American groups, and the explanation for their postwar socioeconomic gains (e.g., Wong, 1982).

Over the past twenty years, sociologists' examination of inequality in the U.S. has progressed from the initial status attainment model (Duncan and Hodge, 1963), to more detailed accounts of status attainment processes (e.g., Sewell and Hauser, 1975), to class analyses (e.g., Wright and Perrone, 1977), and the study of labor market segmentation in terms of detailed occupations (e.g., Stolzenberg, 1975) and more general sector distinctions (e.g., Hodson, 1978). A consensus that has emerged with this literature is that it is necessary to consider the employment circumstances of individuals in some detail when attempting to understand processes of earnings-allocation.[1]

The labor market and occupational concentrations of Asian Americans may be exceptionally important in determining earnings. Scholars have stressed the 'middleman minority role' of Asians in status attainment processes (Loewen, 1971; Kitano, 1974). Some have argued that the strength of kinship ties and ethnic institutions provide Asian Americans with both the cultural predisposition to middlemen minority roles and the comparative advantages to succeed in small businesses (Light, 1972). Bonacich (1973) has maintained that the structural position of a 'sojourner community' gives rise to the ethnic solidarity that promotes the building of an ethnic economy and perpetuates an orientation to middleman roles. But the fact that Filipino and Mexican sojourners have not developed strong ethnic economies, whereas recent Korean immigrants have, raises doubt about the importance of sojourning in the emergence of immigrant enclave economies. Others have argued that the exclusion of Asians from most jobs left them with no alternative but to concentrate in small businesses in ethnic enclaves (Li, 1977). Whatever the interpretation of the causes of Asian concentration in ethnic enterprise, Chinese and Japanese Americans have historically been concentrated in small businesses (Broom and Riemer, 1973; Glick, 1980).

Scholars have analyzed the importance of ethnic economies in reinforcing ethnic hostility and segregation (Bonacich and Modell, 1980), in suppressing earnings by creating an urban political economy in which ethnic enclaves provide a source of cheap labor for outside firms (Nee and Nee, 1973), and in sustaining stereotypes that work against the acceptance of Asians in jobs outside of the ethnic economy (Lyman, 1977). Wilson and Portes (1980) point out that an immigrant enclave economy must be seen as distinct from both the primary and secondary labor markets. Enclave economies provide immigrant/minority groups with advantages in generating higher returns on human capital investments through entrepreneurship. Though workers in the enclave economy have low-wage jobs similar to the secondary economy, ethnically controlled avenues for economic mobility in the enclave may result in benefits not available to workers in the secondary economy. For example, a seamstress may organize her own garment shop with limited capital in an environment where such opportunities are fostered by the existence of an ethnic garment subcontracting industry; whereas a stoop agricultural laborer has little alternative but to continue selling his labor at low wages. Thus whether or not immigrant/minority groups are incorporated into an enclave economy can be decisive in determining whether socioeconomic mobility will be achieved. However, socioeconomic mobility also appears to be open to immigrant/minorities who acquire credentials (e.g., a college degree) that allow them to obtain jobs in the primary labor market (Portes, 1981).

An important debate in the literature on Asian American status attainment is whether cultural or structural factors are decisive in explaining the socioeconomic gains of Asian Americans. Scholars have argued that Asian values are, in effect, similar to the Protestant Ethic and encourage behavior similar to that of the white middle class (Kitano, 1969; Peterson, 1966, 1971; Caudill and De Vos, 1965; Schwartz, 1971). Such cultural explanations have been criticized by sociologists more sensitive to historical and structural explanations of socioeconomic mobility (Lieberson, 1980). Recent studies, however, have sought to reconcile cultural perspectives through comparative historical analysis emphasizing cultural and labor market transformations in both the sending and receiving societies (Nee and Wong, 1984).

Historical background

Asian immigrants were drawn to America in the latter part of the nineteenth century by the demand for cheap labor to build the industrial and agricultural infrastructure of the West Coast. Chinese first came to America to take part in the California Gold Rush, but soon became the major source of cheap labor for early California entrepreneurs in the construction of the transcontinental railroad, in land reclamation and irrigation, mining, and in manufacturing industries. The Chinese were predominantly male peasants who came as 'sojourners' with the intention of saving capital while sending remittances back to their families and, eventually, retiring to their native villages. Few Chinese established families or permanent residence during the first half-century of settlement in America. The willingness of the Chinese to work for low wages ignited violent conflict with white laborers which culminated in 1882 with the passage of the Chinese Exclusion Act. This law curtailed further large-scale immigration of Chinese laborers to the U.S.

Japanese immigrants arrived on the West Coast and in Hawaii shortly after the termination of Chinese immigration. The Japanese were also male sojourners, but due to differences in village culture, which resulted in weaker ties to family and village than in the case of Chinese sojourners (Nee and Wong, 1984), Japanese laborers soon brought wives to the U.S. After the establishment of families, many Japanese immigrants left low-wage labor to start truck farms and other small businesses that utilized household labor (Yanagisako, 1979). Opposition to Japanese immigration gradually increased as economic competition intensified, and resulted in the exclusion of additional Japanese immigrants following the Gentlemen's Agreement with Japan in 1909 and the passage of the Immigration Act of 1924.

With the closure of Japan as a source of cheap labor, American capitalists turned to the Philippines and Mexico. Large scale immigration of Filipino male laborers began in the 1920s, and like previous Asian migrants Filipino laborers were sought to fill labor demand for stoop agricultural work and other low-wage jobs. As in the cases of the Chinese and Japanese, white opposition to Filipino immigration resulted in the exclusion of this group by the Tydings-McDuffie Act in 1934.

Prior to World War II, Chinese and Japanese Americans were concentrated in ethnic economies while Filipino Americans were concentrated in low-wage jobs in the secondary labor market. The evolution of a second-generation of Chinese and Japanese Americans accelerated the acculturation of these groups as their communities acquired a more settled character. Despite the high educational attainment of the native-born Chinese and Japanese, it was not until the end of World War II that Asian Americans began to break through the barriers established by institutional racism and acquire jobs in the primary labor market (Bonacich and Modell, 1980; Nee and Nee 1973).

Large-scale immigration of Asians to the U.S. resumed following the passage of the Immigration Act of 1965. The Act established quotas of 20,000 immigrants per year for each country in both the Eastern and Western hemispheres. As a result of this more recent immigration, with the exception of Japanese Americans, foreign-born Asian Americans now outnumber their native-born counterparts. The character of immigration since 1965 has changed dramatically from earlier immigration in that the new immigrants from Korea, Hong Kong, Taiwan, and India are predominantly urban families with a high percentage of college-educated professionals and white-collar workers. However, entirely new Asian American ethnic groups including Vietnamese, Hmong, Thais and other Southeast Asian nationalities are now emerging in American society. Asian and Pacific Island immigration now constitutes the largest source of legal immigration (44 percent in 1983) to the United States (Fawcett *et al.*, 1984). California continues to be the major end-point of immigration from Asia.

The study

The study focuses on the labor market and occupation profiles of Chinese, Japanese, Filipino and white Americans, and how these labor force characteristics affect earnings. We also attempt to distinguish earning disadvantages asssociated with immigration from earning disadvantages more closely linked to ethnicity. We do not study new Asian American ethnic groups such as Koreans and Vietnamese, because the native-born of these groups have not yet entered the labor market in large numbers.

As the most common end-point of Asian migration, California provides a natural social laboratory for studying how immigrants from Asia and native-born Asian Americans compare to whites in earnings. Not only do large native- and foreign-born populations reside in the state, Asian subcommunities and ethnic economies also exist. These are characteristics seen almost nowhere else on the mainland of the U.S. especially on the scale that exists in California. In 1980, approximately 40 percent of all Chinese, 37 percent of all Japanese, and 46 percent of all Filipino Americans lived in California. At this time, there were 322, 262, and 358 thousand Chinese, Japanese and Filipino Americans residing in California.

We restrict the study to California because only in such a setting is it possible to capture the 'extra' cost of discrimination that hypothetically may be encountered by minorities who are geographically concentrated rather than widely dispersed. In theory, the concentration of Asian Americans in California may give rise to discrimination from whites who perceive themselves to be threatened economically (or otherwise) by large groups of 'outsiders' (Allport, 1954; Williams, 1947). On the other hand, it is plausible that the relatively large numbers of Asian Americans in California may contribute to lower levels of discrimination due to increased contact and interaction between whites and Asians. To the degree that Robert Park's (1950) contact-hypothesis is accurate, and to the extent that the necessary conditions of the hypothesis (i.e., equal intergroup status, a sharing of goals, cooperative interaction, and a supportive environment) are reasonably well met, Asian Americans in California may enjoy greater social acceptance than elsewhere.

Another reason to concentrate on California is that since approximately 40 percent of all Asian Americans compared to less than 10 percent of all whites in the U.S. live in California, the favorable income position of Japanese and Chinese Americans observed at the national level (e.g. Chiswick, 1980) may partly be an artifact of the relatively high per-capita income of Californians. In 1980, per capita income in California was fourth highest among all states. Californians typically earned 18 percent more than residents of the median income states of New Hampshire and Oregon (Statistical Abstract of the United States, 1982/83:427).

The model

The model contains two dummy variables that differentiate workers by sectors of employment. One variable distinguishes public sector workers. These include federal, state, and municipal employees. The second variable combines all private sector salary- and wage-earners, including both highly paid professionals and skilled workers in the primary labor market and low-wage earners in the secondary labor market. Though it would be desirable to distinguish between primary and secondary labor markets in the sector variables, we think it is unlikely that such distinctions can be made accurately from census data. The reference group is made up of self-employed workers. This 'omitted' sector consists predominantly of owners of small businesses. While there are a few large business owners in this category, the variable is a sound indicator of small business ownership — especially among Asian Americans, because Asian American enterprises in California are virtually all small businesses (Light, 1972).[2]

To take into account variation across occupations, we use the thirteen-category standard occupational classification system developed in 1977 and revised in 1980 by the Office of Federal Statistical Policy and Standards.

This system substantially differs from previous classifications developed by the U.S. Census Bureau. Given the recent and profound changes in labor markets due to the rise of high-tech industries, and the decline of heavy industry, other measures that distinguish workers' 'places' in the labor market, like the 1970 based socioeconomic index (SEI), are probably less appropriate.[3]

We also model several other individual characteristics generally recognized as essential to the accurate specification of an earnings equation. Earnings tend to increase more swiftly in the early and middle career than in the later career. To capture this relationship, we include both age and age squared in the equation. If our analysis documents the expected nonlinearity, the age coefficient will be positive and the age squared coefficient will be negative. With a single dummy variable, we compare persons who are presently married and living with their spouse to all others because of the tendency for married men to earn more than other men. While much of this difference is accounted for by the generally higher educational attainments and greater labor force participation rates of married men, a net married versus unmarried difference appears to remain. Though the social psychology of the relationship is not thoroughly understood, the relationship has been observed for some time. We expect the direct relationship between education and earnings to approximate a positive linear function. Therefore, we include years of schooling in the equation.[4] Since earnings are also influenced by how much one works, the number of weeks worked in 1979 is multiplied by the number of hours worked weekly when employed to yield a single variable representing the amount of time spent working.[5] We model the relationship as linear, and of course expect it to be positive. Because the inability to communicate effectively in English is likely to restrict employment opportunities, we expect that English speaking ability and earnings are also related. To examine this hypothesis, we include a five-point Likert-type measure of English speaking skills, assuming interval scaling. High values on this variable represent poor English skills.

For immigrants, we also consider whether U.S. citizenship has been acquired and we distinguish 'early immigrants' from 'new immigrants.' Dummy variables are used to make these comparisons. Citizenship presumably widens workers' opportunities in the labor market and may thus lead to higher earnings. We define the new immigrants as those who migrated to the U.S. no earlier than 1965, when the immigration law allowing large-scale immigration from Asia was enacted.

It is important to distinguish between the dislocation effects experienced in immigration and costs attributable to ethnicity. Recent immigrants, especially those from non-English-speaking cultures, experience difficulties in adjustment to their new society, particularly in obtaining jobs commensurate with their education and work experience. This may be especially true of professional and white-collar immigrants who received their training and education abroad. Immigrant groups that are incorporated into ethnic economies also experience dislocations, as is evident in the case of Korean immigrant professionals who open small businesses because they are unable to gain jobs in their areas of expertise (Kim, 1981). The lack of informal social networks and cultural skills needed to get ahead in the mainstream American economy and society is a disadvantage shared by most recent immigrant groups, and should not be confused with disadvantages associated with ethnicity.

Controlling for immigrant status, in conjunction with ethnicity, helps us to disentangle costs of immigration from costs of ethnicity. A pattern wherein income-returns across the four native-born (or immigrant) groups are more similar to one another than the income-returns of the immigrants and native-born of the same ethnicity, would be consistent with the cost of immigration explanation. Alternatively, a tendency for the native-born and immigrant groups of each ethnicity to be more similar in earning-returns than the native-born (or immigrants) across the four ethnic groups would be consistent with the cost of ethnicity explanation.[6]

Data

The data for Asian Americans are from the 5 percent 1980 U.S. Census public use sample of residents of standard metropolitan statistical areas (SMSA) in the state of California. SMSAs are populated predominantly by urban dwellers but rural areas are also included. We use the 1 percent 1980 Census sample for whites. The sampling procedures for the 1 and 5 percent samples are identical, therefore the comparative nature of our study is unaffected by the use of different samples for Asian Americans and whites. Because Asian Americans in California are predominantely SMSA dwellers, the emphasis on SMSA residents should not be a liability. In fact, approximately 95 percent of all Californians reside in SMSAs. The data reflect self-reports and adjustments made by the Census Bureau.[7]

The analysis is restricted to civilian men aged 25 through 64 who were employed in 1979. Earnings are measured as the sum of 1979 wages, salaries, and self-employment income in dollars. Although we acknowledge the importance of household income (paid and unpaid), and the limitations of considering only the labor market earnings of male adults, we have not yet resolved, to our own satisfaction, the additional theoretical and methodological considerations required of a study that integrates entire households into one model.

Socioeconomic characteristics

Asian Americans make up a heterogeneous population with significant diversity between ethnic groups and between the native-born and immigrants of each group. As seen from Table 1, native-born Chinese have the highest level of education of any group we study, with an average educational attainment of 17.2 years compared to the native-born white average of 16 years. Chinese immigrants average 15.1 years of schooling compared to 13.5 for white immigrants. The standard deviation in years of schooling suggests that immigrant Chinese Americans ($s = 5.3$) are more heterogeneous in educational attainments than their native-born counterparts (s = 3.0). By contrast, native-born and immigrant Japanese Americans are similarly educated with mean educational attainments of 16.4 and 16.7 years respectively. Native-born Filipino Americans are less educated than native-born whites, but Filipino immigrants, who have a mean educational attainment of 16.2 years, tend to have more education than white and Chinese American immigrants.

In general, Asian Americans appear to be highly educated groups, and have achieved parity with whites in educational attainment, with the exception of native-born Filipinos. Indeed, if present trends continue, Asian Americans will exceed whites in educational attainment, particularly in fields, such as engineering, computer science, and the natural sciences. At the major campuses of the University of California (Berkeley and Los Angeles), Asian Americans currently make up one-fifth of all enrollments. We can see the effect of high educational achievement on occupational distribution most clearly in the case of native-born Chinese Americans. Fifty percent of the native-born Chinese in our sample are in administrative, professional and technical occupations. This compares to 38 percent among native-born whites. Immigrant Chinese are also more likely than white immigrants to have these occupations. Chinese immigrants are unlike other groups in that fully one-fourth of the Chinese immigrants are concentrated in the business and household service sector. Native-born Chinese are also unique in that one-third of this group works in the public sector. Perhaps surprisingly, immigrant Chinese and whites are just as likely to be self-employed, and native-born whites are more likely to be self-employed than native-born Chinese.

Native-born Japanese and whites are similarly concentrated in high-status administrative, professional and technical jobs (40 percent and 38 percent respectively), however Japanese Americans are less concentrated in semi-skilled occupations than whites. As would be expected from the similar educational attainments of both the native-born and immigrant Japanese, their occupational profiles are similar. However, Japanese immigrants are more likely to be in administrative and managerial positions, possibly due to the large number of Japanese firms represented in California. Both the native-born and immigrant Japanese are more highly concentrated in self-employment than any other group we study. In part, this reflects Japanese American participation in truck farming, an area where Japanese Americans have been concentrated since the early decades of the twentieth century (Broom and Riemer, 1973).

It is interesting to note that both Chinese and Japanese Americans are concentrated in jobs that are less vulnerable to the decline of America's heavy industrial base than are whites. Filipino Americans, on the other hand, appear to be more of a working-class ethnic group, with greater occupational concentration in semi-skilled jobs. Compared to the other Asian groups, Filipinos are less represented in high-status occupations. The higher educational attainments of immigrants, however, probably accounts for their somewhat lower concentration in manual labor jobs than the native-born Filipino Americans. The critical difference between the Filipino and the Chinese and Japanese

Table 1. *Means and percentages by subgroups.*

Variables	Whites		Japanese		Chinese		Filipinos	
	Native-born (N = 34,687)	Immigrants (N = 4,540)	Native-born (N = 1,266)	Immigrants (N = 304)	Native-born (N = 818)	Immigrants (N = 1,773)	Native-born (N = 405)	Immigrants (N = 1,596)
Individual income (1979)[b]	21505.89	17957.53	20163.54	20310.07	20841.36	15674.75	15482.10	14058.48
Age[b]	41.06	40.77	44.66	37.60	39.71	41.00	35.32	40.13
Age squared[b]	1814.97	1784.85	2134.31	1500.59	1697.96	1797.56	1334.14	1719.32
Education[b]	16.02	13.52	16.35	16.65	17.23	15.06	15.27	16.15
Married	.72	.78	.71	.68	.67	.80	.66	.83
Hours worked in 1979[b]	2032.80	1990.64	2093.86	2076.92	2016.72	1965.76	1901.55	1837.31
Self-employed	.16	.15	.23	.21	.13	.16	.06	.04
Public sector employment	.16	.07	.23	.09	.32	.12	.23	.22
Corporate sector employment	.68	.78	.54	.70	.56	.72	.71	.74
Executive, administrative and managerial	.18	.12	.15	.22	.16	.14	.10	.09
Professional specialties	.16	.12	.19	.18	.26	.19	.10	.09
Technicians	.04	.03	.06	.04	.08	.05	.06	.07
Sales	.11	.08	.09	.09	.11	.08	.08	.04
Administrative support including clerical	.07	.05	.10	.04	.13	.08	.13	.20
Protective services	.03	.01	.01	.01[a]	.02	.00[a]	.02	.03
Business and household services	.04	.08	.03	.12	.04	.25	.08	.16
Farming, forestry and fishing	.02	.06	.14	.10	.00[a]	.01	.05	.05
Precision production and craft	.20	.22	.13	.11	.11	.11	.18	.12
Operators	.05	.13	.04	.04	.03	.05	.08	.08
Transportation	.06	.04	.03	.03[a]	.03	.01	.07	.03
Laborers	.03	.05	.03	.02[a]	.02	.02	.06	.03
English skills[b]	1.02	1.74	.51	1.67	.76	1.95	.38	1.38
U.S. citizenship	—	.43	—	.32	—	.52	—	.55
New immigrants	—	.49	—	.59	—	.67	—	.78

a n < 10

b Means, otherwise the values are percentages (in decimal form). For example, 72% of the native-born whites are married.

American ethnic groups may be the very low level of Filipino small business ownership. On the other hand, Filipino immigrants are considerably more concentrated in government jobs than Chinese and Japanese immigrants. It may be that many Filipino immigrants are able to use their work experience with the U.S. Navy to gain civil service jobs. In every case, immigrants reported working fewer hours than the native-born, suggesting that underemployment may be a problem for immigrants. It should also be noted that within both the native-born and immigrant subgroups, the Japanese reported the most work time while Filipinos reported the least work time.[8]

The effect of the resumption of large-scale immigration from Asia can be seen in the rapid growth of the immigrant population for Chinese and Filipino Americans. Over 68 percent of the Chinese Americans in our sample are immigrants, 67 percent of whom have arrived since 1965. Almost 80 percent of the Filipino American sample members are immigrants, 78 percent of whom have arrived since 1965. By contrast, Japanese immigration has been low, which is reflected in the higher proportion of native-born in the Japanese American sample. Less than 20 percent of the Japanese American sample members are immigrants. Japanese Americans are the most settled Asian group due to the small size and homogeneous character of the new Japanese immigration, and the more dispersed residential pattern of both the native — and foreign-born. While over half of the Chinese and Filipino immigrants are citizens of the U.S. fewer than one-third of the Japanese immigrants are U.S. citizens.

Four groups reported distinctly high earnings in 1979. On the average, native-born whites and Chinese Americans, and both native-born and immigrant Japanese Americans reported earnings in excess of 20 thousand dollars. Chinese American immigrants and native-born Filipino Americans reported earning well over 15 thousand dollars while Filipino American immigrants reported earning just over 14 thousand dollars. In contrast, average earnings among white immigrants were approximately 18 thousand dollars. To some degree this pattern of earnings follows what would be anticipated from the relative educational and occupational achievements of the various groups. However, there are apparent anomalies that suggest that income-returns to schooling, occupation, and possibly other characteristics may vary substantially across the eight subgroups. For example, among immigrants, whites are considerably less educated than Asian Americans and the occupational profile of whites compares unfavorably to that of the Chinese and Japanese, yet the average earnings of whites rank second to the Japanese. In the following section, we examine the extent to which variations in income-returns exist.

Determinants of labor market earnings in 1979

One of the most notable findings from the regression analyses reported in Tables 2 and 3 is the impressive return on education that native-born whites, Japanese, and Chinese Americans receive. Respectively, these groups gain on the average of 904, 900 and 770 dollars in earnings for each year of schooling. Native-born Japanese and whites appear to benefit the most in direct monetary rewards for educational attainment. Native-born Chinese also receive a 'good' return to schooling, but native-born Filipinos appear to receive no direct return to schooling. The returns on education for Asian immigrants are substantially lower than the returns of native-born whites, but this may partially reflect costs to immigration inasmuch as white immigrants also receive much lower returns to education than native-born whites. However, educational related costs of immigration appear to be overcome by those who obtain a college degree. In each of the four ethnic groups we study, native-born and immigrants with a minimum of four years of college attendance averaged similar earnings. To the contrary, for those with less than a college degree, immigrants typically earned substantially less than their native-born ethnic group counterparts. However, a rank-ordering of earnings exists between the four ethnic groups among college degree-holders. College educated whites typically earned in excess of 25 thousand dollars in 1979. Similarly educated Japanese Americans averaged about 23 thousand dollars, Chinese Americans averaged 21 thousand dollars, and Filipino Americans averaged just over 16 thousand dollars in earnings during 1979.

The returns to education received by Filipino Americans are unusually modest. To a lesser extent, this is also true of Chinese Americans. It might be that these patterns reveal costs of ethnicity. But if this is so, how can we account for the relatively high returns to education enjoyed by the native-born Japanese, while Japanese immigrants seem to get no direct returns to education? One possible explanation is that immigrants from Japan, especially 'new immigrants,' so often benefit from employment opportunities provided by contacts with businesses headquartered in Japan, that education per se does not directly determine their earnings in the U.S. Notwithstanding, that Filipinos have such poor income-returns to schooling suggests that this group may be a special case among the Asian Americans we study. Filipinos appear to be unsuccessful in using their educational credentials to gain equal earnings with similarly educated Chinese or Japanese Americans. In sum, our findings pertaining to education and earnings suggest that costs to ethnicity and costs to immigration may operate differently across the various ethnic and immigrant/native-born lines.

The importance of ethnic enterprise in Asian American economic achievement is clearly suggested in our analysis. Self-employment among Asian Americans is generally associated with high earnings. This is seen most clearly in the case of Chinese and Filipinos, and less so for the Japanese. The concentration of Chinese and Japanese Americans in small business ownership implies the existence of an enclave economy. This in fact has been documented in many of the case studies cited earlier. We note, however, that the extent to which Asian American small businesses exist outside of Asian enclave economies is an empirical issue that requires further research. Ethnic economies provide opportunities for entrepreneurs to benefit from a supply of low-wage

Table 2. *OLS estimates of 1979 Income-returns for the native-born samples.*

Variables	Native-born whites B	Native-born Japanese B	Native-born Chinese B	Native-born Filipinos B
Intercept	-38329.80	-45055.10	-23503.60	-20907.10
Age	1626.96***	1912.23***	749.57**	1189.01***
Age squared	- 16.37***	- 19.86***	5.24	- 12.99***
Education	903.64***	899.81***	769.72***	216.63
Married	3546.61***	4196.14***	2376.44***	2209.41***
Hours worked in 1979	6.23***	3.95***	6.42***	6.29***
Public sector employment	- 5501.73***	- 2520.90***	- 4510.61***	- 1801.80
Private sector employment	- 2794.34***	452.82	- 2715.23**	- 3434.01**
Professional specialities	- 1741.09***	389.22	1081.13	- 2589.12
Technicians	- 2075.16***	- 1217.73	- 2256.00	- 2074.48
Sales	- 3265.00***	- 2066.57	- 1034.73	- 3235.70
Administrative support including clerical	- 5893.21***	- 3784.88***	- 3052.84**	- 2234.33
Protective services	- 5232.00***	- 1742.94	- 1872.03	- 114.56
Business and household services	- 9428.30***	- 8080.77***	- 7848.02***	- 4139.10**
Farming, forestry and fishing	- 7629.91***	- 6544.84***	- 13954.50**	- 5909.06***
Precision production and craft	- 4388.35***	- 3421.57***	601.97	420.18
Operators	- 6043.32***	- 4783.88***	- 4415.46	- 303.34
Transportation	- 4905.41***	- 3556.08*	- 1145.76	- 2965.59
Laborers	- 5952.11***	- 4395.37**	- 3310.77	- 1471.90
English skills	- 651.60	- 622.83	- 480.35	- 589.74
R^2	.27	.25	.27	.34

* $p \leqslant .10$, two-tail test
** $p \leqslant .05$, two-tail test
*** $p \leqslant .01$, two-tail test

Note: The regression coefficients (B) are unstandardized. Since most of the regressors are dummy variables, standardized coefficients are

Variables	White Immigrants B	Japanese immigrants B	Chinese Immigrants B	Filipino Immigrants B
Intercept	-19708.10	-3287.40	-14172.40	- 7393.90
Age	1221.45***	2214.25***	988.22***	731.05***
Age squared	- 12.83***	- 22.28***	- 11.13***	- 8.21***
Education	493.77***	28.60	333.96***	299.77***
Married	2753.22***	4278.57***	1306.24**	1850.86***
Hours worked in 1979	5.06***	4.50***	4.80***	3.75***
Public sector employment	- 4318.83***	3297.57	- 2432.74**	- 4231.15***
Private sector employment	- 2841.71***	2286.21	997.85	- 4581.33***
Professional specialties	619.53	- 4794.80**	3528.88***	3502.08***
Technicians	- 3420.64***	- 4897.57	- 1538.66	104.87
Sales	- 2411.09***	- 7211.07***	- 2745.07***	- 1982.73**
Administrative support including clerical	- 6274.55***	- 9624.81**	- 3761.92***	- 2928.41***
Protective services	- 4271.35**	- 16859.20*	831.44	- 5049.88***
Business and household services	- 7347.44***	- 11479.40***	- 6109.94***	- 4469.76***
Farming, forestry and fishing	- 7137.76***	- 7150.49***	- 7486.12***	- 5310.57***
Precision production and craft	- 3716.76***	- 10173.80***	- 2498.45***	54.99
Operators	- 5505.63***	- 14278.10***	- 4832.85***	- 1864.84**
Transportation	4512.25***	- 10630.00**	3292.58	2413.96***
Laborers	- 5404.30***	- 8792.41	- 3758.96**	1140.72
English skills	- 1203.39***	- 2128.02**	1381.82***	192.39
U.S. citizenship	1386.10***	5754.83***	2455.23***	1911.32***
New immigrants	- 1030.73**	3927.66*	- 2307.07***	- 2226.75***
R^2	.31	.34	.36	.33

*   p≤ .10, two-tail test

**   p≤ .05, two-tail test

*** p≤ .01, two-tail test

workers. Though many enclave workers share the same type of dead-end, low-wage jobs characteristic of the secondary labor market, ethnic entrepreneurs utilize the cheap labor to better compete with outside firms. Like Asian Americans, self-employed whites tend to have earning advantages over whites in the public and private sectors. The return for being self-employed for whites is comparable to that of Asian Americans, and to the extent it might be slightly higher may be attributed to the likelihood of larger and better capitalized white owned small businesses.

While the sector variables account for a great deal of income for all groups, one limitation is that private sector jobs include a wide range of occupations in both the high-paying primary labor market and low-wage secondary labor market. For this reason it was necessary to bring into our equation a more detailed measure of occupation. The results obtained from the breakdown of occupational categories follow what would be expected. Occupations conventionally viewed as having high status are typically associated with higher net returns in earnings than are occupations commonly viewed as low in prestige. Clearly, what type of occupation one holds carries considerable weight in determining earnings. One finding that may be of special importance is that in each of the eight subgroups, the relative earning-returns to occupation received by laborers, operators, and most other low- and semi-skilled workers often associated with declining heavy industry exceed those of business and household service workers, an area of expanding employment.

English skills among immigrants are associated with higher earnings. Being a U.S. citizen is also associated with a substantial advantage in earnings for immigrants. Moreover, Filipino and Chinese immigrants who entered the U.S. subsequent to the immigration reforms of 1965 tended to have a net disadvantage in earnings of over 2,200 dollars in 1979. The earnings disadvantage associated with being a 'new immigrant' was roughly 1,000 dollars for white immigrants. On the other hand, the newer immigrants from Japan tend to earn almost 4,000 dollars more than Japanese Americans who immigrated prior to 1965. This reflects a major difference between the old and new Japanese immigration. The new Japanese immigrants are largely Japanese students who have pursued careers in the U.S. and persons associated with the Japanese business community in the U.S., the counterpart to the U.S. multinational community in Japan. This group is derived from the Japanese elite, whereas the earlier immigrants came from peasant stock.[9]

Discussion and conclusion

Our study suggests the importance of small business ownership for providing Asian Americans with an ethnically controlled avenue of economic mobility. We can see the benefits associated with the development of ethnic economies in the cases of Chinese and Japanese Americans. Both groups have been noted for the strength and vitality of their respective ethnic economies. In 1979, the self-employed of these groups clearly enjoyed relatively higher earnings than workers in the private and public sectors. The existence of a strong ethnic economy supports a middle-class based in ownership of small businesses for immigrant/minority groups.

Filipinos remain a disadvantaged minority group in the U.S. They appear to get negligible returns to education, have a comparatively low mean income, and are concentrated in occupations that give this group a distinctly working class character. An interesting study would be to compare Filipino Americans with Mexican Americans, since both groups share a common Hispanic cultural tradition. More importantly, both groups have been incorporated into the secondary labor market where they are locked into low-paying, dead-end jobs with few of the opportunities for advancement available to ethnic minorities with enclave economies.

Our findings challenge Wong's (1982) conclusion that Japanese and Filipino Americans have gained parity with whites in earning-returns, whereas Chinese Americans continue to pay a substantial cost to ethnicity. We find that Chinese Americans do receive somewhat lower returns to education than whites, but it is Filipino, not Chinese Americans that are most disadvantaged in income-returns to variables such as education. Indeed investment in education has provided the most important mechanism for status attainment among Chinese and Japanese Americans. The high payoff they receive for years of schooling helps to explain the fact that over 90 percent of college-age Chinese and Japanese American youth are in institutions of higher education.

The lower aggregate earnings of Chinese Americans must be seen largely as a cost of immigration rather than ethnicity. On average, native-born Chinese earn 30 percent more than Chinese immigrants. This finding is consistent with the low wage structure of enclave economies which benefits ethnic entrepreneurs, allowing them to compete more effectively by using cheap immigrant labor. Japanese immigrants, especially more recent arrivals, tend to avoid immigration costs due to their links to the Japanese economy. Indeed, Japanese immigrants earn substantially more than other immigrants in California. This is consistent with our contention that the major distinction between Chinese and Japanese Americans in earning power is not that Chinese Americans incur greater costs of ethnicity, rather it is that Japanese immigrants have lower immigration-costs.

This brings us to another point of contention with past studies. At the national level, native-born Chinese and Japanese Americans typically report higher earnings than native-born whites (e.g., Chiswick, 1980). As we suspected, this apparent comparative disadvantage of whites is an artifact of the concentration of Chinese and Japanese Americans in a state where earnings are unusually high. Comparing the earnings of Asian Americans who are concentrated in California to whites who more often reside in states where earnings are typically lower gives the false impression of higher earnings for Asian Americans. In California, native-born whites typically report slightly higher earnings than native-born Chinese and Japanese Americans.

In a broader sense, our analysis supports the view that Asian Americans, as a group, are on the road to assimilation in the U.S. The status attainment processes of Chinese and Japanese Americans appear to be similar. Both groups developed strong enclave economies in which many immigrants establish a beachhead, providing the resources and stability for the second generation to acquire more schooling than whites. This in turn, appears to be leading to a more complete economic assimilation among Chinese and Japanese Americans.

By comparison, Filipino Americans have not developed small business bases. Instead, they have been absorbed into largely low-wage private sector jobs. Further, the educational attainments of native-born Filipinos trail those of native-born Japanese and Chinese. It is therefore not surprising that the average earnings of Filipino Americans do not approach those of the other groups we have studied. However, we have also found that native-born Filipinos get lower returns to schooling than other native-born workers. Even the receipt of a college degree does not enable native-born Filipinos to reach the plateau of earnings common to native-born whites, Chinese and Japanese.

Overall, Filipino Americans do not seem to be on the same road as Chinese and Japanese Americans. Filipinos' low income-returns to schooling appear to be consistent with a cost of ethnicity explanation. However, why this group would be harmed by discrimination to such a greater extent than Japanese or Chinese Americans is unclear. It might be argued that Filipino Americans are perceived more as Hispanic than Asian in California and that prejudices against Hispanics are greater than those against Asians. It could also be that Filipinos, more so than other Asian American groups, are perceived as a working class minority and may receive fewer opportunities for advancement than seemingly more middle-class Chinese or Japanese Americans. In this sense, the apparent more costly discrimination received by Filipinos could reflect class discrimination rather than ethnic discrimination per se. Again, a comparative study of Filipino and Mexican Americans might be informative. We believe that much of the distinction between Filipinos and the other Asian American groups we have studied is due to historical differences in small business ownership. As of yet, Filipino Americans have been unable to establish ethnically controlled avenues for socioeconomic mobility. It is possible that this situation will continue to hinder the economic advancements of Filipino Americans.

Notes

*We wish to acknowledge the useful suggestions provided by Richard Alba, William Bielby, Leonard Broom, and Don Mar, and the secretarial assistance of Laura Omi of the Asian American Studies Program at UCSB.

1. Others (e.g. Baron and Bielby, 1980) contend that work arrangements within firms are so crucial to the allocation of earnings that the organization of work rather than the labor market positions of individuals should be focused upon in order to better understand income-inequality.

2. Note that non-family wage-earning employees of ethnic enterprises are not in the self-employed sector, rather they are in the private sector. Our subsequent discussion of the enclave economy, which includes both bosses and workers, should not be equated with the self-employed small business sector.

3. To control for variation in occupations, we include eleven dummy variables in the model. The reference category includes executives, administrators, and managers, those who are conventionally considered to hold the highest-status occupations. We pooled household and business service occupations (except protective services) because of the number of common jobs (e.g., cooking) across the two categories and due to the small number of household service workers. Hence the eleven dummy variables represent: (1) professional specialties, (2) technicians, (3) sales, (4) administrative support including clerical, (5) protective services, (6) business and household services, (7) farming, forestry and fishing, (8) precision production and craft, (9) operators, (10) transportation, and (11) laborers.

4. Years of schooling is coded as: (0) no schooling, (1) nursery school, (2) kindergarten, (3) first grade, etc.

5. An alternative way to specify an earnings equation that takes into account weeks worked and the nonlinear relationship involving age (or labor market experience) is referred to as the human capital earnings function. This strategy produces elasticity estimates (the metrics are in terms of percentages) of weekly earnings. See Becker and Chiswick (1966) for details.

6. Initially we estimate the model with the three Asian American groups combined. Two sets of estimates (with and without dummy variables distinguishing the three groups) were obtained. A modified Chow test (without interactions) was conducted from these analyses and an F-ratio of 13.43 was obtained. This result supports our substantive preference for analyzing the Asian American groups separately. We then conducted four additional Chow tests (with interactions) to help us judge whether separate analyses of the native-born and immigrants of each ethnic group were warranted. The F-ratios obtained were: 2.06 (Japanese), 3.25 (Chinese), 2.78 (Filipinos), and 5.79 (whites). Each of these F-ratios are also statistically significant at the .01 level. Consequently, we analyzed the model for eight subgroups. These include the native-born and immigrants of each of the four ethnic groups.

7. We did make one adjustment to the data. A few men reported working more than eighty hours per week. Believing that there is a good chance that these reports were exaggerated, we recoded hours worked to equal eighty. For the Asian Americans, we analyze a 60 percent sub-sample from the census tapes.

8. To gain a general impression of the degree to which the occupational profiles of Asian Americans compare to whites, we calculated indexes of dissimilarity for the immigrant and native-born subgroups. For native-born Americans, approximately 20 percent of each Asian group would have to change occupations in order to have the same occupational profile as whites. Among immigrants, the occupational profiles of Asian Americans and whites are even less alike. While the overall level of dissimilarity between whites and Asian Americans varies little across the three Asian groups, the detailed occupational differences that make up the overall degree of dissimilarity demonstrate the existence of important distinguishing characteristics in the occupational profiles of each Asian group.

9. It may be instructional to examine the predicted earnings of hypothetical workers who have typical values on the independent variables. Let us consider married, private sector workers who are 40 years old, have 16 years of schooling, worked 2,000 hours, and speak English well (English = 1). Native-born professional specialty workers typically earned 26.4 (whites), 26.2 (Japanese), 31.3 (Chinese), and 17.2 (Filipinos) thousand dollars. By comparison, native-born precision production and craft workers typically earned 23.7 (whites), 22.8 (Japanese), 31.3 (Chinese), and 17.2 (Filipinos) thousand dollars. Using the identical characteristics for immigrants who are U.S. citizens and 'new' immigrants, we find the following. Immigrant professional specialty workers typically earned 25.8 (whites), 30.6 (Japanese), 26.1 (Chinese), and 21.6 (Filipinos) thousand dollars. Immigrant precision production and craft workers typically earned 22.1 (whites), 25.3 (Japanese), 20.1 (Chinese), and 18.1 (Filipinos) thousand dollars. These estimates provide further demonstrations that native-born Chinese often compare

favorably in earnings to other native-born Americans, that Japanese immigrants typically have earning advantages over other immigrants, and that Filipinos are generally the most disadvantaged group we study.

References

ALLPORT, GORDON 1954 *The Nature of Prejudice*. Reading, Massachusetts: Addison-Wesley.

BARON, JAMES, and WILLIAM BIELBY 1980 'Bringing the firms back in: stratification, segmentation, and the organization of work.' *American Sociological Review* 45: 737–65.

BECKER, G., and B. CHISWICK 1966 'Education and the distribution of earnings.' *American Economic Review* (proceedings) 66: 358–69.

BLAUNER, R. 1972 *Racial Oppression in America*. New York: Harper & Row.

BONACICH, E. 1973 'A theory of middleman minorities,' *American Sociological Review* 38: 503–94.

BONACICH, E., and J. MODELL 1980 *The Economic Basis of Ethnic Solidarity: Small Business in the Japanese American Community*. Berkeley: University of California Press.

BROOM, L., and R. RIEMER 1973 *Removal and Return: The Socio-Economic Effects of the War on Japanese-Americans*. Berkeley and Los Angeles: University of California Press.

CAUDILL, W., and G. DEVOS 1965 'Achievement, culture, and personality: The case of the Japanese-Americans.' *American Anthropologist* 58: 1102–26.

CHISWICK, BARRY 1980 'Immigrant earnings patterns by sex, race, and ethnic groupings.' *Monthly Labor Review* 103 (October): 22–5.

DUNCAN, O.D., and R. HODGE 1963 'Education and occupational mobility: a regression analysis.' *American Journal of Sociology* 68: 629–44.

FAWCETT, J., F. ARNOLD, and U. MINOCHA 1984 'Asian Immigration to the United States: Flows and Processes.' Unpublished paper.

GLICK, C. 1980 *Sojourners and Settlers: Chinese Migrants in Hawaii*. Honolulu: University of Hawaii Press.

HIRSCHMAN, CHARLES 1983 'America's melting pot reconsidered.' *Annual Review of Sociology* 9: 397–423.

HIRSCHMAN, CHARLES, and MORRISON WONG 1981 'Trends in socioeconomic achievement among immigrant and native-born Asian-Americans, 1960–1976.' *The Sociological Quarterly* 22: 495–513.

HODSON, RANDY 1978 'Labor in the monopoly, competitive, and state sectors of production.' *Politics and Society* 8: 429–80.

KIM, ILLSOO 1981 *New Urban Immigrants: The Korean Community in New York*. Princeton: Princeton University Press.

KITANO, HARRY 1969 *Japanese Americans: The Evolution of a Subculture*. Englewood Cliffs, N.J.: Prentice-Hall.

KITANO, HARRY 1974 'Japanese Americans: The development of a middleman minority.' *Pacific Historical Review* 43: 500–19.

KUO, W., and N. LIN 1977 'Assimilation of Chinese-Americans in Washington, D.C.' *Sociological Quarterly* 18: 340–52.

LEE, ROSE 1960 *The Chinese in the United States of America*. Hong Kong: Hong Kong University.

LI, PETER 1977 'Ethnic businesses among Chinese in the United States.' *Journal of Ethnic Studies* 4: 35–41.

LIEBERSON, S. 1980 *A Piece of the Pie: Blacks and White Immigrants Since 1880*. Berkeley: University of California Press.

LIGHT, IVAN 1972 *Ethnic Enterprises in America*. Berkeley: University of California Press.

LOEWEN, JAMES 1971 *The Mississippi Chinese: Between Black and White*. Cambridge Mass.: Harvard University Press.

LYMAN, S. 1974 *Chinese Americans*. New York: Random House.

MIYAMOTO, F. 1939 'Social Solidarity among the Japanese of Seattle.' *University of Washington Publications in the Social Sciences* 11:57–130.

MONTERO, D. 1981 'The Japanese Americans – changing patterns of assimilation over three generations.' *American Sociological Review* 46: 829–39.

MONTERO, D., and R. TSUKASHIMA 1977 'Assimilation and educational achievement: The case of the second generation Japanese-American.' *Sociological Quarterly* 18:490–503.

NEE, VICTOR, and HERBERT WONG 1984 'Strength of family bonds in Asian-American socioeconomic mobility.' Unpublished manuscript.

NEE, VICTOR, and BRETT DE BARY NEE 1973 *Longtime California: A Documentary Study of an American Chinatown.* New York: Pantheon Books.

PARK, R. 1950 *Race and Culture*. Glencoe, Ill: Free Press.

PETERSON, WILLIAM 1966 'Success story, Japanese-American style.' *New York Times Magazine*, January 9.

PETERSON, WILLIAM 1971 *Japanese Americans*. New York: Random House.

PORTES, A. 1981 'Modes of structural incorporation and present theories of labor immigration,' in M. Kritz, C. Keely, and S. Tomasi (eds.), in *Global Trends in Migration: Theory and Research on International Population Movements*, pp. 279–97. New York: Center for Migration Studies.

SCHWARTZ, AUDREY 1971 'The culturally advantaged: A study of Japanese-American pupils.' *Sociology and Social Research* 55:341–53.

SEWELL, WILLIAM, and ROBERT HAUSER 1975 *Education, Occupation, and Earnings: Achievement in the Early Career*. New York: Academic Press.

SHIBUTANI, TAMOTSU, and KIAN KWAN 1965 *Ethnic Stratification: A Comparative Approach*. New York: Macmillan.

SOWELL, T. 1981 *Ethnic America: A History*. New York: Basic Books.

STATISTICAL ABSTRACT OF THE UNITED STATES 1982/83 *National Data Book and Guide to Sources*. U.S. Department of Commerce, Bureau of the Census. Washington D.C.: U.S. Government Printing Office.

STOLZENBERG, ROSS 1975 'Occupations, labor markets, and the process of wage attainment.' *American Sociological Review* 40:645–65.

WARNER, L., and LEO SROLE 1945 *The Social Systems of American Ethnic Groups*. New Haven: Yale University Press.

WILLIAMS, ROBIN 1947 *The Reduction of Intergroup Tensions: A Survey of Research on Problems of Ethnic, Racial and Religious Group Relations*. New York: S.S.R. Council.

WILSON, K., and A. PORTES 1980 'Immigrant enclaves: An analysis of the labor market experiences of Cubans in Miami.' *American Journal of Sociology* 86:295–319.

WONG, MORRISON 1982 'The cost of being Chinese, Japanese and Filipino in the United States 1960, 1970, 1976.' *Pacific Sociological Review* 25:59–78.

WRIGHT, ERIK, and LUCA PERRONE 1977 'Marxist class categories and income inequality.' *American Sociological Review* 42:32–55.

YANAGISAKO, SYLVIA 1979 'Family and household: The analysis of domestic groups.' *Annual Review of Anthropology* 8:161–205.

5 The structure of pluralism: 'We're all Italian around here, aren't we, Mrs. O'Brien?'*

William L. Yancey, Eugene P. Ericksen and George H. Leon
Temple University

The subtitle of this paper is the punch-line of a story told by a perceptive observer of American ethnicity, Richard Juliani, who was being led through one of the 'all Italian' blocks in South Philadelphia. It summarizes in a sentence the many contradictions found in the literature on ethnicity. Here is evidence of a melting pot, assimilation, cultural pluralism, and what Greeley (1974) has labeled 'ethnogenesis' — the emergence of new forms of ethnicity in America which have little relationship to national origins.

Richard Alba has asked us to comment upon the extent and trajectory of ethnic and racial differences in the last quarter of the twentieth century. In order to make guesses as to the future of ethnicity, it is not only necessary to understand contemporary ethnicity, but we must also understand its past. If historical research indicates ethnicity has been constant, i.e., an apparently unchanging primordial characteristic immunized from industrial urbanization, then our job is easy — we may expect no change. By contrast, if ethnicity has been systematically eroded by the forces of industrial modernism, again our job is easy — we can simply make projections into the future, following the established historical curves.

The problem is that there is strong evidence supporting both the assimilation and cultural pluralism hypotheses. Residential segregation of national origin groups from native Whites has declined. The largest national origin group reported in the 1980 census of Philadelphia were those with 'multiple' ancestry. Yet, assimilation is neither 'straight line' nor is it complete. Some groups have been maintained, others have been formed. As Hirschman has recently suggested, we must 'advance beyond the debate over whether ethnicity matters, to learn how and why ethnicity matters' (1983: 416).

In order to make such advances it is necessary to maintain the distinction between categories and groups. In simplest terms, a category is a set of people with common characteristics, such as age, socioeconomic status, national origin, or hair texture. A group is people who interact. Having some inherited trait is not sufficient for group membership. Yet, when we use the terms 'ethnicity' and 'ethnic groups' we often fail to make clear whether we are discussing an ethnic category or an ethnic group. An ethnic group is composed

94

of individuals with some common characteristic who associate with one another.

Group boundaries are fluid; group membership is problematic. Ethnicity is not an ascribed trait which either remains constant or is slowly eroded away. Rather there are identifiable historical conditions which are related to the crystallization and maintenance of ethnic groups. By identifying these conditions and characteristics, as well as assessing the impact of membership on ethnic identity and behavior, we will be able to determine whether similar conditions and characteristics are likely to exist for the next twenty-five years. The future of ethnicity is not dependent upon the ethnics themselves, but on the structural conditions which are related to the emergence, erosion or maintenance of ethnicity.

This paper, reporting the results of an investigation of ethnic groups in Philadelphia, Pennsylvania, is organized around two general issues. First, we focus on the historical and structural problem of identifying the boundaries of groups and examining the relationship between the formation of ethnic groups and the city's economic and ecological structure. Second, is an analysis of the 'micro-level' issues of the antecedents and consequences of group membership.

The ecology of residential segregation 1850–1980

Historical information on the formation and boundaries of ethnic groups is largely limited to patterns of residential settlement or segregation. The settlement patterns of race and ethnic populations have changed considerably. In order to understand patterns of settlement it is necessary to consider the economic and ecological conditions which different groups faced.

The walking city of the early nineteenth century was characterized by considerable population density, centralized economic activity and little spatial differentiation of land. In the 'street-car city' of 1890–1930, bedroom suburbs emerged on the outermost concentric zones of the city's northern and western sectors. The manufacturing and wholesale activities in the north-eastern and southern sectors provided the basis for stable working-class communities (see Warner, 1968). The 'automobile' city of the mid-to-late twentieth century experienced a precipitous decline of its manufacturing economy, abandonment of the street-car suburbs, and growth of a relatively centralized professional-service economy. Population density has declined systematically over the last 130 years. Industrial employment which reached its peak in 1900, with the exception of a resurgence of war-related industries in the 1940s, has declined.

Levels of ethnic segregation found in nineteenth-century cities were low, reflecting the density of settlement, centralized industrial employment and constraint of walking to work. The Irish and Germans were never highly segregated from native whites. Blacks were less segregated in 1850 than were the immigrants from southern and eastern Europe arriving around the turn of the century.

By the turn of the century, the increased size and decentralization of manufacturing, coupled with the decentralization of residential populations (following the development of the street-car suburbs), provided the structure of housing and employment that made it possible for immigrants to form ethnic communities in the 'zone of transition' and near decentralized concentrations of industrial employment (Greenberg 1981).

Different national origin groups came with different skills. The passenger manifests of the immigrant ships show how immigration from Europe was informally organized. Individuals and families followed migration chains of friends and relatives (Wolfe, 1983). The result of differential skills and social networks was different groups being concentrated in different occupations (Ericksen and Yancey, 1979).

As Pratt (1911) has shown for New York, the occupational concentrations of immigrants were important determinants of their residential locations. We find that dissimilarities between ethnic group occupations in 1900 and dissimilarities of residence in 1910 were correlated .81. When we eliminate blacks from these data the correlation is .94. Although segregated and concentrated near manufacturing, few blacks were employed in manufacturing (Ericksen and Yancey, 1979).

Since 1910, levels of segregation of new immigrants — especially for the Poles and Italians, have declined. In contrast to the white ethnics, segregation of blacks has increased. There was a slight decline between 1960 and 1970, apparently resulting from the temporary 'integration' of several neighborhoods undergoing racial change. In 1980 black segregation was higher than it had been at any previous time in the city's history.

The stability of ethnic communities is also linked to the city's industrial economy. Ethnic neighborhoods which were characterized by high levels of industrial employment in 1930 were likely to be the location of the same national origin groups in 1970. The stability of these communities reflects the stability of nearby industrial employment as well as the 'entrapment' of industrial workers whose home values have not kept up with inflation, and who have neither the resources nor the youth associated with new mortgages. A very different scenario held for communities which were not near manufacturing. The clearest examples are the old street-car suburbs. With higher status populations not tied to nearby manufacturing employment, these communities were abandoned following the development of the automobile suburbs after World War II (Leon, 1984).

Patterns of black movement in the city between 1930 and 1980 reflect the investment and disinvestment in the city's neighborhoods. Blacks moved into the abandoned street-car suburbs, away from manufacturing locations (Ericksen and Yancey, 1979) and, more recently, from centers of professional-service employment (Goldstein and Yancey, 1984).

The historical research suggests two general conclusions. First, the residential patterns of immigrants are best understood in terms of the structural stage in which groups entered and subsequently played out their ethnic heritages. To a considerable degree differences between groups, often attributed to their cultural origins, were generated within the American urban scene. Second, group boundaries, as reflected in residential segregation, are associated with the structural inequality characterizing the city's economic order and the position of groups within that order. As the structure has changed so too have the boundaries between ethnic groups. Some become more ambiguous as in the case of the white ethnics, while others have become increasingly clear, as in the case of blacks.

The structure of contemporary ethnic groups

While the 1980 census question on national ancestry provides a means of identifying national origin groups regardless of generation in the country, the inability to identify religious affiliations makes it impossible to determine the degree to which religion, rather than race or national origin, is the criterion defining ethnic group membership.

In order to examine the impact of religion on group boundaries, we must forego historical analyses and rely on contemporary social surveys. Laumann's research on Detroit provides an important example of such a strategy. Laumann found, with a sample of white Protestants and Catholics, that patterns of association followed religion and social-economic status.

Using a methodology similar to Laumann's, with a probability sample of the Philadelphia Urbanized Area, we have addressed the questions of which ethnic groups were there, the relative importance of ethno-religious criteria as determinants of association, and the degree to which the structure of ethno-religious affiliation was related to other dimensions of the city's social and economic structure.[1]

Using the three criteria of race, religion, and national origin we divided the sample into fifty-four ascriptive categories. These ranged in size from such large groups as the Italian Catholics (n = 240) Irish Catholics (n = 217) Black Baptists (n = 141) and Russian Jews (n = 123), to relatively small groups such as Irish Presbyterians (15) Black Muslims (7) German Jews (9) Russian-Ukrainian Catholics (15) and Puerto Rican Protestants (8). Although we sought to avoid making assumptions concerning the manner by which ascriptive criteria were used as the basis of group membership, it was necessary to combine some respondents into larger categories as was the case of Eastern European Protestants (25) and non-European Jews (3).

Following Laumann, the distribution of the friendship choices of each ethno-religious category across the categories was obtained. Similarity in the distribution of friends across race, religious, and national origin indicates similarity of social networks. Conversely dissimilarity in the distribution of friends indicates separate networks. Indices of dissimilarity were calculated between the distributions of each pair of groups.

The result is a relatively large matrix of indices of dissimilarity – each of the fifty-four categories against all others. These range from such high values as .978 between Canadian Protestants and Polish Jews and .967 between Black Muslims and Irish Catholics (indicating almost total separation of friendship choices), to such relatively low values of .298 between Black Methodist and Black Baptist and .268 between Rumanian Jews and Russian Jews.

To facilitate our understanding of these data, the matrix was submitted to smallest space analysis, a scaling program which attempts to '*portray graphically* the interrelationships of a set of points whose proximity is a function of the degree to which two points are found together relative to *n* other points. The purpose is to provide a graphic portrayal of a data matrix which will be simple yet faithful to the data matrix in the sense of monotonicity' (Laumann, 1973:16).

The result is presented in Figure 1 showing the two-dimensional model of friendship choices across race, religious, and national origin categories. The picture that emerges is relatively clear. We find four clusters: blacks who are closely associated regardless of religion, Jews who apparently ignore national origin, Puerto Ricans who disregard differences in religious affiliation, and a large cluster of Protestants and Catholics of various national origins. The pattern for this cluster is similar to what Laumann found in Detroit. Laumann's characterization of these categories applies: 'Group "boundaries" are simply too permeable — that is, are too often "breached" by members choosing outsiders as intimates' (1973: 82). Religion, not national origin,

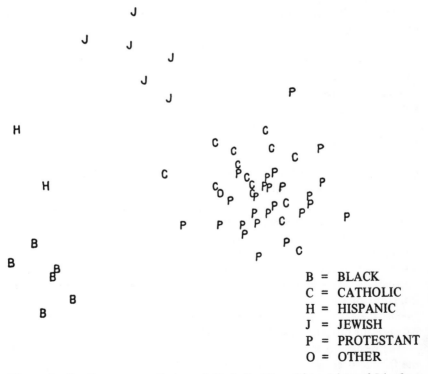

B = BLACK
C = CATHOLIC
H = HISPANIC
J = JEWISH
P = PROTESTANT
O = OTHER

Figure 1. *Smallest space solution of dissimilarities of friendship of 54 ethnoreligious categories.*

appears to differentiate this social space. For example, Irish Protestants are more likely to associate with German Protestants than with Irish Catholics, while Irish Catholics are closer to German Catholics and Italians. We conclude that there are four, perhaps five – depending on the significance attributed to the Protestant-Catholic division – ethnic groups represented in this sample.

In order to simplify further analyses, we combined the small categories appearing within these clusters. We ended up with twelve categories: British-Irish Catholics, British-Irish Protestants, German-Austrian Catholics, German-Austrian Protestants, Italian Catholics, Polish Catholics, Jews, Other Catholics, Other Protestants, Blacks, Puerto Ricans, and Others.

Smallest-space analyses were completed on dissimilarities of friendship and marriage with these twelve categories. The results (shown in Figures 2 and 3) largely duplicate the pattern found with fifty-four categories. Catholics and Protestants are clustered together, although separated by religion, and distant from Blacks, Jews, and Puerto Ricans. There is a very high correlation (.945) between the dissimilarities of friendship and of marriage. Both of these measures of group membership suggest similar group structures.

Social structure and ethnic structure

Having established the structure of ethno-religious groups in the city, the next question focused on the relationship between the social structure of ethno-religious groups and the economic and residential structure of the city. Laumann (1973) and Mayhew (1968) have suggested that groups widely distributed across the occupational structure should exhibit relatively little solidarity. Blau (1977) has argued that the structural differentiation and relative size of groups are the basic parameters determining opportunities for intra-ethnic association. Bonacich and Modell have shown the 'link between small-business concentration and the retention of ethnic group ties, and conversely, when class concentration dispersed, ethnic ties tend to weaken' (1980:34). Structural concentration, whether by socioeconomic status, occupation (Hechter, 1978) industry (Pratt, 1911) or residence (Lieberson, 1961, 1963), has been shown to be associated with ethnic solidarity.

The size of groups has been shown to have both substantive effects on the relationships between groups as well as mathematical effects on the index of dissimilarity. Large groups have greater opportunity for self-selection (Laumann, 1973). Thus, rates of intramarriage are directly related to the size of groups (Blau, 1977). Small groups which, even if randomly distributed, may not be found in all categories of the nominal variable in question. Thus, the indices of dissimilarity may be increased.

In order to test for the effect of structural differentiation on the social distances between ethnic groups we calculated dissimilarities of the distributions of these groups across educational status, industrial-occupational categories, and residential areas. The resulting sets of matrices were then

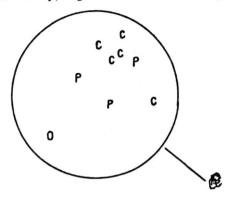

H

J

B = BLACK
C = CATHOLIC
H = HISPANIC
J = JEWISH
P = PROTESTANT
O = OTHER

B

Figure 2. *Smallest space solution of dissimilarities of* friendship *of 12 ethnic categories.*

correlated. The results are given in Table 1. Also given (below the diagonal) are the partial correlations, controlling for group size.

As can be seen, the correlations between social distances measured by friendship or marriage and the structural differentiation of these groups, as indicated by their dissimilarity of education, occupation, and residence are high – ranging between .444 and .945. Controlling for group size increases the strength of these correlations.[2] The data speak for themselves. *Ethnic association and group membership is related to the structural differentiation of groups in the city.*

Table 1: *Correlations between dissimilarities of friends, marriage, residence, occupation and education for ethno-religious groups (zero order correlations above diagonal; partial correlations below).*

	Friend	Spouse	Resi-dence	Indust. Occupat.	Edu-cation
Friend	.XXX	.945	.940	.513	.595
Spouse	.947	.XXX	.862	.444	.505
Residence	.962	.900	.XXX	.644	.735
Indust. Occupat.	.760	.746	.758	.XXX	.905
Education	.805	.752	.832	.868	.XXX

Based for ethno-religious groups on the 66 paired comparisons of dissimilarities.

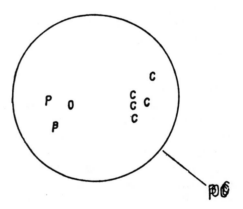

B = BLACK
C = CATHOLIC
H = HISPANIC
J = JEWISH
P = PROTESTANT
O = OTHER

Figure 3. *Smallest space solution of dissimilarities of* marriage *of 12 ethnic categories.*

The above analyses have been based upon measures of ethnic structure of entire groups and have ignored possible variations in social networks within groups. It remained to be determined whether or not ethno-religious criteria were as important as socioeconomic status in determining patterns of association. In order to explore this issue each ethnic group was subdivided into two categories depending on whether a person had graduated from high school. The patterns of friendship of these 'eth-classes,' to use Milton Gordon's (1964) term, were then submitted to a similar procedure, i.e., calculation of the distributions of friendship choices and smallest-space analyses of the resulting matrices of dissimilarity.

The results are shown in Figure 4. The clusters which appeared in the original analysis remain. In addition, we find relatively clear patterns as to the impact of social status (crudely measured) on patterns of association. Blacks and Jews associate with themselves and are separate from all others regardless of social status. Because all Puerto Ricans included in our samples had less than high school educations, we cannot draw a conclusion about the effect of status within this group.

A very different pattern is found among Protestants and Catholics – the large central group. This cluster is differentiated by religion and status. High-status Catholics have friendship choices which appear to be as similar to those of high-status Protestants as they are to lower-status Catholics. The large differences in friendship appear between comparisons crossing both religious and status boundaries. Given these results, one is tempted to conclude either that there are only four ethnic groups in the city, i.e., Blacks, Jews, Puerto Ricans and Whites, or there are seven. Whites form four eth-classes.

Whether we conclude that white Protestants and Catholics form one or four groups depends upon the social distances within this cluster. We repeated the smallest space analysis after removing Blacks, Jews and Puerto Ricans. This procedure allows the smallest space program to generate the more detailed picture of the relationships between these groups shown in Figure 5. In addition to the basic divisions of religion and status, we also find that the lower-status groups are more highly clustered than are the higher-status groups. Religion and national origin appear to be less important determinants of friendship choice among the lower-status white Protestants and Catholics than among those with higher status.

The antecedents and consequences of group membership

The foregoing analysis has indicated both the structure of ethnic groups in the city and the means in which the structure of ethno-religious social networks reflect the distribution of group members in the city's occupational and residential structure. It remained necessary to examine the impact of ethnicity on behavior.

The research design usually followed in addressing this question is illustrated by the works of such social scientists as Duncan and Duncan (1968)

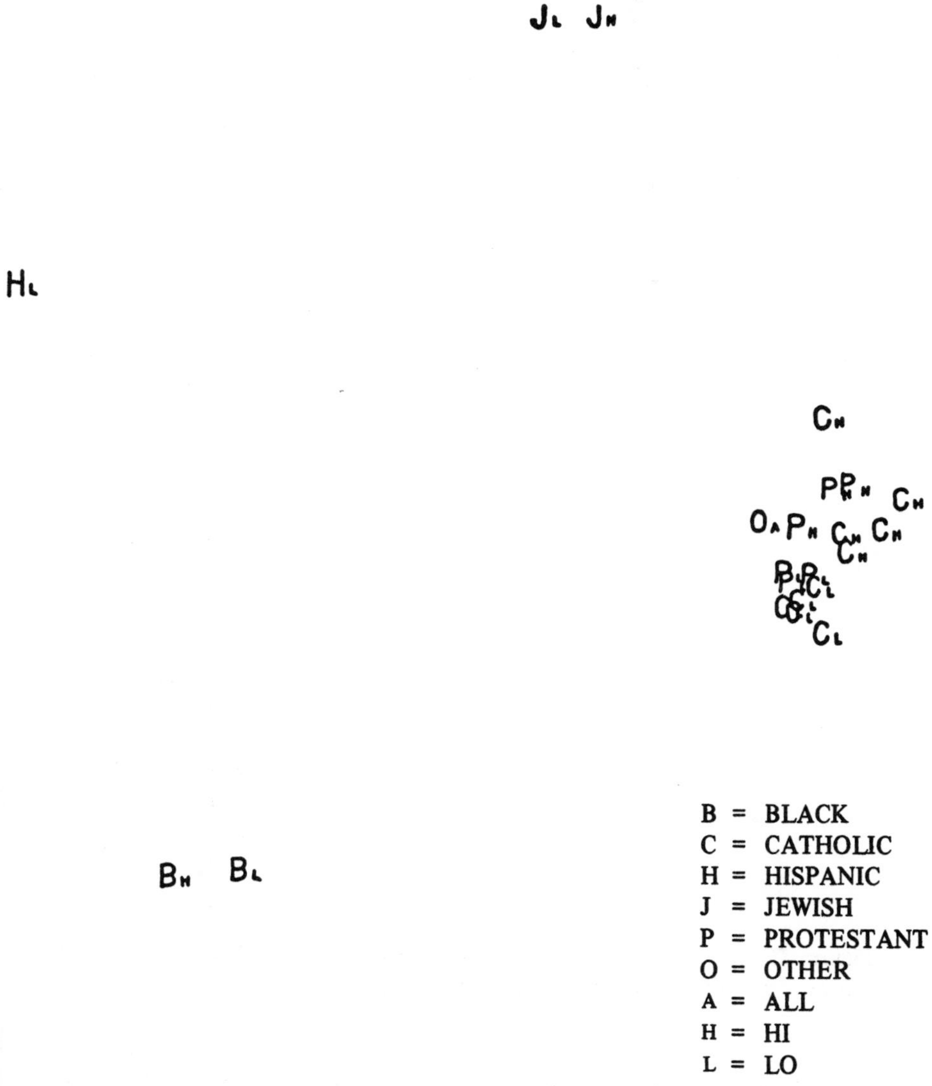

J_L J_H

H_L

C_H

P^P_H C_H
O_AP_H C_H C_H
C_H
P_LP_LC_L
O_LC_L
C_L

B = BLACK
C = CATHOLIC
H = HISPANIC
J = JEWISH
P = PROTESTANT
O = OTHER
A = ALL
H = HI
L = LO

B_H B_L

Figure 4. *Smallest space solution of dissimilarities of friendships for eth-classes.*

and Greeley (1974). Whether individuals with a given inherited characteristic exhibit distinctive behavior is determined by multi-variate analyses in which dummy variables, marking ethnic categories, are used, along with relevant structural variables such as age, social status, or marital status, to predict the dependent variable in question. When the ethnic dummy variables are found to be significant, the conclusion is drawn that the transplanted primordial trait has been passed across generations (Greeley, 1974; Schooler, 1976).

The problem with this research strategy is that it assumes individuals

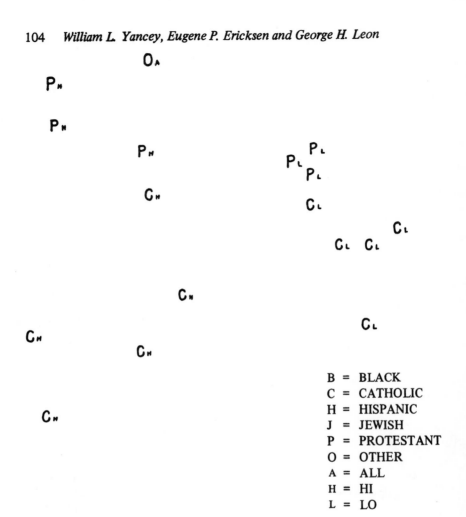

Figure 5. *Smallest space solution of dissimilarities of* friendship *of eth-classes – excluding Jews, Blacks, and Puerto Ricans.*

falling into a given ethno-religious category are members of the ethnic groups. Rather than simply testing for the effect of specific ethnic categories, it is also necessary to identify factors associated with group membership and test for the effect of group membership on the distinctive trait. For example we must determine if Italians who live in Italian neighborhoods differ from other Italians. In short, we must answer the question of whether there is a structural basis of cultural pluralism.

Existing literature contains a series of hypotheses relevant to these issues. First are the basic arguments suggested by Mayhew, Laumann, and Blau concerning the effects of group size and structural differentiation. Individuals who are members of relatively large categories are more likely to affiliate with others with similar traits, than are those in small categories. Whether a given individual is in a structural position dominated by others with similar traits, i.e., those who are 'ethnically embedded' (to use Mark Fried's term) are also expected to be members of the ethnic community.

The traditional paradigm of ethnicity suggests that the relatively poor and/or working-class immigrants are most likely to depend upon the supportive social networks of relatives and friends in the ethnic ghetto (Fitzpatrick, 1956). Indeed, it has been argued that ethnic culture is most likely to be crystallized and maintained among the urban working class (Yancey, Ericksen and Juliani, 1976). As Gans (1956) has pointed out, much of what is considered white ethnic culture is a product of the opportunities and constraints of urban working-class life. To the extent that the ethnic revival of the 1970s was more than a 'media event,' it appears to have been based on white working-class resentment of the civil rights and poverty movements (Gans, 1979; Kronis, 1978).

In contrast to the traditional model of working-class ethnicity, Etzioni (1959) suggested that ethnicity may operate in a variety of contexts from the extreme of a geographically based 'totalistic community' with predominantly local patterns of interaction and primary dependence on local institutions to the other extreme of a residentially dispersed group 'maintained by communication and active in limited social situations.' Patterns of interpersonal association vary by social and economic status (Laumann, 1973) and the character of the residential community (Bell and Force, 1956; Reiss, 1959; Fischer, 1977). Personal networks characterized by weak ties (Granovetter, 1974) which are open-ended and cosmopolitan are associated with voluntary associations and with higher-status populations. Where such networks are ethnically homogenous and supplemented by organizational memberships which are ethnically orientated, it is possible to maintain a viable community despite geographic dispersion (Breton, 1964). Indeed, Zald and Ash (1963) and Granovetter (1974) suggest that weak and cosmopolitan networks are associated with successful political interest groups.

Herbert Gans (1979) has suggested a parallel argument. He points out that the third generation of assimilated ethnics who no longer face the constraints of working-class life are 'less interested in their ethnic cultures and organizations − both sacred and secular − and are instead more concerned with maintaining their ethnic identity, with the feeling of being Jewish, or Italian, or Polish, and with finding ways of feeling and expressing that identity in suitable ways.'

We have examined these issues with the Philadelphia sample, using residential embeddedness, participation in ethnic organizations, and the ethno-religious homogeneity of marriage and friendship networks as indicators of group membership. Our research strategy involved two steps. First, we identified the correlates of group participation. Second, we examined the impact of ethnic membership on a series of attitudes and behaviors associated with ethnic cultures.

The basic findings of the first of these analyses are given in Table 2 showing the results of a correlation and regression analysis of network and marital homogeneity, organizational membership, and residential embeddedness. Independent variables include level of education, residential stability of the census tract, generation in the United States, relative size of the respondent's group in the sample, and a variable we call 'status embeddedness.' It is a measure of the degree to which each respondent's social status is dominated by others of his/her ethnic category. We assigned the percentage of the respondent's educational level which was of the same ethnic group as the respondent. This is analogous to our measure of residential embeddedness, in which we assigned the percentage of the census tract population composed of the respondent's national origin or race.

Although we regard the homogeneity of the contemporary friendship networks as the primary measure of group membership, we were interested in the other dimensions and found it impossible to make convincing arguments as to causal ordering. For example, it is likely that many were induced by their friends to join and maintain membership in ethnic organizations, while other friends were met in organizations. Similarly, homes may have been found through established networks, and friendships made after moving into neighborhoods. We have presented both the zero order correlations between these four variables and the partial correlations controlling for the independent variables included in the equations.

For each of the measures of group membership, we have presented the results of two regressions. The first includes only structural variables: group size, status-embeddedness, education, the stability of the local community, and a dummy variable marking foreign birth. The second equation includes dummy variables for Catholics, Jews, Blacks and Puerto Ricans.

Several conclusions are suggested by the results. First, the four measures of ethnic group membership are interrelated. The relationships between organizational membership and both residential embeddedness and marital homogeneity are weak. After we control for relevant structural variables and ethnic category, the relationships are weaker.

Table 2. *Zero order and partial correlations between ethnic membership and participation.*

	Residential embedded- ness	Marital homogen- eity	Organiz. member	Friendship homogen- eity
Res. embeddedness	XXXX	.392	.090	.510
Marital homog.	.140	XXXX	.164	.544
Ethnic organization	.059	.072	XXXX	.205
Friendship homog.	.217	.219	.109	XXX

Note: Zero-order correlations above diagonal. Partial correlations below. Controls include: group size, status embeddedness, community stability, education, foreign birth, and dummy variables for Catholics, Jews, Blacks, and Puerto Ricans.

Multiple regression analysis: antecedents of group membership

	Residential embeddedness		Organizational membership		Marital homogeneity		Friendship homogeneity	
Status-embedded	.066	n.s.	.115	n.s.	.171	n.s.	.202	.050
Group size	.275	.068	−.056	n.s.	.242	.205	.301	.207
Comm. stability	.069	.118	−.045	n.s.	−.069	n.s.	−.054	n.s.
Education	−.156	−.080	.081	n.s.	−.031	n.s.	−.020	n.s.
Foreign birth	.143	.067	.120	.154	.186	.139	.210	.153
Catholic		.113		.092		n.s.		.106
Jew		.219		.371		.392		.405
Black		.645		.144		.342		.480
Puerto Rican		.188		−.083		.392		.132
R^2	.147	.451	.023	.133	.158	.306	.226	.460

The regression analyses indicate that those respondents who were members of large categories, and who were structurally embedded, were more likely to live in ethnically embedded neighborhoods and have homogenous friendship networks and marriages. Foreign birth had a consistent positive effect on group participation. We found no support for 'Hansen's Law' of the resurgence of ethnic solidarity among the third generation (Hansen, 1938; Goering, 1975). There is only marginal support for the model suggesting that the working-class urban village is the crucible of American ethnicity. Respondents with less education and those living in stable communities are more likely to be residentially embedded; the effect of educational status on organizational membership, marital homogeneity, and friendship is negligible.

When we introduce ethnic group dummy variables the effects of the basic variables are reduced, explained variance increases, and there are significant ethnic effects. Blacks are most likely to be residentially embedded. Jews are associated with organizational membership. Black, Puerto Rican, and Jewish networks are far more homogeneous than Protestant or Catholic.

The previous analyses, indicating there were four ethnic groups in the city − Blacks, Puerto Ricans, Jews and white Protestants and Catholics − raises the question as to whether the antecedents of group membership were similar across these groups. Ignoring the possible reciprocal relationships involved, we included organizational membership and residential embeddedness as independent variables in a series of analyses designed to explore the question of whether the correlates of group membership were different for these major groups.

Differences were found (see Table 3). Little variation was found in the homogeneity of black networks. The few blacks living in predominantly white neighborhoods are likely to have white friends. Puerto Rican networks are also largely homogenous. Although none of the variables included in the regression were significant, with the small sample of Puerto Rican respondents (n = 32) it is difficult to draw conclusions.

Table 3. Multiple regression analysis of friendship network homogeneity within ethnic groups.

	Total	Black	Puerto Rican	All whites	White Lo Ed	non-Jew Hi Ed	Jew Low Ed	Jew Hi Ed
Mean number of friends with R's ethnicity	1.17	2.66	2.09	1.01	.85	.70	2.32	2.42
Group size	.191	n.s.	n.s.	.206	.170	.471	—	—
Status embeddedness	.172	n.s.	n.s.	.062	.116	n.s.	n.s.	n.s.
Foreign birth	.133	n.s.	—	.114	.124	.212	.149	.153
Resident. embedded	.386	.159	n.s.	.177	.260	n.s.	.162	n.s.
Ethnic organization	.145	n.s.	n.s.	.087	n.s.	n.s.	n.s.	.408
Catholic	.076			.083	.107	n.s.		
Jew	.341			.414				
Black	.351							
Puerto Rican	.098							
R^2	.392	.045	—	.367	.222	.189	.092	.183

Among the three white groups — Protestants, Catholics, and Jews — there were interactions with social status and the antecedents of group membership. Taken together, those who were members of large groups, embedded by status and residence, and who were members of ethnic organizations, had more homogeneous networks. Social status had no effect on network homogeneity.

When we divided whites into these three religious categories additional differences are found. Among non-Jewish whites (both Protestants and Catholics), those who were members of large groups, and were foreign-born, had homogeneous networks. Participation in ethnic organizations was not related to network homogeneity among these groups. While educational status had no direct effect on network homogeneity, there is an interaction between status, ethnicity, and the antecedents of group membership. The effects of structural embeddedness — by social status and residence — were found only among lower-status whites. Lower-status Catholics have more homogeneous networks than Protestants. Among the higher-status Protestants and Catholics only group size and foreign birth were related to network homogeneity.

For Jews, the correlates of group membership also vary by educational status. Lower-status Jews living in Jewish neighborhoods had Jewish friends, yet membership in Jewish organizations was not related to friendship homogeneity. The opposite pattern was found among higher-status Jews whose networks were not affected by residential embeddedness but strongly correlated with organizational participation.

While causal ordering is impossible, the results suggest multiple paths to ethnic group membership. One is associated with blacks and Puerto Ricans whose friendship networks were homogeneous and only marginally affected by other factors. The second, associated with lower-status whites, conforms to the traditional model of ethnic group membership based on the local community. The third, associated with higher status Jews and organizational membership, conforms to the model of cosmopolitan ethnicity suggested by Etzioni (1959) and Gans (1979).

The appearance of these three models of ethnic organization raises the question of the degree to which they are a function of the history of these groups. Thus, one may speculate about the heritage of slavery and Jim Crow, and the provincialism of Ireland, Southern Italy, or Poland, or the rootlessness of Jews as explanations of the solidarity of the black community, the localism of Catholics, and the cosmopolitan character of Jews. We suggest that a somewhat different conclusion is warranted.

Blacks are concentrated in segregated ghettos, Jews in middle-class suburbs, and Catholics are overrepresented among the working-class urban villagers. The differential location of these groups in the urban social structure has a direct effect on their organizational character. Thus, the factors which are associated with ethnicity among lower-status whites are characteristics associated with stable working-class communities (Young and Willmott, 1957, Gans, 1956). Similarly, the factors associated with ethnicity among higher-status Jews — organizational membership and networks which are not tied to the local community — are characteristics associated with the upper-middle-class suburban cosmopolites (Gans, 1962). The striking and unvarying homogeneity of black social networks suggests the overriding importance of race. The overall pattern suggests that whatever cultural propensities found among these groups toward isolation, provincialism, or cosmopolitanism, have been reinforced by the structural positions within which they are concentrated.

Ethnic community and culture

We are now in a position to examine the impact of ethnicity on behavior and attitudes. The distinction which we have made concerning ethnic groups and ethnic categories is central to the issue of whether there are behavioral or attitudinal differences between ethnic groups that may be attributed to cultural heritage. To test for the effects of ethnic heritage it is not only necessary to control on structural factors — such as social status — which are related to the behavior or attitude in question, but it is also necessary to examine the degree to which subcultural characteristics are dependent upon the presence and participation in the ethnic community. The central hypothesis is that those who were members of ethnic groups, i.e., had ethnically homogeneous friendship networks, were most likely to manifest distinctive traits.

We have examined this issue using a series of dependent variables: White Racial Prejudice, Protestant Ethic Work Values, Economic Liberalism, Social Class Identification, and Political Affiliation (Democratic-Republican). Some of these have been explicitly tied to the cultural heritage of ethnic groups such as the Protestant Ethic; others are more clearly linked to the historical experience of ethnic groups in America.

We have asked three questions. First, are there significant differences between ethnic categories in the degree to which they exhibit these characteristics? Second, are these differences found among all members of ethnic categories, or only among those who are members of the ethnic community? Third, are the differences the results of differences in the social and economic characteristics of the groups? Thus, we included variables such as education, occupation, union membership, and the character of the local neighborhood, which had been shown in previous research to affect the attitude or behavior in question.

For each of the dependent variables, six regressions were completed. First, a regression using only the dummy variables identifying ethnic category: Protestant, Catholic, Jew, Puerto Rican, and Black. The sample was then divided into those with ethnically homogeneous and heterogeneous networks. Each of these regressions was repeated with the addition of relevant structural variables. The results of these equations are presented in Table 4 showing the beta weights associated with each of four dummy variables — Catholics, Puerto Ricans, Jews, and Blacks.

The results of these repeated analyses follow relatively clear patterns. First,

Table 4. *Ethnic effects on attitudes: results of multiple regressions (beta weights) total sample and controlling for network homogeneity and relevant structural variables.*[3]

| | | | | With structural controls | | |
	Total	Friend-ship Homog.	Network Hetero.	Total	Friend-ship Homog.	Network Hetero.
Democratic political orientation						
Catholic	.301	.341	.292	.233	.254	.242
Puerto Rican	.154	.233	.088	.112	.173	.072
Jews	.231	.323	.162	.226	.294	.143
Blacks	.376	.541	.152	.278	.414	.107
R^2	.136	.103	.059	.181	.133	.152
Economic liberalism						
Catholic	.133	.214	.105	.093	.184	n.s.
Puerto Rican	.070	.134	n.s.	n.s.	.097	n.s.
Jewish	.132	.226	.072	.161	.239	.098
Blacks	.294	.447	.159	.241	.401	.118
R^2	.068	.055	.050	.097	.096	.068
Identification with higher class						
Catholic	−.121	−.160	−.122	n.s.	n.s.	n.s.
Puerto Rican	−.174	−.094	−.094	−.048	n.s.	−.094
Jews	.161	.239	.098	.078	.174	n.s.
Blacks	−.219	−.252	−.201	−.141	−.170	−.147
R^2	.080	.131	.052	.164	.150	.214
White racial prejudice						
Catholic	.072	.132	n.s.	n.s.	n.s.	n.s.
Puerto Rican	−.091	−.108	−.083	−.118	−.135	−.101
Jews	n.s.	n.s.	n.s.	n.s.	n.s.	n.s.
R^2	.018	.092	.069	.092	.113	.096
Protestant ethic work values						
Catholic	−.066	−.127	n.s.	n.s.	n.s.	n.s.
Puerto Rican	−.097	−.098	−.086	n.s.	n.s.	n.s.
Jews	.132	.226	.079	n.s.	n.s.	n.s.
Blacks	−.116	−.190	n.s.	n.s.	n.s.	n.s.
R^2	.016	.018	.003	.095	.088	.104

there were significant differences between ethnic groups using the total sample, with no controls. Second, the differences were greater among those respondents with ethnically homogeneous networks. Third, when we introduce relevant structural variables, the differences between ethno-religious groups were reduced. In some cases, as with the Protestant Ethic and Racial Prejudice, structural controls largely eliminated ethnic effects. In others, although structural variables explained a majority of the variance, the differences which remained were particularly marked among those who were members of ethnic communities.

The evidence is relatively clear. While there may be differences between ethnic groups in attitudes and behavior, much of these differences are the result of the economic and social circumstances which group members face. When substantial numbers of individuals with the same ethnic origins are concentrated in similar social, economic and ecological positions, the result is the development of distinctive life styles which are reinforced by participation in the ethnic community. Laumann made the point a decade ago when he wrote: 'We regard social structural differentiation as a necessary corollary of cultural differentiation (different styles of life for different groups) because it provides the crucial structural mechanism by which group differences may be developed and sustained' (1973:208).

The future of ethnicity

It is impossible, given this analysis of ethnicity in Philadelphia, to resolve the arguments between assimilation, cultural pluralism, and 'ethnogenesis' — the emergence of new ethnic groups. Our evidence supports all three.

Assimilation, viewed as a process of declining levels of differential association with others with similar origins, and corresponding erosion of interest in these origins, is suggested by those findings showing significant effect of foreign birth. Cultural pluralism is suggested by results which indicate religion and race have independent effects on group membership, ethnic interests, and political-economic attitudes. The effect of religion and race are not independent of the structural position of these groups and the subsequent character of ethnic community organization. There is also evidence suggesting the emergence of a new ethnic group, heterogeneous in both religion and national origin, forming among urban working-class whites. The difficulty in reaching a general conclusion results in large part on the misguided attempt to draw a single conclusion about what, in fact, are different processes which have been generated under different circumstances.

White ethnics, especially Catholics, appear to have followed the traditional paradigm of immigrants initially concentrated in ethnic urban villages. Since the establishment of these communities many of their members and their children have left and become assimilated. Those who remained in the ethnic neighborhoods have homogeneous networks and maintain attitudes and behaviors reflecting the social and economic constraints characterizing their communities.

The future of ethnicity among this group remains unclear. With the continued decline of manufacturing cities such as Philadelphia, the structural foundations which generated these communities are being undermined and replaced by homogenization in the secondary sector of the economy. The concentrations of poverty previously associated with the urban black community may become increasingly associated with these residuals of the past.

That lower-status whites ignore differences in national origin and religion suggests that we may be observing the formation of a new ethnic group, with heterogeneous origins, yet common political and economic interests.

Blacks, Puerto Ricans, and Jews are not only different groups, but also the solidarity of these communities is associated with very different factors. Black ethnicity is, in large part, a product of the constraints imposed upon an increasingly segregated community whose members have been excluded from participation in the city's major economic activities. Because blacks have historically been denied industrial employment, the erosion of the city's manufacturing economy may have fewer consequences for the character of the black community. In spite of the substantial variation in the social and economic status of blacks, there is little variation in the homogeneity of black social networks or in the expression of black ethnic interest. Increased residential segregation, and almost universal social isolation, suggest that the significance of race has *not declined*. We see no indication that it will decline in the future.

Our results concerning Puerto Rican ethnicity are necessarily ambiguous given the small number of Puerto Rican respondents included in our sample. That Puerto Rican residential segregation has declined over the last decade, in spite of the growth of this population in the city, suggests the results recently reported by Massey and Mullan (1984) for Los Angeles, indicating that Puerto Ricans have been able to translate socioeconomic advances into residential integration, may also be at work in Philadelphia.

Jewish ethnicity comes closest to approximating the model of 'middleman minorities' suggested by Bonacich (1981). It stands in sharp contrast to the urban village or black ghetto. The distinctiveness of Jews was indicated first by their early mobility out of industrial manufacturing employment into retail trades and the professions. Although successful, Jews have not been widely distributed across the city's occupational structure. Occupational success made it possible for many Jews to move into the street-car suburbs, avoid the entrapment of the industrial working class, and take advantage of the automobile suburbs following World War II. Yet, even the relatively high levels of residential mobility and decentralization have not resulted in the demise of Jewish ethnic solidarity. The higher-status members of the community involved in secular organizations with cosmopolitan social networks are paradigmatic of the third model of the ethnic solidarity.

As a general conclusion, there are two things which we would like to emphasize. First, while the maintenance of ethnic interests and distinctive ethnic values and attitudes are enhanced by the presence of the ethnic community, ethnicity is not a singular social phenomenon, with singular sets of antecedents and processes. Rather, it is a multi-dimensional phenomenon. The future of ethnicity, as its past, depends on the structural location of groups and individuals. Existing groups will be maintained to the degree that they adopt traditions and organizational forms which are consistent with their position in the changing urban macro-structure.

Second, rather than taking ethnic groups as given and asking questions concerning the conditions leading to their demise or solidarity, we must begin viewing ethnic groups as products of the larger urban system. The specific form taken and the historical trajectory which they follow — toward assimilation, pluralism or ethnogenesis — are determined by the structural parameters which generate the groups and define their positions in the political, economic, and ecological structure.

Notes

*This research was supported by a grant from the Center for the Study of Metropolitan Problems, National Institute of Mental Health (Grant R01MH25244). The resources and facilities of the Social Science Data Library, Temple University, have been an essential aid to our efforts. The authors are indebted to the members of the Urban Housing Seminar, Institute for Public Policy Studies, Temple University, who have criticized the analyses of these data and arguments. Nancy Kleniewski and Joane Nagel provided helpful critiques of earlier drafts.
1.   The sample is of the Philadelphia Urbanized Area taken in the spring and summer of 1975. Eligible respondents were adults aged 65 and under. A total of 1,780 respondents were interviewed. Residentially stable census tracts and census tracts with heavy concentrations of foreign stock population were over-sampled. The first set of areas comprises census tracts where at least 30 percent of the household heads had lived at their current address for 20 years or more in 1970. This represented a critical variable, since these are areas which were most similar to the classical 'urban village' described by Gans (1962) and Young and Wilmott (1957). These areas are tied to local industrial jobs, have high proportions of manufacturing workers, and high rates of homeownership. (Yancey and Ericksen, 1979).

The second set of over-sampled areas were other areas where at least 23 percent of the population was of foreign stock. These areas are typically the new bedroom suburbs and are the areas of second settlement of ethnic populations.

The remaining third of the sample was drawn from the remaining areas of the city and were mainly black, Puerto Rican, and newer white areas. One third of the sample was drawn from each of these strata. One-sixth of the population lived in 'stable' areas, one-third in 'foreign-stock' areas, and one-half in the remaining neighborhoods.

2.   Because of the large dissimilarities between blacks and Puerto Ricans and all other groups, we were concerned with the possibility that these high correlations were merely the result of these outliers. The analysis was repeated in which only dissimilarities of Jews, Catholics, and Protestants were included. The resulting matrix of zero order and partial correlations remain similar although slightly weaker. With the full analysis, the average correlation is .770. With the restricted data set, the average correlation is .704.

3.   Structural and control variables used in all of these analyses included level of education received, union membership, age of respondent, and a dummy variable indicating city or suburban residence. In addition, for Political Orientation we included responses to the Economic Liberalism scale; for Social Class Identification, Economic Liberalism, and Protestant Ethnic Work Values, the residential stability of the local community; for White Racial Prejudice, we included measures of the racial composition of the neighborhood. Three categories were identified: (1) racially mixed (2) white areas which were proximate to predominantly black areas and (3) white areas which were not proximate to black areas.

References

ALBA, RICHARD D. 1976 'Social Assimilation Among American Catholic National Origin Groups.' *American Socoiological Review* 41:1030–46.

ALBA, RICHARD D. 1983 'A Preliminary Examination of Ethnic Identification Among Whites', *American Sociological Review* 48:240–47.

BELL, WENDELL, and MARYANNE T. FORCE 1956 'Urban Neighborhood Types and Participation in Formal Associations.' *American Sociological Review* 21:25–34.

BLAU, PETER 1977 'A Macro Sociological Theory of Social Structure.' *American Journal of Sociology* 83:26–54.

BONACICH, EDNA 1976 'Advanced Capitalism and Black/White Race Relations in the United States: A Split Labor Market Interpretation.' *American Sociological Review* 41:34–51.

BONACICH, EDNA, and JOHN MODELL 1980 *The Economic Basis of Ethnic Solidarity: Small Business in the Japanese American Community.* Berkeley: University of California Press.

BRETON, RAYMOND 1964 'Institutional Completeness of Ethnic Communities and the Personal Relations of Immigrants.' *American Journal of Sociology* 70:193–205.

COHEN, ABNER 1974 *Urban Ethnicity*. London: Tavistock.

DUNCAN, BEVERLY, and OTIS DUDLEY DUNCAN 1968 'Minorities and the Process of Stratification.' *American Sociological Review* 33: 356–64.

ERICKSEN, EUGENE, and WILLIAM L. YANCEY 1976 'The Location of Manufacturing Jobs in Philadelphia: Changes in the Pattern, 1927–1972.' Unpublished paper, Temple Univ.

ERICKSEN, EUGENE, and WILLIAM L. YANCEY 1979 'Work and Residence in Industrial Philadelphia.' *Journal of Urban History* 5:147–82.

ERICKSEN, EUGENE, and WILLIAM L. YANCEY 1979 'Immigrants and Their Opportunities: Philadelphia, 1850–1936.' Paper presented to meetings of the American Association for the Advancement of Science, Houston.

ETZIONI, AMITAI 1959 'The Ghetto – A re-evalution.' *Social Forces* 39:255–62.

FISCHER, CLAUDE S. 1977 *Networks and Places: Social Relations in the Urban Setting.* New York: Free Press.

FITZPATRICK, JOSEPH P. 1966 'The importance of community in the process of immigrant assimilation.' *International Migration Review* 1:6–16.

FOLEY, DONALD 1952 *Neighborhoods or Urbanites? A Study of a Rochester Residential District.* Rochester, N.Y.: University of Rochester.

FRIED, MARC 1973 *The World of the Urban Working Class.* Cambridge: Harvard University Press.

GANS, HERBERT 1956 *The Urban Villagers*. New York: Free Press.

GANS, HERBERT 1962 'Urbanism and suburbanism as ways of life: a reevaluation of definitions,' in Arnold Rose (ed.) *Human Behavior and Social Processes*. Boston: Houghton Mifflin, pp. 625–48.

GANS, HERBERT 1979 'Symbolic Ethnicity: The Future of Ethnic Groups and Culture in America.' *Ethnic and Racial Studies* 2.

GOERING, JOHN 1975 'The Emergence of Ethnic Interest: A Case of Serendipity.' *Social Forces* 49.

GOLDSTEIN, IRA, and WILLIAM L. YANCEY 1984 'Projects, Blacks and Public Policy: The Historical Ecology of Public Housing,' in John Goering (ed.), *Racial Integration and Housing Policies*, forthcoming.

GORDON, MILTON 1964 *Assimilation in American Life*. New York: Oxford, University Press.

GRANOVETTER, MARK 1974 'Granovetter Replies to Gans.' *American Journal of Sociology* 80:527–9.

GREELEY, ANDREW M. 1974 *Ethnicity in the United States: A Preliminary Reconnaisance.* New York: Wiley

GREENBERG, STEPHANIE W. 1981 'Industrial Location and Ethnic Residential Patterns in an Industrializing City: Philadelphia, 1880.' in Theodore Hershberg (ed.) *Philadelphia: Work, Space, Family, and Group Experience in the 19th Century*. New York: Oxford University Press, pp. 204–32.

HANSEN, MARCUS LEE 1983 *The Problem of the Third Generation Immigrant.*
Rock Island, Illinois: Augustana Historical Society.
HECHTER, MICHAEL 1975 *Internal Colonialism.* Berkeley: University of California
Press.
HECHTER, MICHAEL 1978 'Group Formation and the Cultural Division of Labor.'
American Journal of Sociology 84:293–318.
HERSHBERG, THEODORE, ALAN N. BURSTEIN, EUGENE P. ERICKSEN,
STEPHANIE W. GREENBERG, and WILLIAM L. YANCEY 1979 'A Tale of Three
Cities: Blacks and Immigrants in Philadelphia, 1850–1880, 1930, 1970.'
The Annals 441:55–81.
HIRSCHMAN, CHARLES 1983 'America's Melting Pot Reconsidered,' in *Annual
Review of Sociology*, Vol. 9, ed Ralph H. Turner and James F. Short, Jr. Palo Alto,
Calif.: Annual Reviews.
KEYS, CHARLES F. 1981 'The Dialectics of Ethnic Change,' in Charles Keys (ed.),
Ethnic Change, Seattle: University of Washington Press, pp. 3–30.
KRONIS, SIDNEY 1978 'Race, Ethnicity, and Community,' in *Handbook of
Contemporary Urban Life*, ed. David Street. San Francisco: Jossey-Bass, pp. 202–31.
LAUMANN, E.O. 1973 *Bonds of Pluralism.* New York: Wiley.
LEON, GEORGE H. 1985 *Ghost Towns, Ghettoes and Gold Coasts: A Structural
Analysis of Housing Abandonment in Philadelphia*. Ph.D. Dissertation, Department of
Sociology, Temple University, Philadelphia, Pa.
LIEBERSON, STANLEY 1961 'The Impact of Residential Segregation on Ethnic
Assimilation.' *Social Forces* 40:52–7.
LIEBERSON, STANLEY 1963 *Ethnic Patterns in American Cities.* New York: Free
Press.
LIEBERSON, STANLEY 1980 *A Piece of the Pie: Blacks and White Immigrants Since
1880.* Berkeley: University of California Press.
MASSEY, DOUGLAS S., and BRENDAN P. MULLAN 1984 'Processes of Hispanic
and Black Spatial Assimilation.' *American Journal of Sociology* 89:836–73.
MAYHEW, LEON 1968 'Ascription in Modern Societies.' *Sociological Inquiry* 38:105–20.
PRATT, E.E. 1911 *The Industrial Causes of Congestion of Population in New York
City.* New York: Columbia University Press.
REISS, ALBERT J. 1959 'Rural-Urban Differences in Interpersonal Contacts.' *American
Journal of Sociology* 65:182–95.
SCHOOLER, CARMI 'Serfdom's Legacy: An Ethnic Continuum.' *American Journal of
Sociology* 81:1265–86.
TAEUBER, KARL, and ANNA TAEUBER 1965 *Negroes in Cities.* Chicago: Aldine.
WARD, DAVID 1971 *Cities and Immigrants.* New York: Oxford University Press.
WARNER, SAM BASS 1968 *The Private City: Philadelphia in Three Periods of Its
Growth.* Philadelphia: University of Pennsylvania Press.
WARNER, SAM BASS, and COLIN BURKE 1962 'Cultural Change and the Ghetto.'
Journal of Contemporary History 4:173–88.
WOLFE, ELAINE M. 1983 *Migration, System Characteristics, and the Division of
Labor: The Case of the United States, 1890–1900.* Ph.D. Dissertation, Department of
Sociology, Temple University, Philadelphia, Pa.
YANCEY, WILLIAM L., EUGENE P. ERICKSEN and RICHARD N. JULIANI 1976
'Emergent Ethnicity: A Review and Reformulation.' *American Sociological Review*
41:391–403.
YANCEY, WILLIAM L., and EUGENE P. ERICKSEN 1979 'The Antecedents of
Community: The Economic and Institutional Structure of Urban Neighborhoods.'
American Sociological Review, 44;253–62.
YOUNG, MICHAEL, and PETER WILLMOTT 1957 *Family and Kinship in East
London*. Routledge & Kegan Paul.
ZALD, MAYER N., and ROBERTA ASH 1963 'Social Movement Organizations:
Growth, Decay, and Change.' *Social Forces* 44:327–41.

6 Jewishness in America: ascription and choice*

Walter P. Zenner
State University of New York at Albany

Introduction

'Ethnicity' and 'race' are terms which cover many sins. Both terms suggest biological relationships between those identified with one or another group or classed together in one category; both terms suggest that there are social and sometimes cultural dimensions. While 'ethnicity' stresses cultural and social features, it also implies some biological kinship among those who share a common identity. It is clear, however, that groups and categories lumped together as 'ethnic' entities are not strictly comparable. The meanings of 'negritude,' Italianness, Arabism, and Jewishness share some components, but each lacks or adds elements foreign to the others. It is easier to compare the economic and political implications or consequences of ethnic group boundaries and the definition of categories than it is to compare the features of the identity itself and the meanings of that identity to both in-group and outgroup members.[1] Not all 'primordial' forces are alike.

In this paper, the changing nature of what it means to be Jewish in America will be discussed. Rather than speaking of Jewish ethnicity, the term 'Jewishness' is preferred because of the importance of the religious component of Jewish identity which makes it quite different from other identities like 'Black' or 'Italian' or 'Native American' (Amerind). At the same time, the ancestral elements are also present, which makes 'Jewishness' different from Protestant and even Catholic definitions of being a 'Christian.' For instance, one hears American Gentiles make statements like 'When I was a Christian' or 'Before I became a Christian,' even though they were born to church-going parents; one rarely hears Jews refer to themselves in this manner. At the same time, one can become a member of a religious group, such as the Jews or the Greek Orthodox church, while ethnic groups in America generally lack formal mechanisms for incorporating or naturalizing those not born into the group. While Judaism generally does not proselytize actively, converts are accepted into the fold. Most Jews are members of the group on account of their ancestry, but proselytes beginning with the Biblical Ruth, have been significant in Jewish history. Since sociology of

117

religion is segregated from sociology of ethnic relations, this facet is often neglected. With regard to Jewish ethnicity in particular it cannot be ignored.[2]

Here I will argue that in present-day America, Jewishness has ceased to be a given for many of those who are born Jews nor is it excluded as an alternative for Gentiles. While the vast majority of those who are born Jews still see themselves as Jewish in terms of an ancestral heritage, their Jewishness is being transformed into a preference, rather than an ascribed status, *à la* caste or race. This transformation follows certain general patterns present in American life. American Protestantism, with its roots in the competition between various established churches and dissenting sects, developed a viewpoint whereby membership in a church was a matter of individual faith, rather than an imposition from parents or the surrounding society. The spirit of capitalism which permeated economics, politics, and the arts made the metaphor of the marketplace applicable to ideas, both religious and secular. Capitalism in its American formulation has encouraged both physical and social mobility to a degree unknown in other parts of the world.

Citizenship and nationality in the United States is conceived in the same terms as religion — as a matter of choice, while the American-born are automatically citizens, no regard is given to their ancestry. Even the children of illegal aliens are automatically citizens. Ideally, all who immigrate to the United States are eligible for citizenship, a fact borne out today when one attends naturalization ceremonies. Becoming an American is achieving a position in the world. Stressing this ideal should not blind us to the opposing ideologies of racism, anti-Semitism, and anti-Catholicism which present an opposite ideal and which continue to exist with varying degrees of manifestation and latency.

This idea of becoming an American by choice fits in very well with urban American values today. Freedom in choosing occupations, neighborhoods, clothing, foods, and sexual partners are highly valued, especially in those places where most American Jews reside. In fact, the great debates of contemporary America are often phrased in terms of conflicts of rights and freedoms, such as the abortion controversy.

The transformation of Jewishness will be described and explained in a number of ways. First, the general trends discerned by social scientific research dealing with American Jewry will be reported. The historical dimensions of the changes will be briefly outlined, in terms of both the European and American backgrounds. Then attention will be turned to certain influences of American culture, particularly those relating to the value of individuality. Next, the manner in which widely accepted retentions and elaborations of Jewish culture themselves illustrate this transformation will be examined. Jewishness in America is also exemplified by those on the margins of the community, either Jews moving out of the Jewish community or trying to combine Judaism and other religions or non-Jews wholly or partially adopting Judaism. The existence of several categories of the marginal in itself tells us about Jewish identity in this period. While most of the studies and reports on which this paper is based demonstrate the erosion of traditional Judaism, it is necessary to remind ourselves that within this general entropy there are regenerative processes. While these also are often products of individuality, they illustrate the complexity of the processes involved in ethnic and religious identifications in America today.

General trends

There are a number of general social trends marking American Jewry as it enters the last fifteen years of the twentieth century. There are approximately 5½ million Jews in the U.S. today. The trends have emerged out of a variety of studies, but they have been well summarized by Cohen (1983).

1. Jews are increasingly attracted to those professions accessible through higher education. Many now work for large corporate entities including the government and universities, although considerable self-employment persists. Jewish participation in the old small business sector, exemplified by mom-and-pop stores, has declined. In part, this is because this sector as a whole has declined; in part, it has been abandoned by Jews for more prestigeful enterprises. There are, of course, new small businesses such as financial advising and consultancy (see Elazar, 1976: 33–6; Cohen, 1983: 76–97; Kuznets, 1975; Zenner, 1980, forthcoming).

2. As the majority of American Jews enter what are the third and fourth generations since immigration from Eastern Europe, one finds a decline in institutional affiliation, both with synagogues and with the philanthropic and defense organizations. More and more later-generational Jews have more and more Gentile friends and spouses, although predominantly Jewish familial and friendship circles continue to have importance.

3. There has been a decline in ritual observance, connected especially with more and more higher education and entry into the professions. This is less true of those who continue in the small business/self-employment sector.

4. Jews have moved away from their early inner-city and Northeastern metropolitan concentrations. Increasing numbers have moved to newer Sunbelt communities and new university centers and other areas where the traditional communal structures are 'underdeveloped.' Even there, however, they have formed new synagogues and other communal structures. As in other areas this follows a general trend.

5. The Jewish family has followed general trends in American society. The average age of marriage among Jews has risen and the fertility rate has declined. Divorces have risen and so has the tendency towards intermarriage. The latter two continue to be below the national averages for other groups but the general curves follow national trends. Communal affiliation among the single, the divorced, and the intermarried is lower than for those in conventional families.

6. Politically Jews have been associated with the Democratic party, at least since the 1930s, and have generally been characterized by left-liberal

sympathies. There have always been, however, Jews who were conservative and Republican. The latter have increased, as indicated by the fact that 40 percent of Jewish voters preferred Reagan in 1980, although it should be added that 60 percent continued to prefer more liberal candidates, notably Carter and Anderson in the same election.

7. As more and more Jews have moved out of the core of the community and become less affiliated with it, the more orthopraxic Jews have gained in confidence and prominence. Occupationally, educationally, and even behaviorally — outside of areas of ritual practice, these 'integral Jews,' as Elazar (1976: 71) calls them, are similar to their 'assimilating' counterparts. Among them as among the Conservative, Reform, and unaffiliated, one finds increasing divorce and alcoholism — although the extent to which this is true may be less. Even intermarriage (although here inevitably accompanied by conversion) is found among orthodox Jews. Herman Wouk (1959), a leading exponent of Orthodoxy in his book *This is My God*, is married to a woman of non-Jewish origin. The existence of the orthodox group among American Jews, is important in that it provides an important core and an alternative for others. By its persistence, adaptability, and rise to prominence, it provides a model.

These trends indicate the general conformity of American Jews to others in the United States, albeit with some twists which are uniquely Jewish.

Historical dimensions[3]

The special characteristics of Jewishness today must be understood in the light of Diaspora Jewish history. While technically open to converts, for the better part of two millennia Jews under Christendom and Islam were forbidden to accept proselytes. While Jews could convert to the majority religion, such conversion involved a total break with one's family and kin, unless they also converted. Since Jews were specialized economically, this often entailed a drastic change in occupation. During this period Jews were subject to rabbinic and secular authorities of the Jewish community. The community in both Europe and the Middle East was a recognized corporate body which collected taxes for itself and the state. Members could be disciplined by fines, ostracism, and other sanctions. Jewish atheists and 'non-Jewish Jews' did not exist in this period.

This pattern was broken in Western Europe during the eighteenth century. In Britain, the Jews had never had an organized community, while in other lands the power of the organized community over its members was broken by official governmental acts. By the 1880s, this 'opening of ghetto gates' extended to the population centers of Eastern Europe (Baron, 1942; Endelman, 1979; Katz, 1963; Hertzberg, 1968).

In this process, Jewishness was transformed from having a close connection with a corporate body in a particular place and with similar communities elsewhere to something vague and ill-defined. Jews could opt out of the organized community, even when it was state-supported, without conversion. They could ignore Jewish institutions in their everyday lives. Now a whole range of people were recognized as Jews from near-converts to Christianity who had not been baptized, and unbelievers, through the inter-married, moderate Reform, Conservative, to ultra-Orthodox Jews who segregated themselves from the others. Increasing numbers of Jews went to school and worked side-by-side with Gentiles though their social lives were often segregated (Sharot, 1976: 63—100; Katz, 1973: 104—222).

In North America, informal and flexible patterns of communal organization developed early on. Judaism was not an established religion. The rigid division between Central European and Spanish—Portuguese Jews was not maintained. American Jews followed the Protestant pattern of organizing on congregational lines. There was nothing to prevent secession, if a faction disapproved of a rabbi on personal, political or religious lines. In the nineteenth century, American Jewry was split between the Reform and the more traditional Conservative—Orthodox groupings. The massive East European migration at the end of that century was itself divided by a variety of ideologies, including socialist, nationalist, Yiddishist, Hebraist, orthodox and atheist. Efforts at forming an umbrella communal structure failed at both the national level and in New York City (Howe, 1976). Only when some of the ideological divisions lessened in importance and the sense of outside danger during the Second World War increased could some successful coordination of effort occur. Still, each organization to this day maintains its autonomy. In addition, any Jew in America can defy the wishes of the community and can probably find some other Jews who will sympathize with him/her. Of course, some issues, such as assertive opposition to the State of Israel, will still call forth a measure of ostracism.

The impact of American individualism and conformity

In dealing with American Jewry, one must weight the impact of general United States culture. Much of this culture is shared with other countries of West European origin, although the degree of competitive individualism is considered more extreme here than even in Canada. Paradoxically the pressures to conform to American ways is also stronger. This is explained by the shared criteria of success found in American society. This individualism has been accepted by American Jews. Mark Glazer (1973)[4] has contrasted the Jews of Chicago with those of Istanbul. In his work he demonstrates the great importance which American Jews give to being American, rather than Jewish, to non-kin acquaintances, and to intimacy limited to spouse and children. As opposed to the Istanbul Sephardic Jews, parents and siblings and certainly cousins are unimportant to the Chicago Jews. While in an American context, Jewish Americans are often seen as having strong kin networks, even forming recreational groups like cousin clubs (Mitchell, 1978), when seen in cross-cultural perspective, their intimate ties resemble those of other 'self-reliant' Americans. Glazer's contrast also shows the integration of American Jewry in Anglophone America, their economic success, and their adoption of American identity. This is unlike their Ashkenazic forbears in Eastern Europe and their Sephardic cousins in Turkey.

Anglo-conformity which marked American cultural policies until recently was particularly successful because it was not imposed by the federal government but through the zeal of English-speaking Americans at every level of society. Immigrants were encouraged to speak English, adopt American dress, and American ways. Even new immigrants within two or three years of arrival found themselves going to public school, eating turkey with dressing on Thanksgiving, and becoming spiritual descendants of the Mayflower Pilgrims. Compulsory education and universal conscription during the two World Wars speeded this process. The public schools and more recently the mass media encouraged conformity in other areas as well, such as the adoption of American dating patterns. The trend towards 'sexual liberation' which became so clear during the 1960s was, in fact, a logical consequence of premarital patterns of dating and the choice of marital partners on the basis of sexual attraction, characteristic of America since the 1920s. Except for the Hasidim and, to a lesser extent, among Middle Eastern Jews, such mores have been accepted by most segments of American Jewry.[5]

American individualism is often expressed by everyone wanting to do their own thing with the least amount of restriction possible, even though it may mean conforming to what one's neighbour is doing. There is also fierce competition on both an individual and collective level. 'Grantsmanship' — the competition for public funds — is an expression of this even though it involves redistribution of revenues. This individual competitiveness fits very well into the vocabulary of freedom and rights.

From 1840 to 1950, there was intense competition by Jews in forming congregations, philanthropic groups and communal organizations. Often these groups worked at cross-purposes, even during the tragic period of the Second World War. Since 1950, the competition has abated though the old organizations persist. New groups continue to be formed. These include the radically separatist and militantly rightwing Jewish Defense League, the formation of gay synagogues, the various moderate and radical leftwing groups, the havurot, feminist circles, and organizations which attempt to assert a departure from the Establishment like the Committee for a Safe Israel, Breira, Friends of Peace Now, and the New Jewish Agenda. Many such groups are ephemeral but they may form the cutting edge of a new establishment (e.g., Maibaum, 1971).

The competitiveness of individual entrepreneurship has also entered into the regulation and observance of the dietary laws among traditional orthopraxic Jews. In the traditional community, the rabbi served as judge of the community, not for a voluntarily organized association. Supervision of the slaughter of kosher animals for eating was equally communal; indeed, in most larger communities, the shohet or ritual slaughterer was considered a communal functionary and the proceeds from the sale of kosher meat went into the community's treasury (Baron, 1942: 107–10 and 256–60). A quite different situation prevails in the United States. There is no official communal or governmental supervision, except insofar as the government may provide some protection against fraud. In addition, new complications have arisen. One is the fact of long-distance slaughter and shipment of meat, so that butchers in community X must depend upon slaughterhouses far away. Another is that people rely more and more upon previously prepared foods and only obtain information about ingredients and the presumed propriety of the food from labels.

While local kashrut councils still exist, individuals may choose to buy kosher or non-kosher meat. Those who observe the dietary laws may either buy locally butchered meat or meat prepared hundreds of miles away under the supervision of rabbis whom they trust. There is competition between different orthodox factions for which group has the most trustworthy supervision. This is especially the case with regard to products for the Passover when the strictest laws apply and when many who are indifferent to kashrut during the rest of the year buy prepared foods which are proper for that holiday (Shenker, 1979).

In the realm of food there have been other influences as well. The possibility of synthetic foods which look like what they are not and the introduction of new tastes have left their mark on the orthopraxic. As far as the former is concerned there are now products which appear to be dairy but which can be served with meat, like Dairy Cream, and the reverse, such as artificial bacon bits. The international styles which mark American cuisine today can be found in a kosher form, such as French, Italian and Chinese.

Traditional Jewish retentions and their elaborations

The word 'retention' must be defined, for it refers to traits present in a culture or subculture which are historically traceable to a previous period, but which may have a new function. Many whose social scientific training is post-functional or Marxist mistakenly see such a usage as synonymous with 'survival' as used by Fraser and other evolutionists. To anyone with historical knowledge of Jewish ritual, it is obvious that Jewish ritual even in the attenuated form practiced by large numbers of American Jews is a retention. The services in a Reform synagogue, for instance, still are structurally based on the same prayers as that of the Orthodox synagogues and the text of the prayers, albeit, altered, abridged and reinterpreted is recognizably from the same source.

Priorities in observance have changed. Previously minor rituals and ceremonies have been given much wider observance. So Hanukkah, a once minor holiday, has become a visible sign of Jewishness, obviously because it is parallel to Christmas and it is suited to Zionism and American ideas of religious liberty. The Bar Mitzvah ceremony which only developed during the late Middle Ages and its half-century old companion, the Bat Mitzvah ceremony, now mark a crucial rite between childhood and adolescence for American Jewish youth. These ceremonies have even replaced the once widely observed Confirmation ritual of the Reform which was based on a Lutheran model. Yom Kippur and the Passover Seder remain central observances. Other ceremonies and holidays have declined in importance and are often not observed by the multitudes of non-orthodox Jews, such as Sukkot (the Feast of Tabernacles, which comes five days after Yom Kippur).

The synagogue, home observances of festivals, Jewish community centers and the like help demarcate a Jewish symbolic arena in both time and space. While many, if not most, Jews only move in and out of the arena a few times a year, others remain in the arena for a wide range of activities. While there is no corporate Jewish body, the activities within the arena and the movements through it indicate that American Jewry retains its vitality.

One important activity within the arena has been fundraising. The importance of fundraising and giving has been related to the traditional Jewish value of *sedaqah* or charity (Elazar, 1976: 86–95; S. Cohen, 1983: 46–75, 56–75, 61–2, 128–9, 144, 156). Fundraising shows the overlap of Jewish and American values and norms. In addition to the value of *sedaqah* or charity, Jewish communal life has often been marked by intense competition for having the honor of giving large sums of money for synagogues, burial societies and the poor. Such competitiveness has been found in communities from Germany to Iran (Loeb, 1978). In the United States, such traditional patterns of giving have been utilized by the highly professional and sophisticated fundraisers of the United Jewish Appeal and other organizations.

So far our concern has been with central symbols and values which transcend specific Jewish culture areas and speech communities. Jewishness in America, however, has an association with the former Yiddish-speaking Ashkenazic Jews from Eastern Europe, who form the vast majority of American Jews. Some identifiable art-forms and styles representing this culture persist. Woody Allen, for instance, shows that an assertively New York Jewish comedian can become a star. In recent years, there has been a revival of *klezmer*, an improvisational form of music from Eastern Europe, albeit performed today primarily for Jewish audiences. Generally, however, American Jews increasingly share the tastes of other Americans. Bagels are becoming as American as pizza, frankfurters, chop suey and apple pie, while younger Jews are often giving up corn beef for alfalfa sprouts. The differences in styles and tastes between Jews and their neighbors are diminishing, as the East European influence becomes more and more diluted.[6]

The marginally Jewish

In America today, the boundary between Jew and non-Jew is not a clear one. There are those who identify as Jews who would be excluded by Jewish law. These include the children of Jewish men by non-Jewish women (now accepted as Jews by the Reform), judaizing Christians who observe Jewish ritual, and members of Black sects which define themselves as Hebrews or Israelites but are not necessarily accepted as such by Jews. There are also people born as Jews but excluded from the community because of their conversion and participation in other religions, both Christian and non-Christian. Finally there are Jews who do not consider themselves Jews because of their lack of belief in Judaism and their non-participation in the Jewish community. These may include the children of Jewish women by non-Jewish men. Several of these categories deserve further discussion.

The intermarried and their children are obviously the largest and most important category here, whether we are dealing with Jewish men marrying non-Jewish women, or Jewish women who marry non-Jewish men. Conversions may occur in either direction or no religious conversion or affiliation may be the result. There has been a steady and inexorable increase in intermarriage which has undergone sociological scrutiny, although the study of the children of the intermarried has only recently begun to receive the attention it deserves.

Despite considerable effort by Jewish sociologists, the actual rate of intermarriage between Jews and non-Jews is impossible to calculate accurately. One national study had as its findings for the period 1966–72 that *c.* 9 percent of Jews were intermarried, but that in the period 1966–72 the number intermarrying was *c.* 32 percent (Temkin, 1982). Steven Cohen's heading 'Intermarriage Ever Upward' (1983: 122) expressed an indubitable consensus among social scientists. The increasing integration and dispersion of American Jewry can only increase this rate. About one-quarter of non-Jewish spouses (especially females) report conversion to Judaism, although again this should not be taken too literally.

In terms of outcome, the increasing secularization of the society has possibly resulted in less concern with religious conversion altogether, but rather with an accommodation. For the non-religious Jew and non-Jew, this may result in a compromise of general non-observance, possibly including both Christmas and Hanukkah. Thus a child may light the Hanukkah candles and get a visit from Santa Claus.[7] Even the converted may have double religious experiences. In one large American metropolitan area, a Greek woman married a Sephardic Jew and converted to Judaism. She participates in the activities of an orthodox synagogue, sends her children to a Hebrew day school, but on Sundays her children attend Greek school at the local Orthodox church. A Jew who agreed to raise his children as Catholics goes with his family each year to his parents' Passover Seder. On his return home, Barry Rosen, one of the Embassy hostages in Iran, attended a mass at St. Patrick's Cathedral with his Catholic wife. Then he went to Temple Emanu-El and asked to hold the Torah scroll in his arms as a sign of thanksgiving (Blair, 1981).

Such anecdotes may be multiplied.[8] A recent study of the children of intermarriage show that those whose non-Jewish parent converted have a stronger identity as Jews than those whose parents did not. However, for both categories Jewishness is seen as an individual religious preference; they do not perceive it as a primordial non-contingent commitment (Mayer, 1980, 1983a; Lazerwitz, 1971). All this leads to a diminution of the Jewish community as one built on kinship and descent.

As indicated above, the 'non-Jewish Jews' are an important component of modern Jewry, even though they lie outside the organized community for the most part. They certainly overlap with the intermarried and often provide recruits for other religions. Many Jews have been attracted to Asian religions, including Hare Krishna, the Maharishi movement, and groups linked to other gurus, as well as to the Unification Church. The interaction between Judaism and Christianity continues to be the most significant one for Americans.

The shifting boundaries between 'Christian Jews' and 'judaizing Christians' involve small numbers in a religiously sincere form, but are significant for their possible ramifications. Since the Enlightenment, European Jews have participated in a Christian-based culture, however secular it may seem. Jewish writers, like the Yiddish novelist Sholem Asch (1966), the Hebrew-Zionist historian Joseph Klausner, and the American Reform biblical scholar, Sanford Sandmel have written sympathetic books on Jesus and his followers. Chagall painted murals for churches, while Leonard Bernstein, whose career started with a very Jewish *Jeremiah* symphony has also written a very idiosyncratic Mass.

While the 'christianity' and apostasy of those who joined established churches has always been clearly recognized by both Christian and Jew, it is common for converts to Christianity to assert that for them Christianity is the highest form of Judaism (K. Stern, 1951). Most of these converts, still, throw off the practice of Jewish ritual with their conversion to Catholicism and Protestantism. Since the nineteenth century, however, a number of organizations, often under missionary auspices have sprung up which have combined Christian doctrine with the use of Hebrew and of Jewish ritual. The 'Jews for Jesus' who preach what they call 'Messianic Judaism' are a recent variety. Most Jews see such organizations as mere fronts for Protestant missionary activity and are not ready to accept such 'Messianic Jews' as members in good standing in the community. Still students who are members of evangelical Jews for Jesus groups may return home to attend their families' Seders at Passover. Bob Dylan has gone through phases of Zionism and a born-again Christianity, thus exemplifying these trends.

Besides converts to Christianity and individuals who convert to Judaism, there are also judaising trends within the Christian churches. Such 'heretical' groups have existed since the separation between Judaism and Christianity in the first century. On a certain level, a sect like the Seventh Day Adventists who switched from the observance of Sunday to Saturday as the Sabbath can be seen as such a group. Some of their equivalents actually moved into the Jewish fold.[9]

In America, one finds the mainstream churches being more open to Jewish influences than in the past. Both Protestants and Roman Catholics today acknowledge the Jewish roots of Christianity. This has been symbolized in particular by Christian celebrations of the Passover Seder prior to Easter. There have also been judaizers. A few years ago, a group of Lutheran ministers were accused of subordinating Christian doctrine to Jewish practice. These Lutheran ministers and their followers on Long Island adopted Jewish practices, including a strict observance of the Sabbath and dietary laws. In fact, the main service was held on Sunday night, so members did not have to drive their cars on the Sabbath. Yet they were still believers in the divinity of Christ and came from Gentile families (Molotsky, 1977). More recently, they have reformed their congregations into a kind of Christian synagogue with a Hebrew name (*New York Times*, 1983). While coming from a different direction, such groups can be seen as merging with the 'messianic Jews.'

Like converts to other religions, converts to Judaism come from a variety of backgrounds and for many different reasons. A particularly noteworthy case was that of James Eli Mahan, Jr., an American Protestant who was a Vietnam war veteran and son of a professional soldier. He converted to Reform Judaism and then to orthodoxy before joining a group of ultra-nationalists in Hebron on the West Bank, where he became a martyr for Israel's right wing as Eli-Hazeev (Taubman and Shipler, 1980).

Judaism among blacks in the United States must be considered separately. There are several categories of Black Jews in the United States. One group consists of black, mixed-race and Asian children who have been adopted by Jewish families and who like their white counterparts are converted to Judaism. Another are individuals who convert to one or another mainstream branch of Judaism, either because of marriage to a Jew, for personal religious reasons or both. Sammy Davis, Jr., is a prominent member of this grouping. Again, there is no essential difference between these and White converts, although it is obvious that race aggravates the difficulty for acceptance of converts by ethnic Jews.

Black Jewish sects are a separate phenomenon, in some ways, resembling other judaising sects. Black Jews historically and sociologically are similar to the Black Muslim groups and the Rastafarians. All of these sects represent a search for a new identity and for roots among the descendants of African slaves in the New World. Like the Muslims, many of these black Jews assert that their true identity is that of Hebrews and thus they claim Jewishness as a birthright, as authentic as that of the white Jews. Such an assertion challenges the white Jews, especially since they perceive the Jewish ritual practiced by the blacks as flawed. For the most part white Jews see such blacks as neither sincere converts nor as true Jews.

There are further nuances to this process, however. Black Jewish groups range from those which are syncretistic, combining African, Christian, and other elements with Jewish traits to those who seek to conform to orthodox Judaism. Groups and individuals which do so conform have succeeded in being accepted by other orthodox Jews. One example is the son of a black rabbi who became a star basketball player for the Orthodox Jewish Yeshiva University.[10]

All of these cases indicate a blurring of formerly clear ethnic/religious boundaries. Many different kinds of choices regarding religion and ethnic identity are being made. Simultaneously the central organizations are unable to control these choices, whether it is Conservative congregations which permit the intermarried to participate in the congregation or the Reform rabbinical organization which cannot discipline rabbis who conduct mixed marriages without conversion of the Gentile party.[11] Thus boundary maintenance, often seen as an essential quality of ethnicity (Barth, 1969), becomes extremely difficult.

Regenerative processes[12]

Most of the emphasis here has been on how individualism has contributed to assimilation and the erosion of Jewish ethnicity and religiosity. Few social processes are clearly unidirectional. The emphasis has been on those processes indicating disintegration. There are also aspects, however, which indicate that American Jewry has the ability to maintain and reproduce Jewish cultural forms, particularly but not solely in the religious sphere.

Scholars and rabbis are now trained in North America as well as being imported. The Reform and the Conservative no longer rely on defectors from orthodox families for congregational rabbis. Jewish day schools have grown in numbers since the 1940s and exist in small and peripheral communities such as Dayton, Ohio, and Bangor, Maine, as well as in large metropolitan areas. They serve non-orthodox as well as orthodox Jews for a variety of reasons, but one of the motives must be the continued desire of Jewish parents for a Jewish schooling for their children. The orthodox day schools have contributed to the maintenance and growth of orthodox Judaism in the past two decades.

The continuing desire of Jews to express themselves as Jews persists. This is as true of leftist radicals as of neo-conservatives and mainstream liberals. Thus, an atheist rabbi in the 1970s founded a Society for Humanistic Judaism, whereas in the nineteenth century a rabbi had formed the non-ethnic Society for Ethical Culture. Jewish feminists organized their own circles and their own journal, *Lilith*. There are Jewish organizations which have combined left-liberal and radical programs, often critical of Israel and the American Jewish community, such as the New Jewish Agenda. The organizers of these groups include both religious and secular Jews. In addition, many *havurot*, or informal prayer and discussion groups, have been formed by non-orthodox religious Jews.

The fact that Judaism, is a religious tradition with profoundly ethical, philosophic, and mystical strains makes it possible for individuals to find paths to self-fulfillment within it, on a level not possible to a primarily ethnic tradition. Those who find such comfort within Judaism include a wide range of people, even though their numbers are small. For instance, a woman from an orthodox family, married to a university professor, has found her niche by active membership in a Reform congregation. She has made her family much more observant of the Sabbath and other rituals, but not in an orthopraxic way. Another woman, born to a radical non-Jewish family, was married to a Jew. She did not convert at marriage. Since she divorced her husband, she has formally converted to Judaism and now considers herself a traditionalist. She is not alone in this (Mayer, 1983b). Such individuals strain relationships within their families, although Judaism is a familistic religion.

There are also revivalist efforts within the Jewish community, which utilize various forms of missionary activity to attract Jews to more traditional forms of Judaism. Some of these rely primarily on traditional forms like that of the *yeshiva* (Talmudic academy), while others utilize evangelical techniques adapted from Protestant models to Jewish purposes. The yeshivot, primarily in Israel,[13] for *baale teshuvah* (penitents, returnees – the Jewish term for such individuals) are examples of the former approach (Aviad, 1983). The rebbetzin Esther Jungreis is an exemplar of the latter, while the Chabad (Lubovicher) Chassidic movement combines a variety of techniques.

Most of these approaches, however, are individualistic. They bear on separate persons, not on the groups. As Sheingold has pointed out, they often involve intra-familial tensions. A 'return to Judaism' whether of an orthodox or non-orthodox variety is often difficult to sustain without a family or traditional support group (Handelman, 1984; Sheingold, 1981).

Jewishness and ethnicity in America

In this discussion of Jewish ethnicity, I have stressed the religious aspect of Jewishness, rather than a more general cultural aspect or the material basis for ethnic solidarity. Anyone examining the sociological literature on Jews will be struck by the importance of ritual observance. This connection between religion and ethnicity is not confined to Jews. Basic assumptions regarding the nature of the world reside in most ethnic ideologies which mobilize people to action, whether it is the connection of blood, language, and soil that underlies much modern nationalism or the Orthodox liturgy of many Balkan nationalities. Among Jews, for a variety of reasons the ethnic or descent element was bound more intimately with the religious than in other groups. Yet in modern times, this bond was partially, but only partially, severed.

If we consider the Jews in America, in contradistinction to other ethnic groups of similar vintage, such as the Irish, the Italians, and the Poles, we find that they, unlike the latter, have a mechanism for accepting new members. It is conversion; yet only religions convert, ethnic groups do not. Thus one may see a possible course which Jewishness is America is likely to follow and in which it may persist. This was, of course, the dominant form of Jewish identity for a long time in America, outside of New York City. Now, however, it may be based more on choice by individuals of both Jewish and non-Jewish origin than it was in the past.

The religious forms of Judaism, whether traditionalist or modernist, will, however, have to compete with each other and with alternative claimants. These may include secularism and 'Hebrew Christianity.' If ethnic identity is a matter of ascription, then Jewish identity as a choice will have lost much of its ethnic character. Such a transformation requires many radical changes, but they are within the realm of possibility against the background of American individualism. The content of Jewishness in America combines retentions with forms and meanings which are infused with North American values. This, of course, replicates a process which has recurred in many places throughout Jewish history. What makes this process different today is that while there are many Jewish arenas, it is often hard to pinpoint real communities in a structural sense. Again it is permeated by individual activity.

This transformation can be seen as a triumph of the Enlightenment which sought to replace the old tribalisms with a sense of universal brotherhood. Yet when a particular moment is examined, Americans continue to have fierce particularistic loyalties, including devotion to their professions and disciplines, but they can be persuaded to throw these off when the economic climate and the winds of fashion change. What has happened is that many former life-long commitments, including those relating to kinship and ethnicity, have become commodities. Whether such a transformation is one which portends more freedom for the individual or totalitarian tyranny is hidden from our sight.

Notes

*Richard Alba asked me to write this paper and has made many valuable suggestions. Robert Jarvenpa read and commented on an earlier version. The many syntheses of studies of American Jewry which I read influenced my own interpretation of the limited aspects presented here. Important among these are those by Liebman (1973), Heilman (1982), and Cohen (1983). My own participation in the community and my research are also reflected here. I take full responsibility for the viewpoint herein expressed. To preserve anonymity details in several examples used in the paper have been altered.

1.   I have dealt with these implications for American Jews in Zenner (1980, and forthcoming), ch. VIII. For an attempt to compare different groups and categories, see my forthcoming book, especially chs. III, VI, and VII.

2.   Obviously those who posited the 'triple-melting-pot' thesis in the 1950s looked at the interplay for the full spectrum of White ethnic groups. (See Herberg, 1960.)

3.   I am following here the modernization perspective which is a dominant one in Judaic social history and sociology. For examples, see Katz (1961, 1973), Sharot (1976), Elazar (1976), S.M. Cohen (1977). An alternative would be to view these changes as acculturation to a West European cultural pattern.

4.   Glazer (1973) is testing the hypotheses of Frances Hsu (1971).

5.   Syrian Jews are a partial exception to the trend in that their adoption of American

patterns seems slower than that of other groups. See Zenner (1983), Sutton (1979).
On other Sephardic Jews, see Fredman (1982) and S. Stern (1977).
6.   See Duker (1960) for a discussion of these patterns. Duker's description of main-stream American Jewish culture should be followed up. Also see Carolyn L. Weiner
(1972) and Epstein (1978).
7.   For the meaning of Christmas to assimilated American Jews, see Matz (1963).
Also see Roiphe's personal account (Roiphe, 1981).
8.   For an account showing the 'Jewishness' of Felix Rohatyn an intermarried member
of the 'ruling elite' see McClintick (1984).
9.   On 'Hebrew Christians' in the past, see S. Sharot (1968), B.Z. Sobel (1974), Marton
(1971).
10.   On black Jewish sects which originated in the United States, see H. Brotz (1964),
R. Landes (1967), Pieter van Bennekom (1979) and Morris Lounds (1981).
11.   There is one effective central organization in the world which can define Jewishness
on certain levels. That is the Israeli government, which for purposes of the Law of
Return, must define who is a Jew. The Law of Return is that law which permits
any Jew to immigrate to Israel; it does not exclude the immigration of non-Jews who are
admitted on another basis. In general, the Israeli government follows traditional halakhah
in defining who is a Jew in terms of being born to a Jewish woman or converted in an
orthodox legal fashion. But, even for Israel, this does not resolve the problem, since
there are problematic categories such as Ethiopian Falashas, the Bene Israel from India,
American Black Hebrews, non-Jews who pass as Jews, native Israelis who are 'Jews
for Jesus,' children of mixed Jewish-Christian couples, etc. Some of these are recognized
as Jews, while others are not. The large non-traditional secular sector, while not
necessarily the majority has the same essential openness as do non-orthodox Jews in
the U.S. (Roshwald, 1970); on the problem of defining a Jew in a more general sense,
see Berofsky (1983).
12.   Robert Jarvenpa suggests that processes like regeneration contradict our efforts
to measure assimilation and acculturation in a linear fashion.
13.   *Aliyah* or immigration to Israel itself is an attempt to regenerate one's Jewish
roots. It certainly can affect the family left behind in America. In many cases, going
to Israel and returning is a process of many comings and going (see Avruch, 1982).

References

ASCH, SHOLOM 1966 *One Destiny – An Epistle to Christians*. New York: G.P. Dutton.
AVIAD, JANET 1983 *Return to Judaism*. Chicago: University of Chicago Press.
AVRUCH, KEVIN 1982 'On the "Traditionalization" of Social Identity: American
Immigrants in Israel.' *Ethos* 19(2): 95–116.
BARON, SALO W. 1942 *The Jewish Community*. Philadelphia: Jewish Publication
Society of America.
BARTH, FREDRIK 1969 *Ethnic Groups and Boundaries*. Boston: Little, Brown.
BEROFSKY, BERNARD 1983 'Jewish Self-Definition and Exile,' in E. Levine (ed.),
Diaspora: Exile and the Jewish Condition. New York: Jason Aronson, pp. 101–25.
BLAIR, W.G. 1981 'St. Patrick's Resounds to Cheers for Ex-Hostage.' *New York
Times*, January 30, B–1; B–6.
BROTZ, HOWARD 1964 *The Black Jews of Harlem*. New York: The Free Press.
COHEN, STEVEN 1983 *American Modernity and Jewish Identity*. New York and
London: Tavistock.
DAVIS, MOSHE 1960 'Jewish Religious Life and Institutions in America', *in* L.
Finkelstein (ed.), *The Jews: Their History, Culture and Religion*. New York: Harper,
3rd ed., pp. 488–587.
DUKER, ABRAHAM 1960 'Notes on the Culture of American Jewry.' *Jewish Journal
of Sociology* 2(1): 98–102.

ELAZAR, DANIEL 1976 *Community and Polity*. Philadelphia: Jewish Publication Society.

ENDELMAN, TODD 1979 *Jews in Georgian England: Tradition and Crises in a Liberal Society*. Philadelphia: Jewish Publication Society.

EPSTEIN, A.L. 1978 *Ethos and Identity: Three Studies in Ethnicity*. Chicago: Aldine.

FREDMAN, RUTH G. 1982 *Cosmopolitans at Home: Sephardic Jews of Washington, D.C.* Ph.D. dissertation, Anthropology, Temple University, Philadelphia.

GLAZER, MARK 1973 *Psychological Intimacy among the Jews of North Metropolitan Chicago and the Sephardic Jews of Istanbul, Turkey*. Ph.D. dissertation, Northwestern University. Ann Arbor: University Microfilms Order No. 73, 30, 591.

GLAZER, NATHAN 1957 *American Judaism*. Chicago: University of Chicago Press.

HANDELMAN, SUSAN 1984 'The Honeymoon is Over: Ba'alei Teshuvah after Ten Years'. *Melton Journal*, No. 18 (Summer 1984): 6–8, 18.

HEILMAN, SAMUEL 1982 'The Sociology of American Jewry.' *Annual Review of Sociology* 8: 135–60.

HERBERG, WILL 1960 *Protestant, Catholic, Jew*. New York: Doubleday Anchor.

HERTZBERG, ARTHUR 1968 *The French Enlightenment and the Jews*. New York: Columbia University Press.

HOWE, IRVING 1976 *The World of Our Fathers*. New York: Harcourt Brace Jovanovich.

HSU, FRANCIS L.K. 1971 'Psychosocial Homeostasis and *Jen*: Conceptual Tools for Advancing Psychological Anthropology.' *American Anthropologist* 73: 23–44.

KATZ, JACOB 1961 *Tradition and Crisis*. New York: Schocken.

KATZ, JACOB 1973 *Out of the Ghetto*. Cambridge, Mass.: Harvard University Press.

KUGELMASS, JACK 1982 'Cultures in Contact: Jews and Blacks in the South Bronx.' Paper presented at the Annual Meeting of the American Anthropological Association, Washington, D.C., December 6.

KUZNETS, SIMON 1972 *The Economic Structure of U.S. Jewry*. Jerusalem: Hebrew University Institute for Contemporary Jewry.

LANDES, RUTH 1967 'Negro Jews in Harlem.' *Jewish Journal of Sociology* 9(2): 175–90.

LAZERWITZ, B. 1971 'Intermarriage and Conversion: A Guide for Future Research.' *Jewish Journal of Sociology* 13(1): 41–64.

LIEBMAN, CHARLES 1973 *The Ambivalent American Jew*. Philadelphia: Jewish Publication Society.

LOEB, LAURENCE D. 1978 'Prestige and Piety in the Iranian Synagogue.' *Anthropological Quarterly* 51: 155–61.

LOUNDS, MORRIS 1981 *Israel's Black Hebrews*. Washington: University Press of America.

McCLINTICK, DAVID 1984 'Life at the Top.' *New York Times Magazine* (August 5): 22–6, 48–62.

MAIBAUM, MATTHEW 1971 'The Berkeley Hillel and the Union of Jewish Students: The History of a Conflict.' *Jewish Journal of Sociology* 13: 153–72.

MARTON, Y. 1971 'Bezidul Nou.' *Encyclopaedia Judaica* 4: 970–1.

MATZ, MILTON 1961 'The Significance of the Christmas Tree to American Jews.' *Jewish Journal of Sociology* 3: 129–37.

MAYER, EGON 1980 'Processes and Outcomes: Marriages Between Jews and Non-Jews.' *American Behavioral Scientist* 23: 487–518.

MAYER, EGON 1983a *Children of Intermarriage*. New York: American Jewish Committee.

MAYER, EGON 1983b 'Jews by Choice: Some Reflections on Their Impact on the Contemporary American Jewish Community.' Paper presented at the Annual Meeting of the Rabbinical Assembly, Dallas, Texas, April 12.

MITCHELL, WILLIAM E. 1978 *Mishpokhe: A Study of New York City Jewish Family Clubs*. The Hague: Mouton.

MOLOTSKY, J. 1977 'Two Long Island Churches Hold Christian and Jewish Services.' *New York Times* (November 7): 1: 21.

NEW YORK TIMES 1983 'Update on the News.' November 13.

ROIPHE, MARION R. 1981 *Generation without Memory: A Jewish Journey in Christian America*. Boston: Beacon Press.

ROSHWALD, MORDECHAI 1970 'Who is a Jew in Israel?' *Jewish Journal of Sociology* 12: 233–66.

SHAROT, S. 1968 'A Jewish Christian Adventist Movement.' *Jewish Journal of Sociology* 10: 35–46.

SHAROT, S. 1976 *Judaism – A Sociology*. Newton Abbot: David & Charles.

SHEINGOLD, CARL 1981 'Jewish Rejuvenation.' Paper presented at the Conference on the Evolving Jewish Family, New York, Queens College, June 21.

SHENKER, ISRAEL 1979 'With Them It's Strictly Kosher.' *New York Times Magazine* (April 15): 32–42.

SKLARE, M. 1971 *America's Jews*. New York: Random House.

SKLARE, M. 1974 *Jews in American Society*. New York: Behrman House.

SOBEL, B.Z. 1974 *Hebrew Christianity – The 13th Tribe*. New York: John Wiley.

STERN, KARL 1951 *Pillar of Fire*. New York: Harcourt Brace.

STERN, STEPHEN 1977 *The Sephardic Jewish Community of Los Angeles: A Study in Folklore and Ethnic Identity*. Ph.D. thesis, Indiana University Folklore. Ann Arbor: University Microfilms International No. 77–22, 676.

SUTTON, JOSEPH A.D. 1979 *Magic Carpet: Aleppo-in-Flatbush*. Brooklyn, N.Y.: Thayer, Jacoby.

TAUBMAN, P., and D. SHIPLER 1980 'Martyr for Israel's Hard-Liners Sprang from Extremism in U.S.' *New York Times* (May 12): A–1, A–14.

TEMKIN, SEFTON 1982 'Jewish Life in the U.S., 1972–1982.' *Encyclopedia Judaica* supplement.

VAN BENNEKOM, PIETER 1979 'New cult makes political waves in Guyana.' *Albany Times-Union*, (November 25): D1 (U.P.I. dispatch).

WEINER, CAROLYN L. 1972 'A Merger of Synagogues in San Francisco.' *Jewish Journal of Sociology* 14: 2: 167–96.

WOUK, HERMAN 1959 *This Is My God*. New York: Doubleday.

ZENNER, WALTER P. 1980 'American Jewry in the Light of Middleman Minority Theories.' *Contemporary Jewry* 5(1): 11–30.

ZENNER, WALTER P. 1983 'Syrian Jews in New York Twenty Years Ago', *in Fields of Offerings: Studies in Honor of Raphael Patai*. New York: Herzl Press, pp. 173–196.

ZENNER, WALTER P. forthcoming *Minorities in the Middle*. Philadelphia: ISHI Publications.

7 The twilight of ethnicity among Americans of European ancestry: the case of Italians*

Richard D. Alba
State University of New York at Albany

The course of ethnicity in advanced industrial societies continues to be debated without satisfactory resolution. Earlier social theorists, inspired by a vision of the erosion of traditional structures under the impact of a tide of modernization, tended to see ethnicity as receding. More recently, sociologists and others have proclaimed the resilience of ethnicity; for some, this is because ethnicity is an affiliation apart, primordial and only superficially modified by currents of modernization, while for others, it is due to ethnicity's moorings in durable structures of inequality.

Proponents of the view that ethnicity is resilient are the dominant voice in contemporary discussions, but their dominance is by no means assured, since the conceptual groundwork for interpreting ethnicity remains unsettled. There is in fact no consensus on the proper vantage point from which to view ethnicity, 'assimilation' having been dethroned as the crowning concept of the field over the last two decades (Blauner, 1972; Greeley, 1977).

This paper examines some of the interpretative difficulties surrounding ethnicity through the experiences of one group, Italian Americans. In particular, Italians are taken to constitute a strategic test case for some reigning assumptions in the study of ethnicity of European-ancestry groups in the United States. I will argue that the Italian experience demonstrates the importance of boundary-shifting processes, as opposed to assimilation at the individual level only, and that these shifts require for their explanation the invocation of historical contingencies, rooted in structural changes external to the group.

Assimilation and ethnic boundaries

For a long time, assimilation appeared as one of the most successful and important concepts for the study of ethnicity; this status is reflected in its classic treatment at the hands of Milton Gordon (1964). But much recent writing on ethnicity rejects or avoids assimilation as a focus of major concern. At least part of the reason appears to lie in an implicit model of assimilation, which is ahistorical, individualistic and incrementalist – which, in other words, does not connect assimilatory processes to macrostructural dynamics,

134

but instead conceives of them as individual decisions played out against a static background. Such a conception naturally places the emphasis on social psychological constructs, including the acceptability of a group's members to the majority or core and, perhaps more importantly, their motivation to merge with the majority. At the same time, it is implicitly one-directional: assimilating individuals are affiliating with a new group, thereby dropping the cultural and other garb of their original one.

This individualistic conception makes it easier to understand why assimilation has slipped out of the inner circle of concern. Since it assumes that assimilation hinges on the willingness of individuals to surrender to the majority, then the importance of assimilation would appear to decrease as this willingness does. And this is precisely what seemed to happen during the 1960s, in what appeared to many as a revival of ethnicity among American groups, both the racial minorities and, somewhat surprisingly, those of European ancestry. The revival meant, to use a characterization that, with minor variations, rings throughout the literature on ethnicity in America, that the ethnics were refusing to assimilate (e.g., Novak, 1972).

One difficulty with this diminishing of the importance of assimilation as a concept is that statistical indicators, such as intermarriage rates (Alba and Chamlin, 1983), suggest the cresting of assimilatory processes in recent decades. The apparent contradiction with the presumed ethnic revival indicates the limitations inherent in the individualistic conception of assimilation and the need to reconceptualize it in a way that allows it to be linked to structural processes of group formation and dissolution. One way to achieve this is to explicitly include the notion of group boundaries within the focus of assimilation. Group boundaries in this context refer to the recognition of ethnic distinctions in interaction, and thus are premised upon 'criteria for determining membership and ways of signalling membership and exclusion' (Barth, 1969: 15). Ethnic distinctions are socially maintained by such boundary markers as language, speech mannerisms, food, culture more broadly, and physical appearance, all of which can serve to identify group members to each other and to outsiders.

Reexamining the concept of assimilation with the notion of group boundaries in mind forces the recognition of two ideal types of assimilation. One is the type envisioned by the individualistic conception described above: namely, an individual moves across an ethnic boundary, transferring allegiance to another group, but without any change to the boundary itself. Assimilation of this kind can be viewed as a sort of population trade between different ethnic blocs (e.g., Newman, 1973; Greeley, 1971). Research advancing such an interpretation has emphasized such consequences of intermarriage as the conversion of one spouse to the religion of the other (Newman, 1973: 162–4). The consequences of this kind of assimilation for ethnic change are problematic; it can be plausibly argued that it does not weaken ethnicity.

The second kind is a group form: it is assimilation accomplished through a change in ethnic boundaries, either through a weakening to reduce their salience or through a shift that removes a previously recognized distinction.

By definition, such boundary changes mean changes to ethnicity as well. That they may occur is made plausible by the much noted observation that the coincidence of ethnic and other boundaries, such as those of occupation and residence, tends to enhance ethnic solidarity (Glazer and Moynihan, 1970; Hechter, 1978; Yancey *et al.*, 1976); consequently, a dilution through mobility of ethnic considerations in particular occupational strata or neighborhoods might be expected to weaken ethnic boundaries.

Empirically, of course, there is not necessarily a sharp distinction between the two types. Nonetheless, a separate recognition for the second type is valuable because it forces attention to the structural factors that may enhance or detract from ethnic solidarity, such as those stemming from the cultural division of labor (Hechter, 1978), group size (Blau, 1977), and the institutional completeness of ethnic communities (Breton, 1964).

The type of assimilation at the group level also underlines the cardinal importance of studying interethnic relations, since they provide a means of detecting ethnic boundaries and the changes that occur to them. The same does not hold true for the 'content' of boundaries, i.e., the cultural and other signs of group membership, which may change without change to the boundaries themselves (Barth, 1969); for this reason, the study of culture by itself is not decisive for resolving questions of ethnicity. The occurrence, even the frequent occurrence, of interethnic relations also need not contradict the existence of an ethnic boundary, but the maintenance of such a boundary requires that interethnic contacts be asymmetric in some fundamental way, as would be true of relations between members of groups of unequal status (Barth, 1969). Interactions structured by ethnicity help to maintain ethnic distinctions. This is generally not the case for symmetric, nonsegmental relations, such as those of friendship and marriage. A change in the pattern of such relations is a signal of a change in ethnic boundaries.[1]

A case in point: the Italian Americans

Italian Americans provide an intriguing example of the significance of boundary-shift processes as well as a litmus test for the most frequently advanced interpretations of ethnicity. Thus, those who argue for the persistence or revival of ethnicity generally point to white ethnic groups such as the Italians to support their arguments. In this view, Italians remain entrenched in ethnicity partly because of their recency of arrival and partly because their core values — in particular, the values embodied in the family — have enabled them to maintain solidary ethnic communities, manifest for example in vital urban neighborhoods.

These contemporary arguments find an echo in older ones. Few argued on behalf of the assimilability of the Italians at the time of their arrival, for they entered as one of the most despised of European immigrant groups (Higham, 1970). The bulk of the Italian immigration before the close of mass immigration in the 1920s came from the rural villages of the south, or Mezzogiorno, although because of the imprecision of both American and Italian statistics, it is not possible to estimate precisely the proportion from southern provinces (Sori, 1979).[2] The available statistics, however, do clearly support the well-known overall picture of an immigration swollen with a dislocated peasantry. For example, tabulations published by the Immigration Commission of 1911 reveal that in the crucial period 1899–1910, when 2.22 million Italian immigrants arrived on American shores (44 percent of the total from 1820 to 1970), 32 percent of those with European work experience described themselves as farm laborers and an additional 43 percent as laborers (Kessner, 1977: 33–4). The general category of 'laborer,' or *bracciante* in Italian, included many who had only recently been forced out of agricultural work (Sori, 1979).

The experiences of southern Italians hardly constituted preparation for integration into an urban, industrial society. The Mezzogiorno presents a classical picture of an underdeveloped society where the penetration of capitalist markets of land and labor created severe dislocations, uprooting peasants from the land and transforming them into a rural proletariat. By the latter part of the nineteenth century, many rural dwellers were forced to work the land of others, frequently under share-cropping or other tenancy arrangements that gave them little return for their efforts. Patterns of land holding and land use, combined with unfavorable climate and topography, produced an agriculture of scarcity, characterized by chronic shortages of work and food (Covello, 1972; Schneider and Schneider, 1976; Sori, 1979). And the nature of the work bore little relation either to farm or industrial work in the United States. The tools were primitive, so that, according to the immigrant writer, Constantine Panunzio, 'When they come to America, the work which comes nearest to that which they did in Italy is not farming or even farm labor, but excavation work' (Panunzio, 1928: 78; quoted by Kessner, 1977: 39).

The cultural values engendered by the social and material contours of the Mezzogiorno also did not mesh well with the exigencies in the United States. In such a landscape of scarcity, a supreme value was placed on the family. It has been observed many times that the family, not the individual, was the basic social atom of Mezzogiorno society; in the well-known words of Robert Foerster,

> Life in the South exalts the family. It has been said of Sicily that the
> family sentiment is perhaps the only deeply rooted moral sentiment that
> prevails. (Foerster, 1924: 95)

This was not, however, the 'amoral familism' of Banfield (1958), which portrays Mezzogiorno life as a Hobbesian war pitting each nuclear family against all others. Southern Italian social structure was constituted in good part from filaments of family-like relations extending beyond the nuclear family, such as extended kinship, fictive kinship created through the institution of godparentship (*compareggio*), and friendship (*amicizia*) (Chapman, 1971; Schneider and Schneider, 1976).

An aspect of the southern Italian ethos with repercussions for Italians in America lay in the presumption that family interests should take precedence over individual ones. A well-known instance of this occurred in relation to marriage. Since the position of a family was affected by the marriages of its members, families attempted to exert considerable control over the choice of a spouse, to the point that many marriages were arranged. Family control was enhanced by the sexual provisions of the Mezzogiorno's code of honor, which drastically restricted contact between eligible men and women (Chapman, 1971). A second instance lay in the economic value attached to children. In peasant families, children were generally expected to make an economic contribution as soon as they were able to work, beginning usually during adolescence. The early initiation to work brought an abrupt transition to adulthood. It also generally spelled the end of formal schooling. This was in any event in accordance with the family-centered culture, in which education was regarded with suspicion, as a potential danger to family solidarity (Covello, 1972: 257; Gambino, 1974).

This occupational and cultural background powerfully shaped the niche the immigrants were able to establish for themselves. The majority of Italian immigrants sought work in urban labor markets, in part because they frequently intended to repatriate after earning enough money to improve their position and this limited them to places where employment was readily available. But immigrants fresh from the peasantry discovered upon their arrival that only 'peek and shuvil' work, as Panunzio described it (quoted by Kessner, 1977: 58), was open to them. In 1905 in New York City, i.e., at the height of immigration in the city with the largest concentration of Italians in the United States, nearly 60 percent of Italian household heads did unskilled or semiskilled manual labor, working on construction gangs or as rag pickers and longshoremen (Kessner, 1977: 52–9). The reasons were not limited to a shortage of skills that could be applied in the industrial sector. Culturally engendered expectations about the nature of work, carried from the Mezzogiorno, also constrained occupational possibilities. That many immigrant men took jobs in construction or on the docks was partly a result of a preference for outdoor work, an attempt to reproduce familiar work cycles and conditions. This preference tended to consign Italians to seasonal work outside the regular channels of blue-collar mobility, which were found in factories (Yans-McLaughlin, 1977: 35–44).

Culture also limited the work horizons of women. One of Mezzogiorno's strongest prohibitions was directed against contact between women and male strangers, and this powerful norm went far toward defining what was an acceptable work situation for women. Work in the home was strongly preferred. Some took in boarders (generally relatives or paesani in order not to compromise the family honor), and others homework such as laundering or the manufacture of artificial flowers. One instance where Italian women did work outside the home occurred in the New York City garment industry, where women could work among other women (Yans-McLaughlin, 1977: 50–4).

Immigrant adjustment was complicated by the intention to repatriate. The number who ultimately returned to the Mezzogiorno is uncertain, but clearly it was large; one estimate is that 1.5 million Italians returned from the United States in the years between 1900 and 1914 (Caroli, 1973: 41). The sojourner's orientation toward the homeland, felt undoubtedly also by many who stayed, delayed such important adaptations as the acquisition of citizenship and the learning of English.[3] Lieberson's study of ten cities, for example, shows that in 1930, at a point when new immigration had all but ceased, Italians had the highest percentage of foreign-born who did not speak English in nine of the cities (they ranked second highest in the other); and they had the first or second highest percentages of immigrants who were not citizens in eight (Lieberson, 1963: 206–18). Obviously, this retarded adaptation had a large impact on the group, disadvantaging it relative to other immigrant groups who arrived around the same time (particularly in relation to Jews, who did not wish to return to the European societies from which they fled (Kessner, 1977: 167)).

The prospects for Italians seemed bleak also on the basis of American reactions to them. The Italian group arrived in a period when racial ideologies were widespread in the United States; and its arrival served to stimulate their further development, as Italians became a focus for explicitly racist thinking and stereotypes. The Italians were perceived as prone to crime, both organized and that spurred by passion and vengeance, the latter symbolized for Americans by the stiletto (Higham, 1970: 66–7). The Italian distinctiveness was perceived in physical terms as well: the immigrants were 'swarthy' and seemed to bear other signs of physical degradation, such as low foreheads. In the racially conscious climate, at a time when race theoreticians were attempting to draw biological distinctions among European peoples to the disfavor of those from the south and east, the question of color may have been unavoidable. It would go much too far to say that Italians were viewed as non-whites, but their color position was problematic. This is evident in the common epithet for them, 'guinea,' which was derived from a term referring originally to slaves from the western coast of Africa (Mencken, 1963: 373; Craigie and Hulbert, 1940: 1192–3).

The situation in the 1930s

The assimilability of the Italians continued to seem unlikely in the 1930s, after the close of the period of mass immigration. This is not to deny that significant cultural changes had taken place by then; these were especially evident in the transition to the second generation. Important aspects of the family-centered culture of the Mezzogiorno were so attuned to southern Italian situations that they could not be reestablished successfully in the United States. For example, strict control over unmarried daughters was only workable in southern Italian villages, where parents were in a position to evaluate the suitability of all potential suitors. Parental superiority broke down in American ghettos, since more acculturated children were better able to make appropriate matches for themselves. The extent of change in family norms is suggested by Ware's study of Greenwich Village in the early 1930s (Ware, 1935: 180–202). In a survey of its Italian residents, she found clear-cut differences between older and younger respondents, a division that no doubt corresponded well with generational status (i.e., foreign versus native-born). Older Italians were less likely than younger ones to reject such Mezzogiorno family norms as 'girls should not associate with men unless engaged' and parental arrangement of marriages.

But in other ways, the same survey indicates second-generation fidelity to the southern Italian cultural heritage. Only half the younger group rejected the proposition that 'a child should sacrifice his personal ambition to the welfare of the family group'; and only 15 percent denied that 'children owe absolute obedience to parents' (Ware, 1935: 193).

One area in which the remaining power of the family ethos was undeniably manifest was that of education. The conflict between the school system and the family that had existed in the Mezzogiorno was renewed in America. Immigrant families perceived many points of friction in the contact between these culturally alien worlds. These occurred even in seemingly innocuous matters such as school recreation, which immigrant parents saw as creating moral and physical risk for teen-agers, who in their eyes were already adults (Covello, 1972: 325–6). Undoubtedly, the most important conflict centered on the economic contribution expected of children, which was jeopardized by compulsory attendance laws, greatly resented by Italian parents.

As a result of the clash between school and family, Italian children had high rates of truancy and frequently left school as early as the law allowed (Covello, 1972). In fact, during the height of mass immigration, it is estimated that as many as 10 percent of the immigrant children in New York City managed to avoid school altogether (Kessner, 1977: 96). But even as late as 1930, only 11 percent of Italian Americans who entered New York City high schools graduated from them, at a time when over 40 percent of all the city's high school students stayed through to receive their diplomas (Covello, 1972: 285). The obvious consequence was low ultimate educational attainment for second-generation Italians and a channeling of them towards jobs where educational credentials were not important, mostly in the blue-collar ranks.

The ultimate assimilation of the Italians was also put in question by attitudes of the Italians themselves. Two studies of Italian-American ghettos, in Boston and New Haven, offer relevant testimony. Whyte's (1955) classic study indicates a split among Italians in their attitudes towards assimilation. He portrays the division in terms of 'college boys,' oriented toward mobility into the larger society, and 'corner boys,' loyal to their peer groups and held on ghetto corners by that loyalty. Whyte did not provide direct evidence on the relative popularity of these two orientations, but Child's (1943) New Haven study did. Child depicted the attitudes of Italians as defined against a background of virulent prejudice directed at their group, which hedged in the possible choices with the risk of potential losses. Identification with the Italian group meant risking complete exclusion by other Americans and the loss of any prospects for mobility. On the other hand, identification with Americans, and hence a positive valuation of assimilation, risked a double rejection: by non-Italians as a result of prejudice and by other Italians on the grounds of disloyalty to the group. According to Child, the most common response to this double-bind situation was one he labeled 'apathetic': a denial of the meaningfulness of nationality distinctions and of the existence of prejudice against Italians. Individuals displaying the apathetic response remained through inertia within the orbit of Italian-American social and cultural life, for it required deliberate action to break this social gravity and move into non-Italian spheres. Because of the risks involved, few maintained such intentions.

The 1940s and 50s: the watershed

By the end of the 1930s, an analysis based solely on the group's experiences and its cultural and occupational background would seem to have doomed Italian Americans to a perpetual position of inferiority and separateness in American society. But such an analysis would have been misleading because other developments were taking place in the larger society that affected the context within which Italian-American preferences would be played out. These factors came to a head during and shortly after World War II.

Some had been in the background all along, but the war sharpened their effects. One such was the transformation of the occupational structure and the attendant structural mobility. Between 1930 and 1970, for example, the white-collar proportion of the national labor force expanded rapidly from 29.4 to 44.8 percent (all figures are from U.S. Bureau of the Census, 1975: 139); about half this change, moreover, was concentrated in the upper part of the white-collar spectrum, the category of professional and technical workers, whose share of the labor force increased in this period from 6.8 to 13.7 percent. Although the proportion in the combined blue-collar and service occupations hardly changed, within them a significant realignment was taking shape. In particular, unskilled laborers, a category which included many Italian Americans in the earlier part of the century, declined sharply from 11.0 to 4.4 percent. The structural mobility engendered by such shifts in the occupational distribution holds a special significance for disadvantaged ethnic groups because it does not have a 'zero sum' character. Thus, the upward mobility of an individual or group can occur without the complementary downward mobility of another; and as a result, it is not likely to produce a heightened salience of group boundaries among more advantaged groups, intended to keep the disadvantaged in their place.

The effects wrought by structural mobility were most sharply felt in those places where Italian Americans were concentrated: the metropolitan areas of the north. This is made clearest by examining the kinds of jobs that were opening up and closing out in different places in the post-war interval, since it is the changes at the margins that chiefly dictate the occupational options for young people entering the labor force and thus shape intergenerational occupational mobility. Over the period 1940–60, metropolitan areas in general were the places of greatest job growth (Stanback and Knight, 1970). In the older metropolises of the Northeast and Midwest, growth was primarily concentrated in white-collar rather than blue-collar jobs (Berry and Kasarda, 1977: ch. 12).

A corollary of structural occupational shifts during the 1940s and 1950s was another kind of structural mobility: the rapid expansion of higher education and its transformation from a selective system to a mass one. In 1940, only 15 percent of the college-age group actually attended college, but by 1954 the rate of college attendance had climbed to 30 percent; by 1960, it was almost 38 percent (Trow, 1961). This expansion played an important role in reducing status differences because, in addition to propelling occupational mobility, higher education extends a sense of equality among its students through an experience that is viewed as a sharp alteration in status and is sanctified by the selectivity of colleges and universities.

World War II acted as a catalyst for both kinds of mobility. The War helped to drag the United States out of the Depression and open up an era of prosperity and economic growth, signaled by a steady growth in real income beginning in the early 1950s (Miller, 1971); and it specifically fueled the expansion of higher education through the G.I. Bill. But the impact of the war was much wider than the socioeconomic changes it helped to stimulate, for the war had a powerful effect on American perceptions of nationality and national origins.

The crux of the wartime situations during this century is that they have turned ethnic identity into a matter of national loyalty, thereby giving ethnicity a subversive appearance and ultimately hastening a deemphasis on nationality differences. The diversity of the origins of Americans and the substantial proportion of those of recent origins, particularly from combatant nations, have made Americans sensitive to the potential frailty of national solidarity. During World War I, the presence of millions of recently arrived European immigrants provoked intense anxieties about the immediate loyalties of aliens and the potential for subversion from within, leading to overt xenophobia and demands for the 'pressure-cooker assimilation' and '100 percent Americanization' of the immigrants (Higham, 1970). By the 1940s, the flood tide of immigration had receded; the groups with the potential for loyalty to enemy nations were increasingly composed of the native-born, and the responses of Americans were accordingly different.

This is not to say that the war did not stimulate anxieties over national loyalty. The internment of Japanese Americans demonstrates indisputably that it did. In the case of European ethnics, clouds of suspicion gathered early during the war over Germans and Italians, but then largely gave way to a cultivated national unity that was also a response to the wartime strains. The melding of Americans of different nationalities was almost ritualistically promoted by festivals to celebrate the contributions of immigrant groups to America (Polenberg, 1980: 54). More significant, wartime reporting and films about the war made for domestic consumption self-consciously highlighted the spirit of unity among American fighting men from different backgrounds, portraying the armed forces as a melting pot in miniature (Blum, 1976: 63).

The war no doubt served to drive home the perils of too strong an ethnic identification for many ethnics. One of Child's New Haven respondents sharply formulated a general problem:

> Then a lot of times in the show you see Mussolini on the screen and they all start to razz him. Then I feel, 'How the hell do I stand?' (Child, 1943: 88)

A frequent response on the part of the ethnics was a push toward further assimilation. Ethnics had high rates of enlistment in the military, and there was massive adoption of American citizenship by the foreign-born — more than 1,750,000 became citizens in the period 1940—45 (Polenberg, 1980: 57). Movement toward acculturation is evident in the waning of the foreign language press that occurred during the war. The number of radio stations broadcasting in immigrant languages dropped by 40 percent between 1942 and 1948 (Polenberg, 1980: 55).

An ultimate impact of the war was to render the perceptions of the ethnics more fluid and thus open to the possibility of change. One realm in which this influence is visible is in the novels about the war, published during it and afterwards. Norman Mailer's *The Naked and the Dead*, James Jones's *From Here to Eternity*, Harry Brown's *A Walk in the Sun*, and John Hersey's *A Bell for Adano*, which were all popular novels made into successful films, presented a very different version of American society from that which prevailed before the war. Like many wartime films, these novels depicted military groups that contained American ethnic diversity, or more precisely the part of European ancestry, in microcosm, and showed ethnics as the moral equals of those of 'old stock' origins (Blum, 1976). The novels, which served to interpret the war experience for many Americans, signaled a shift in attitudes towards ethnics.

Thus, World War II stands as a watershed for European ethnics, partly because it lies at a fortuitous conjunction of forces — structural transformation of the labor force, demographic transition from the immigrant to the second generation among the ethnics of recent European origins, and a cultural relaxation of the attitudes towards ethnics — that served to fluidify the boundaries separating ethnics from old stock groups. It remains still to confirm that these massive forces actually had an effect on the life chances of ethnics. Relevant evidence is supplied by Lieberson's recent study (1980), which reveals a prodigious socioeconomic leap for the 1925—35 cohort of second-generation South-Central-Eastern European ethnics, which came to maturity during and shortly after the war (Lieberson, 1980: 200—6, 328—32).

The boundary fluidity associated with the large-scale mobility in the aftermath of the war was further advanced by the enormous residential movements of the 1950s and 1960s. In the single decade from 1950 to 1960, the population in the suburbs increased by nearly 50 percent, from 41 to 60 million (Polenberg, 1980: 128). For ethnics and others, the suburban exodus was often directly connected with occupational chances – and not merely the result of increasing affluence – since the bulk of newly created jobs were to be found in the suburban fringes, not central-city areas (Berry and Kasarda, 1977: ch. 12). But the exodus was full of portent for ethnic groups because it disrupted urban ethnic communities and brought many mobile families into an ethnically heterogeneous milieu, a shift with obvious ramifications for the next generation. The residential changes of Italians are exemplified by the group's distribution in the metropolitan region centered around New York City and Newark, which contained nearly a third of the Italian Americans the Census counted in 1970. By then, the second generation had significantly dispersed to the suburbs. According to Census figures, 47 percent were living in the area's smaller places, those with fewer than 100,000 residents; and 41 percent were living in places with fewer than 50,000. These figures are only slightly lower than those for whites generally (50 percent and 45 percent, respectively). However, first-generation Italians remained distinctly more concentrated in the region's larger cities. Only 35 percent were in places smaller than 100,000 in population, and 29 percent in places smaller than 50,000.[4]

Obviously, the changes of the post-war period did not mean a complete dissolution of ethnic communities and subcultures. Gans's (1962) study of Boston's West End in the late 1950s establishes that many, particularly in the urban working class, remained firmly in the grip of ethnic worlds. But a process had been initiated, one that spelled a gradual lowering of ethnic boundaries among European ancestry groups and an upward shift in the life chances of their younger members.

The contemporary situation of Italian Americans

This process of boundary shift has had a profound impact on Italian Americans, and recent evidence points to a convergence with other European ancestry groups, including those of older stock. As one demonstration, consider the educational trajectory across different cohorts of second- and later-generation Italians, compiled in Table 1 from the November, 1979, Current Population Survey.[5] To provide a rigorous yardstick against which to measure change, comparable figures are also provided for third- and later-generation Americans of exclusively British ancestry (defined as those who report ancestry only from England, Scotland, and Wales). Such a comparison group avoids the confusion that might be introduced by including other recent ethnics in the reference group and also compares the Italians to an ethnic category that is indisputably part of the American core, thus underlining the sharpness of the changes. For similar reasons, the focus in the table is exclusively on rates of college attendance and graduation.

What stands out in the table is a pattern of convergence across cohorts. Although the pattern is complicated somewhat by an unsustained peak in college education among British Americans in the 1946–50 cohort (which

Table ... Trends of college education among Italian Americans, by sex, generation, and cohort and compared to those of third-generation British Americans.a

Cohort	Second generation		Third generation		Third-generation British Americans	
	% attended college	% finished 4 or more yrs.	% attended college	% finished 4 or more yrs.	% attended college	% finished 4 or more yrs.
Men						
1951–	56.6	28.9	54.4	25.8	53.2	27.1
1946–50	42.1	32.8	55.9	29.1	66.4	38.1
1941–45	45.4	26.2	51.8	35.7	55.7	38.5
1936–40	42.9	30.3	42.3	22.1	51.5	35.1
1931–35	33.0	18.7	39.0	18.4	50.3	31.3
1926–30	24.9	11.7	31.5	15.2	42.1	27.8
1921–25	22.1	16.0	20.1	7.7	43.9	23.8
1916–20	17.5	3.9	13.4	11.3	35.7	20.1
–15	16.3	7.9	15.2	6.2	30.1	17.4
Women						
1951–	50.4	20.2	46.6	26.3	48.8	24.0
1946–50	35.0	17.1	40.5	20.0	53.5	31.8
1941–45	27.3	13.1	32.1	13.5	44.7	22.5
1936–40	28.3	13.2	18.2	3.9	39.0	21.7
1931–35	9.1	4.4	17.9	10.5	33.2	16.1
1926–30	14.6	5.7	27.6	9.2	41.8	23.0
1921–25	8.2	4.5	22.6	5.1	29.7	14.5
1916–20	7.0	4.2	30.1	20.2	37.6	17.8
–15	5.1	1.8	2.7	0.0	26.5	12.3

Source: My tabulations from November, 1979, Current Population Survey
a Table restricted to individuals older than 22. The 'third generation' contains all native-born group members with native-born parents and thus encompasses the third and later generations.

may be part of a Vietnam era phenomenon revealed by a recent Census report) and by some wandering of the numbers from a simple trajectory of linear change, its basic nature is clear: a gradual narrowing of Italian differences from British Americans and the achievement of parity in the youngest cohort (who were in their mid-twenties in 1979). This convergence holds for both men and women, and indeed what the table also reveals is the relatively greater disadvantage of Italian-American women in the past, especially in the second generation. For this last group, the rise in college attendance (from 9.1 percent to 50.4 percent) across a twenty-year time span, from the 1930–35 cohort to that of 1951–56, is very strong. The convergence also holds for both generations, and underlining the historical nature of the convergence is the fact that the generations do not seem much different, although the third generation shows some tendency to take the lead in rising rates of college attendance.

Evidence of cultural convergence is provided by survey items that tap attitudes and values connected with the stereotypical family-centered ethos presumed to color Italian-American life (e.g., Greeley and McCready, 1975).[6] One widely cited expression of this is greater loyalty to kin groups, purportedly evident for instance in a reluctance to move away from the family (Gambino, 1974; Vecoli, 1978). Another is conservatism on family-related matters, ranging from hostility toward changes in sexual mores and the position of women to a low frequency of divorce (Greeley, 1974; Femminella and Quadagno, 1976).

The thinness of any residual cultural patina among individuals of Italian heritage is evident from Table 2, which reports the analysis of items from the General Social Surveys for the years 1975 through 1980 (the table is a selection from a larger set discussed in Alba, 1985).[7] The comparison is again to those of British ancestry (more precisely: since the General Social Surveys ask for the religion in which a respondent was raised, the comparison group contains those with Protestant ancestry from the British Isles). The table presents the comparison without any controls and also with controls for: current region and size of place as well as those where the respondent was raised; education and occupation of respondent and parents; and sex and age.[8]

On items relating to traditional family roles, Italians are generally quite similar to WASPs. They do not significantly differ from WASPs in terms of acceptance of abortion, for example, although they appear slightly more conservative after controls are applied because of their greater concentration in areas where liberal attitudes prevail.[9] Italians do not differ from WASPs in their acceptance of women outside the home.[10] Similarity between the groups is also found, albeit with an important exception, in attitudes toward the raising of children. Italians have been depicted as emphasizing traditional values, rather than those of self-direction (Rosen, 1959; Schooler, 1976). But in terms of their rating of the desirability of various traits in children, they are not meaningfully different from British Protestants.[11] Worthy of mention for its echo of the Mezzogiorno is one trait on the list, 'that he

Table 2. *Cultural comparison between WASPs and Italian Americans.*

	WASP mean	Italian mean	difference	diff. after adjustment[a]
Anti-abortion scale	1.33	1.42	.09	.20*
Anti-feminism scale	1.26	1.25	−.01	.08
Premarital sex is 'always wrong'	34.5%	22.6%	−11.9*	1.3
Adultery is 'always wrong'	69.8%	58.6%	−11.2*	−3.5
Homosexual sex is 'always wrong'	69.3%	60.4%	−8.9*	−4.7
Ever divorced or legally separated	25.7%	21.9%	−3.8	−4.4
Divorce should be 'more difficult'	50.1%	41.3%	−8.8*	−3.1
Scale of value put on self-direction for children	1.24	1.17	−.07	−.12
Young people 'should be taught by their elders'	37.9%	53.0%	15.1*	19.8*
Reside in same place where grew up	39.5%	53.2%	13.6*	6.6*
Socialize with relatives weekly	33.8%	46.8%	13.0*	10.4*

*Indicates statistical significance.

Source: Tabulations from the NORC General Social Surveys, 1975–80.

[a]Variables for which adjustment has been made include: current region and size of place and those where respondent grew up, education and occupation of respondent and parents, age and sex.

[the child] obeys his parents well.' Just a quarter of the Italian-American respondents prize obedience as one of the most desirable traits in children, a figure not statistically different from that for WASPs (28 percent). The exception to this general similarity concerns whether young people should be taught 'by their elders to do what is right' or 'to think for themselves even though they may do something their elders disapprove of.' About half of Italians agree with the position consistent with the family-centered ethos — namely, that young people should be taught by their elders — compared to 38 percent of WASPs. Nonetheless, the Italian percentage is not far from the one for all Americans, 45 percent of whom favor the traditional option.

Despite their conservative image, Italians are more liberal than WASPs in certain respects, apparently because of their location in the metropolitan northeast, where cosmopolitan outlooks are frequent. They are less likely to condemn adultery, premarital sex, and homosexuality as 'always wrong.' They are also less likely to feel that divorce laws should be tightened to make divorce more difficult to obtain. (The proportion who have ever been divorced or separated is also, incidentally, not statistically different from that found among British Americans.) But in all these cases, the differences disappear after statistical controls are introduced, and an inspection of the regressions indicates that the reduction is chiefly brought about by the controls for place.

Broadly speaking, then, there is little support for the image of a distinctive Italian conservatism on family matters. Where there does appear to be greater evidence for an Italian-American ethos is in terms of loyalty to the family group, but at best its remaining strength seems no more than moderate. This loyalty can be examined through two items in Table 2.

One tests the idea that Italians remain rooted in one place because of their reluctance to move away from family. Indeed, an impressive 53 percent reside in the same place where they grew up; however, the percentage of WASPs who do so also is high, 40 percent. Moreoever, the Italian percentage could be expected to be higher on the grounds that Italians have more frequently grown up in the cosmopolitan magnets that attract others from their hometowns (New York City is the prototype) and also have lower overall educational and occupational attainment, factors associated with less residential mobility. When controls are applied, the difference between the two groups is only modest, 7 percentage points.[12]

Finally, the Italian pattern of socializing with relatives, emphasized by Gans (1962) in his depiction of the 'peer group society,' still persists to some degree. Nearly half of Italians socialize with family members weekly or more frequently, compared to only a third of WASPs. This difference is not explained very much by the background variables, as the tendency to socialize within the family is not much affected by socioeconomic variables, and this is counterbalanced for WASPs by the fact that it is somewhat higher among those who live in smaller places. After controls, Italians are still 10 percent more likely to socialize on a weekly basis with relatives.

Thus, what remains of the family-centered ethos is a slightly greater tendency to remain in the same place, greatly diluted from ancestral peasant rootedness, and a moderately greater willingness to keep company with relatives. The evidence of cultural convergence seems substantial,[13] but there is still more imposing evidence of convergence and assimilation: in intermarriage rates. Intermarriage stands as the cardinal indicator of boundary shift for several reasons (cf. Merton, 1941). To begin with the obvious, because marriage is an enduring and intimate relation, intermarriage provides a stringent test of group perceptions, of the social distance between Italians and others. Moreover, an intermarriage is not simply an isolated crossing of ethnic boundaries but carries far wider ramifications, including most importantly those for the next generation, which will be raised in an ethnically heterogeneous milieu. Finally, the occurrence of intermarriage implies the occurrence of other relations that penetrate ethnic boundaries.

The intermarriage rates of Italians, calculated from the 1979 Current Population Survey, are presented in Table 3. In the case of marriage, it makes little sense to combine individuals of part Italian ancestry with those of wholly Italian parentage, because the social contexts in which the two types are raised are so different that their intermarriage rates are likely to be as well; and consequently, they are shown separately in the table. The marriage rates are also decomposed by generations and birth cohort, and presented separately for men and women.

The table indicates a rapid rise in the intermarriage rate, which has reached the point that, of Italians marrying recently, generally two-thirds to three-quarters, depending on the category of the group, have intermarried. Revealing of the changes is the trend by birth cohort for persons with unmixed Italian ancestry, especially in the second generation. Among those born before 1920, i.e., during the era of mass immigration, about 60 percent of this second generation chose spouses of wholly Italian percentage. But this strict endogamy falls off with each new cohort. Among men, a sharp drop occurs with the cohort born during the 1930s; for women, such a drop occurs with the cohort born in the next decade. This rapid change has, among men, closed the gap between the second and third generations. For both, only about 20 percent of men born since 1950 have chosen wives with all Italian parentage, while another 10 to 15 percent have chosen wives with part Italian ancestry. The gap between the generations is not quite closed among women; second-generation women have the highest rate of endogamy in the youngest cohort, although this may be a statistical aberration, since a small number of cases is involved. In any event, the great majority of Italian Americans in this

Table 3. *Marriage patterns of Italian Americans, by sex, generation, and cohort.*

	Men			
	Second generation		Third generation	
Cohort	Ancestry of spouse is . . .		Ancestry of spouse is . . .	
	wholly	wholly	wholly	wholly
Ancestry type	Italian %	non-Italian %	Italian %	non-Italian %
1950–				
wholly Ital.	20.3	64.1	20.0	70.5
partly Ital.	—a	—a	5.4	78.9
1940–49				
wholly Ital.	30.0	60.0	24.4	69.2
partly Ital.	0.0	82.7	10.7	76.8
1930–39				
wholly Ital.	29.8	62.9	24.1	63.3
partly Ital.	17.8	81.5	6.9	80.1
1920–29				
wholly Ital.	44.6	51.7	38.8	60.9
partly Ital.	15.7	83.7	4.8	90.0
Before 1920				
wholly Ital.	56.7	41.7	42.7	57.3
partly Ital.	—a	—a	15.8	78.6

Table 3. *Continued*

Cohort	Women			
	Second generation Ancestry of spouse is . . .		Third generation Ancestry of spouse is . . .	
	wholly	wholly	wholly	wholly
Ancestry type	Italian %	non-Italian %	Italian %	non-Italian %
1950–				
wholly Ital.	38.7	53.2	23.8	72.7
partly Ital.	—a	—a	10.3	79.1
1940–49				
wholly Ital.	25.7	71.3	31.7	58.4
partly Ital.	20.7	72.1	11.7	77.8
1930–39				
wholly Ital.	38.8	61.0	49.4	46.6
partly Ital.	17.0	83.0	17.2	75.6
1920–29				
wholly Ital.	54.9	44.6	34.6	61.7
partly Ital.	10.3	89.7	18.6	69.3
Before 1920				
wholly Ital.	59.5	37.6	40.8	60.2
partly Ital.	—a	—a	11.5	78.5

Source: My tabulations from November, 1979, Current Population Survey.
aPercent not reported because it is based on 10 or fewer cases (weighted).

cohort belong to the third or later generations, where high intermarriage rates prevail.

Individuals of wholly Italian ancestry provide a conservative estimate of intermarriage rates. Individuals of mixed background have higher intermarriage rates and, moreover, the overall Italian rates will increasingly resemble theirs, since the group is more and more composed of them (this will be made clear shortly). For example, if the two ancestry groups are combined among men, then nearly three-quarters of third-generation men born since 1950 have chosen wives with no Italian ancestry. The comparable third-generation figure among women is nearly identical to that for the men.

It might be argued that these high intermarriage rates do not establish by themselves a relaxing of boundaries between Italians and other groups because they do not show whom Italians marry when they marry outside. Thus, it remains possible that other boundaries, enclosing clusters of culturally and socially similar groups, constrain their choices. It is true that, like other European ancestry groups, Italians are very unlikely to marry Hispanics and non-whites (Alba and Golden, 1984). But this important exception aside, two pieces of evidence damage the thesis of selective intermarriage. One is Alba and Kessler's (1979) analysis of marriage patterns among Catholics, demonstrating that very little selectivity is visible among those who marry across nationality lines. The second emerges from data that reveal fairly high rates of marriage across religious lines. For example, Alba (1985) shows from General Social Survey data that about half of Italian Catholics born since World War II have married Protestants. So, in other words, it appears that the elective affinities of intermarrying Italians are not narrowly channeled to a few groups, but range widely across the spectrum of European ancestries.

The rising rate of intermarriage is bringing about a profound transformation of the Italian ancestry group. The character of this transformation is quite evident when the proportion of individuals with mixed Italian ancestry is displayed by birth cohort, as is done in Table 4.[14] The figures reveal a striking relationship of mixed parentage to cohort, with a percentage change between the oldest and youngest cohorts of over 75 percent. These dramatic figures indicate that a tremendous swing in the nature of the Italian ancestry group is destined to take place by the end of this century, as members of older cohorts, for the most part of unmixed ancestry, die and are replaced by younger persons of mixed parentage. Thus, in the Current Population Survey, persons with only Italian ancestry make up two-thirds of the adult ancestry group, a comfortable majority. But counting individuals of all ages, including children, they were a scant majority; 52 percent. Taking into account the expected mortality in the older group, these figures suggest that individuals with one non-Italian parent will compose a majority of the ancestry group by the end of the next decade.

Table 4. *Type of Italian ancestry by age (1979).*

	% with mixed Italian ancestry
all ages	48.0
65 and over	5.9
55 to 64	11.4
45 to 54	18.5
35 to 44	36.1
25 to 34	48.1
18 to 24	60.5
14 to 17	71.3
5 to 13	77.8
under 5	81.5

Source: November, 1979, Current Population Survey, report in U.S. Bureau of the Census (1982): Table 2.

It is doubtful that even the mild distinctiveness of Italians on matters of family solidarity can withstand such higher intermarriage rates. Intermarriage not only tests the extent of existing cultural differences among groups, but it ultimately alters the cultural boundary. Johnson's (1982) study of kinship contact among Italians in Syracuse, New York, illustrates the general process. She compared in-married and out-married Italians to each other and to Protestants of non-Italian background in terms of the frequency of their contact with parents, siblings, and other relatives. Although contact with the relatives on the Italian side appeared dominant among the intermarried Italians, in the sense that both spouses saw more of them than of the non-Italian relatives, the frequency of contact was diminished; the intermarried group stood intermediate between the in-married Italians, the majority of whom had daily contact with parents and with siblings, and the Protestants, the majority of whom had comparatively infrequent contact with their relatives. Johnson's research implies that high rates of intermarriage are associated with further erosion of what Herbert Gans labeled as the 'peer group society' in the 1950s.

Conclusion

Italian Americans are on the verge of the twilight of their ethnicity. 'Twilight' appears an accurate metaphor for a stage when ethnic differences will remain visible, but only faintly so. The metaphor acknowledges the claims of many (e.g., Glazer and Moynihan, 1970; Greeley, 1977) that indeed ethnicity has not speedily disappeared and, therefore, the optimism of the melting-pot portrayal of American society seems to have been ill-founded. At the same time, it also captures the reality that ethnicity, at least among whites, seems to be steadily receding.

The approach of this twilight may seem deceiving, for when Italians and some other white ethnic groups are observed in the aggregate, their ethnic features still appear prominent. But in the case of the Italians, this happens because earlier generations and older cohorts are quite different from old-stock Americans on such factors as educational and occupational attainment. Hence, it is only when the group is analytically decomposed by generation or birth cohort that the leading edge of change can be discerned.

Properly analyzed, the evidence on behalf of the looming ethnic twilight among Italians appears overwhelming. Despite the widely accepted image of an intense, family-centered Italian-American culture, the group's cultural distinctiveness has paled to a feeble version of its former self. Paralleling this change, the social boundary between Italians and other Americans has become easily permeable; intermarriage, an irrevocable indicator of boundary shifts, takes place quite freely between Italians and those of other European ancestries. Acculturation and social assimilation have been fed by a surge in the educational attainment of Italians, which has brought cohorts born since World War II to the brink of parity with British Americans, the quintessential American group. Moreover, this profound transformation of the Italian group has taken place at a time when the fourth generation, the first generation without direct contact with the immigrant experience, is small (Steinberg, 1982; Alba, 1985). But this generation will grow substantially in size during the rest of this century, and simultaneously, the first and second generations, which presently constitute the majority of the group, will shrink.

In a number of respects, events among the Italians seem to parallel those among other groups descended from European immigrants, although because of differences in their times of arrivals, the specific situations that greeted them, and their occupational and cultural heritages, no two groups are following exactly the same pathways to the twilight stage. Yet among virtually all white ethnic groups, one can observe a progressive, if gradual, dampening of cultural distinctiveness. Core values have been overwhelmed by a common American culture so that even though cultural uniformity has not been the end result, the remaining differences among groups are so mild as to constitute neither a basis for group solidarity nor a barrier to intergroup contact. Additionally, among almost all groups, one can see a spreading pattern of intermarriage, testimony to the minor nature of remaining group differences and guarantee of additional assimilation (e.g., Alba, 1976). The strength of this pattern is confirmed by events among Jewish Americans, who provide the acid test of pervasive intermarriage. Historically, the rate of Jewish-Gentile intermarriage rate has been quite low, but recent studies have confirmed a sharp rise in this rate, starting in the 1960s (Cohen, 1983).

Such pervasive intermarriage suggests the emergence of a new ethnic group, one defined by ancestry from anywhere on the European continent. This need not mean that ethnic differences within this group will disappear altogether, but rather that their character is being fundamentally altered. This appears to be increasingly the case with ethnic identity. As Herbert Gans (1979) has observed, many mobile ethnics attempt to maintain some psychological connection with their origins, but in such a way that this attachment does not prevent them from mixing freely with others of diverse backgrounds. This contemporary form of ethnicity is private and voluntary, intermittent and undemanding; it focuses on symbols of ethnic cultures, rather than the cultures themselves, and tends to be confined to leisure-time activities. There is a wide latitude available for this 'symbolic ethnicity' — for Italians, it can range from a liking for pasta to a repudiation of criminal stereotypes — but the crucial point is that it is the individual who decides on the appropriate form. Such an ethnic identity is, in other words, a personal style, and not the manifestation of membership in an ethnic group.

The impending twilight of ethnicity among those of European ancestry is not matched by equal changes among most of America's non-European minorities. Black Americans stand as the extreme case. Though their socio-economic progress in recent years has been debated, no informed observer claims that they are even close to parity with whites (Farley, 1985). It hardly needs saying, then, that racial boundaries remain salient. Residentially, blacks are still extremely segregated from whites, and the incidence of black-white intermarriage is very small (Heer, 1980).

The position of some other minorities is more ambiguous. Some older non-European groups that were voluntary immigrants to the United States evidence developments like those among the white ethnics, though these are not as far along. For example, Japanese Americans, despite the bitter legacy of World War II internment, have been quite successful in socioeconomic terms, with high rates of college attendance and occupational mobility. In tandem with this upward movement have come increases in intermarriage, frequently with whites (Montero, 1981; Woodrum, 1981). Although in the future it may become appropriate to speak of an ethnic twilight among Japanese Americans, the picture for non-European groups is complicated by the large-scale immigration from Asia, the Caribbean, and Latin America since immigration laws were revised in 1965. Immigrants from Colombia, Cuba, Haiti, Korea, Mexico, the Philippines, Taiwan, Hong Kong, Vietnam, and still other places are adding new parts to the American ethnic tapestry. Thus, although twilight may be descending on those ethnic groups whose forebears came from Europe, ethnicity itself is not subsiding as an issue for American society. In the future, the salient ethnic outlines may stem from non-European origins, just as those of European origins have been prominent in the recent past.

Notes

*A preliminary version of this paper was presented at the 1983 meetings of the American Sociological Association. I am grateful to Robert K. Merton for his comments and to Prentice-Hall for permission to use materials from my book.

1.   This, of course, coincides with the importance that Gordon (1964) attributes to 'structural assimilation,' that is, large-scale primary relations across ethnic boundaries.

2.   Although American immigration authorities began to keep statistics on 'southern' and 'northern' Italians in 1899, the racial intent of the distinction distorted the definition of a 'southern' Italian to include anyone from the 'peninsula proper' (as well as the islands of Sicily and Sardinia). According to the Bureau of Immigration's definition, 'even Genoa is South Italian' (U.S. Senate, 1911: 81)! While American statistics were weakened in this way, Italian statistics depend largely on applications for the *nulla osta*, or exit permit, which required a destination to be stated. But many applicants either did not subsequently leave or went somewhere other than where they stated (Caroli, 1973: 30; Sori, 1979).

Nonetheless, both sources, though imprecise, are broadly consistent.

3.   Jerre Mangione's (1981) memoir of Italian-American life in Rochester paints a very clear portrait of the sojourner's mentality among his Sicilian relatives.

4.   These figures are for the New York, N.Y. Northeastern New Jersey Standard Consolidated Area, which in 1970 contained 1.4 million foreign-stock Italian Americans. The figures are my calculations from Tables 17, 23, and 81 of the *Characteristics of the Population*, Parts 32 and 34 (Bureau of the Census, 1973).

5.   This survey included the same ethnic ancestry question that appeared in the long form of the 1980 Census. This question, 'What is . . .'s ancestry?' is superior to questions asked in previous Current Population Surveys and decennial Censuses, because it does not constrain answers by a predefined list of responses and hence does not eliminate the many individuals with mixed ancestry. However, by the same token, it offers a too inclusive definition of the Italian-American group, since it forces the inclusion of individuals with any reported degree of Italian ancestry, regardless of its magnitude and

of the extent of their identification with the Italian group (for a more detailed discussion, see Alba, 1985).

A virtue of this survey for the study of socioeconomic change is that its large sample size allows for refined breakdowns.

6.   The focus here must be on this ethos, rather than the outward forms of culture, since these tend to wither away within the first two generations. This is true, for example, of the everyday-use of Italian. According to the Current Population Survey, over 4 million claim Italian as a mother tongue, a language spoken in their childhood home, but only 1.4 million (about 12 percent of the group) claim to speak it in their current home (U.S. Bureau of the Census, 1982: 14). Since the total size of the ancestry group is around 12 million and that of the first generation, whose members are very likely to continue to speak their native tongue at home, is 800 thousand, it is clear that only a small part of the second and third generations continues to use the language on an everyday basis. For further analysis of external culture, see Crispino (1980).

7.   The General Social Surveys offer a narrower definition of the Italian-American group than does the November, 1979, Current Population Survey. The GSS ask individuals with mixed ethnic ancestry to identify, if they can, the group to which they feel closer. This is then reported as their ethnic category.

8.   The adjusted difference between the groups reported in the table is the coefficient for the Italian dummy variable taken from a regression analysis. To achieve stable estimates of the effects of the control variables, the regression analysis includes all whites; the comparison to WASPs is effected by making them the omitted category.

9.   The value of the anti-abortion scale is the number of times the respondent would deny a legal abortion in three situations where a presumably healthy pregnancy has resulted from voluntary sexual activity (Davis *et al.*, 1980: 143–4). Such situations are the litmus test for abortion attitudes, as most Americans would allow an abortion for such circumstances as a life-endangering pregnancy, or one resulting from rape.

10.   The anti-feminism scale is a summative scale composed of responses to four questions such as 'Do you approve or disapprove of a married woman earning money in business or industry if she has a husband capable of supporting her?' For the wordings of the other three, see Davis *et al.* (1980: 142).

11.   These items are derived from the well-known ones developed by Melvin Kohn and his colleagues. But there is no pretense here of replicating Kohn's work, since he has explicitly confined the validity of his scale to parents with children in a certain age range (Kohn, 1976). Such a limitation is not feasible here.

The scale I report is calculated by counting a +1 for each time a respondent rated as desirable a trait associated with self-direction and also each time he or she rated as undesirable a trait associated with conformity, and counting a −1 when the reverses occurred. Positive numbers on the scale thus indicate a valence toward self-direction.

12.   Since simultaneous controls for both current and original location amount to controls for mobility itself, one has to be removed from the list of independent variables for this analysis; current location (both region and size of place) has been deleted.

13.   This does not imply that Italians and WASPs are similar in all ways. For one, they differ in their political party allegiances, with Italians notably more tied to the Democratic Party. But the crucial point is that they are similar on many traits bearing on the family-centered ethos. (For more details and discussion, see Alba, 1985).

14.   The 1980 Census yields a somewhat lower estimate of the percentage of Italians with mixed ancestry, 43.5 (versus 48.0), and presumably will show lower rates of mixed ancestry in younger cohorts when tables of ancestry by age become available. Nevertheless, there appears to be good reason to give greater credence to the CPS rather than the decennial census in this case. The markedly lower estimates of mixed ancestry in general in the census suggest that ancestry responses were more cursory to the census's mail survey than to the face-to-face interviewing of the CPS (for further discussion of the differences between the two, see Bureau of the Census, 1983: 4–5).

References

ALBA, RICHARD 1976 'Social assimilation among American Catholic national-origin groups,' *American Sociological Review* 41 (December): 1030–46.

ALBA, RICHARD 1981 'The twilight of ethnicity among American Catholics of European ancestry.' *The Annals* 454 (March): 86–97.

ALBA, RICHARD 1985 *Italian Americans: Into the Twilight of Ethnicity*. Englewood Cliffs: Prentice-Hall.

ALBA, RICHARD, and MITCHELL CHAMLIN 1983. 'A preliminary examination of ethnic identification among whites.' *American Sociological Review* 48 (April): 240–7.

ALBA, RICHARD, and REID GOLDEN 1984 'Patterns of ethnic marriage in the United States.' Paper presented at the annual meetings of the American Sociological Association.

ALBA, RICHARD, and RONALD KESSLER 1979 'Patterns of interethnic marriage among American Catholics.' *Social Forces* 57 (June): 1124–40.

BANFIELD, ROBERT 1958 *The Moral Basis of a Backward Society*. New York: The Free Press.

BARTH, FREDRIK 1969 'Introduction,' pp. 9–38 in Fredrik Barth (ed.), *Ethnic Groups and Boundaries*. Boston: Little, Brown.

BERRY, BRIAN, and JOHN KASARDA 1977 *Contemporary Urban Ecology*. New York: Macmillan.

BLAU, PETER 1977 *Inequality and Heterogeneity: A Primitive Theory of Social Structure*. New York: The Free Press.

BLAUNER, ROBERT 1972 *Racial Oppression in America*. New York: Harper & Row.

BLUM, JOHN MORTON 1976 *V Was for Victory: Politics and American Culture During World War II*. New York: Harcourt Brace Jovanovich.

BRETON, RAYMOND 1964 'Institutional completeness of ethnic communities and the personal relations of immigrants.' *American Journal of Sociology* 70 (July): 193–205.

BUREAU OF THE CENSUS 1973 *1970 Census of the Population, Volume I, Characteristics of the Population*. Washington: U.S. Government Printing Office.

BUREAU OF THE CENSUS 1975 *Historical Statistics of the United States, Colonial Times to 1970*. Bicentennial edition, Part 1. Washington: U.S. Government Printing Office.

BUREAU OF THE CENSUS 1982 'Ancestry and language in the United States: November 1979.' *Current Population Reports*, Special Studies, Series P–23, No. 116. Washington: U.S. Government Printing Office.

BUREAU OF THE CENSUS 1983 *1980 Census of the Population, Ancestry of the Population by State: 1980, Supplementary Report*. Washington: U.S. Government Printing Office.

CAROLI, BETTY BOYD 1973 *Italian Repatriation from the United States 1900–1914*. Staten Island: Center for Migration Studies.

CHAPMAN, CHARLOTTE GOWER 1971 *Milocca: A Sicilian Village*. Cambridge, Mass.: Schenkman.

CHILD, IRVIN 1943 *Italian or American? Second Generation in Conflict*. New Haven: Yale University Press.

COHEN, STEVEN 1983 *American Modernity and Jewish Identity*. New York and London: Tavistock.

COVELLO, LEONARD 1972 *The Social Background of the Italo-American School Child*. Totowa: Rowman & Littlefield.

CRAIGIE, WILLIAM, and JAMES HULBERT 1940 *A Dictionary of American English on Historical Principles*, Vol. II. Chicago: University of Chicago Press.

CRISPINO, JAMES 1980 *The Assimilation of Ethnic Groups: The Italian Case*. Staten Island: Center for Migration Studies.

DAVIS, JAMES, TOM SMITH, and C. BRUCE STEPHENSON 1980 *General Social Surveys, 1972–1980: Cumulative Codebook*. Chicago: NORC.

FARLEY, REYNOLDS 1985 'Recent changes in the social and economic status of

blacks: three steps forward and two back?' *Ethnic and Racial Studies* (January).
FEMMINELLA, FRANK, and JILL QUADAGNO 1976 'The Italian American family,' in Charles Mindell and Robert Habenstein (eds.), *Ethnic Families in America: Patterns and Variations*. New York: Elsevier.
FOERSTER, ROBERT 1924 *The Italian Emigration of Our Times*. Cambridge, Mass.: Harvard University Press.
GAMBINO, RICHARD 1974 *Blood of My Blood*. Garden City, N.Y.: Doubleday.
GANS, HERBERT 1962 *The Urban Villagers: Group and Class in the Life of Italian-Americans*. New York: The Free Press.
GANS, HERBERT 1979 'Symbolic ethnicity: The future of ethnic groups and cultures in America.' *Ethnic and Racial Studies* 2 (January): 1–20.
GLAZER, NATHAN, and DANIEL MOYNIHAN 1970 *Beyond the Melting Pot*. Rev. ed. Cambridge, Mass.: MIT Press.
GORDON, MILTON 1964 *Assimilation in American Life*. New York: Oxford University Press.
GREELEY, ANDREW 1971 *Why Can't They Be Like Us?* New York: Dutton.
GREELEY, ANDREW 1974 *Ethnicity in the United States: A Preliminary Reconnaisance*. New York: Wiley.
GREELEY, ANDREW 1977 *The American Catholic: A Social Portrait*. New York: Basic Books.
GREELEY, ANDREW, and WILLIAM McCREADY 1975 'The transmission of cultural heritages: The case of the Irish and the Italians,' pp. 209–35 in Nathan Glazer and Daniel Moynihan (eds.), *Ethnicity: Theory and Experience*. Cambridge, Mass.: Harvard University Press.
HECHTER, MICHAEL 1978 'Group formation and the cultural division of labor.' *American Journal of Sociology* 84 (September): 293–318.
HEER, DAVID 1980 'Intermarriage,' in Stephan Thernstrom, Ann Orlov, and Oscar Handlin (eds.), *Harvard Encyclopedia of American Ethnic Groups*. Cambridge, Mass.: Harvard University Press.
HIGHAM, JOHN 1970 *Strangers in the Land: Patterns of American Nativism 1860–1925*. New York: Atheneum.
JOHNSON, COLLEEN LEAHY 1982 'Sibling solidarity: its origin and functioning in Italian-American families.' *Journal of Marriage and the Family* (February): 155–67.
KESSNER, THOMAS 1977 *The Golden Door: Italian and Jewish Immigrant Mobility in New York City 1880–1915*. New York: Oxford University Press.
KOHN, MELVIN 1976 'Social class and parental values: another confirmation of the relationship.' *American Sociological Review* 41 (June): 538–45.
LIEBERSON, STANLEY 1963 *Ethnic Patterns in American Cities*. New York: The Free Press.
LIEBERSON, STANLEY 1980 *A Piece of the Pie: Blacks and White Immigrants since 1880*. Berkeley: University of California Press.
MANGIONE, JERRE 1981 *Mount Allegro: A Memoir of Italian American Life*. New York: Columbia University Press.
MENCKEN, H.L. 1963 *The American Language*. Abridg. ed. New York: Knopf.
MERTON, ROBERT 1941 'Intermarriage and the social structure: fact and theory.' *Psychiatry* 4 (August): 361–74.
MILLER, HERMAN P. 1971 *Rich Man, Poor Man*. New York: Thomas Y. Crowell.
MONTERO, DARREL 1981 'The Japanese Americans: Changing patterns of assimilation over three generations.' *American Sociological Review* 46 (December): 829–39.
NEWMAN, WILLIAM 1973 *American Pluralism: A Study of Minority Groups and Social Theory*. New York: Harper & Row.
NOVAK, MICHAEL 1972 *The Rise of the Unmeltable Ethnics*. New York: Macmillan.
PANUNZIO, CONSTANTINE 1928 *The Soul of an Immigrant*. New York.
POLENBERG, RICHARD 1980 *One Nation Divisible: Class, Race, and Ethnicity in the United States*. New York: Viking.

ROSEN, BERNARD 1959 'Race, ethnicity, and the achievement syndrome.' *American Sociological Review* 24 (February): 47–60.

SCHNEIDER, JANE, and PETER SCHNEIDER 1976 *Culture and Political Economy in Western Sicily*. New York: Academic Press.

SCHOOLER, CARMI 1976 'Serfdom's legacy: An ethnic continuum.' *American Journal of Sociology* 81 (May): 1265–86.

SORI, ERCOLE 1979 *L'emigrazione italiana dall' Unita alla seconda guerra mondiale*. Bologna: Il Mulino.

STANBACK, THOMAS, and RICHARD KNIGHT 1970 *The Metropolitan Economy*. New York: Columbia University Press.

STEINBERG, STEPHEN 1982 *The Ethnic Myth: Race, Ethnicity, and Class in America*. Boston: Beacon Press.

TROW, MARTIN 1961 'The second transformation of American secondary education.' *International Journal of Comparative Sociology* 2: 144–66.

U.S. SENATE 1911 *Reports of the Immigration Commission: Dictionary of Races or Peoples*. Washington: Government Printing Office.

VECOLI, RUDOLPH J. 1978 'The coming of age of the Italian Americans.' *Ethnicity* 5 (June).

WARE, CAROLINE 1935 *Greenwich Village, 1920–1930*. Boston: Houghton Mifflin.

WHYTE, WILLIAM FOOTE 1955 *Street Corner Society*. Sec. ed. Chicago: University of Chicago Press.

WOODRUM, ERIC 1981 'An assessment of Japanese American assimilation, pluralism, and subordination.' *American Journal of Sociology* 87 (July): 157–69.

YANCEY, WILLIAM, EUGENE ERICKSEN, and RICHARD JULIANI 1976 'Emergent ethnicity: a review and a reformulation.' *American Sociological Review* 41 (June): 391–403.

YANS-MCLAUGHLIN, VIRGINIA 1977 *Family and Community: Italian Immigrants in Buffalo 1880–1930*. Urbana: University of Illinois.

8 Unhyphenated whites in the United States*

Stanley Lieberson
University of California, Berkeley

It is the thesis of this paper that a major and extraordinarily important ethnic population exists in the United States, one that is barely recognized or understood. Yet, in my estimation, this population is likely to expand considerably in the years ahead. This new white group is characterized by several features:

There is a recognition of being white, but lack of any clearcut identification with, and/or knowledge of, a specific European origin. Such people recognize that they are not the same as some of the existing ethnic groups in the country such as Greeks, Jews, Italians, Poles, Irish, etc. It is assumed at this point that the vast bulk of persons meeting these conditions are of older Northwestern European origins, but I also assume that there are some persons from newer European sources of immigration shifting into this group. Indeed, for reasons to be given below, I would expect more to do so in the years ahead.

One has some difficulty finding an appropriate name for this group. The term 'WASP' is inappropriate for several reasons: first, it is often used in a pejorative sense; second, it is not clear that this new group is restricted to persons of Anglo-Saxon origin or to Protestants. One also has a certain difficulty in deciding whether this newly developing entity should be called a *group* or simply a *population*, the former term implying more organization and coherence than may be appropriate. I assume that both we-feelings and organizational unity may well fluctuate through the years and there is no point trying to prejudge the matter here. At any rate, for lack of an appropriate alternative, I will refer to this group as 'Unhyphenated whites' – as distinguished from all whites.

This conclusion about a new ethnic group stems from several factors that, in my estimation, are not as widely appreciated as they might be. First, a tendency exists to see ethnic and racial categories as static unchanging entities – a perception that is probably correct on the short term, but radically in error when viewed through the years. To be sure, it is widely recognized that the degree of identification with an ethnic group may fluctuate over time as a function of various social conditions (see Yancey, Ericksen, and Juliani, 1976). But less clearly understood is the fact that the group categories themselves may shift over time and, moreover, short-term vacillations in identification may well be hiding strong long-term shifts. Second, there is not

159

an adequate understanding of the mechanisms that permit shifts in ethnic classification and identification. Third, there are fundamental causes of changes that have not been recognized. Finally, there are data that are at least consistent with this thesis about a newly forming ethnic group, but which have not been interpreted in this way.

Ethnic and racial groups in flux

Racial and ethnic groups should be viewed not merely as static entities, but also as products of labelling and identification *processes* that change and evolve over time. Obviously, differentials in fertility, mortality, and migration will affect the size of a group. Beyond this, gradual shifts occur in the sets and subsets of groups found in a society such as to lead to both new combinations and new divisions. This continuous process of combining and recombining means that the very existence of a given group is not to be taken for granted; groups appear and disappear. Ethnic groups such as Mexicans or Puerto Ricans are essentially very recent in nature, resulting from inter-ethnic contacts only since the expansion of Europe into the New World. In similar fashion, the Coloured population in South Africa is a recent group. But it would be the case for many older ethnic groups as well; the English ethnic population in the United Kingdom, for example, is obviously a hybridized population descending from contact and expansion involving a number of groups.

What we have then are processes which run counter to the goals and desires of both census takers and quantitative researchers. These processes can be so gradual that they may run for hundreds of years before anything close to a complete shift occurs (an estimate that is probably conservative). Through both inter- and intra-generational shifts of a non-random nature, it would mean *inconsistency* and *less than full reliability* — terms that are counter to the goals of most empirical instruments. Ethnic origin, from this point of view, is both a status and a process. At any given time, we are more likely to see the state of affairs reported by the population — it is less easy to see the process of ethnic change that is also going on. Indeed, some of the difficulties that researchers and census takers experience in using data on racial and ethnic groups are due not to problems of instrumentation or execution, pure and simple — such as might occur if a question was constructed incorrectly through, say, some vagueness or ambiguity of meaning. Rather some of the difficulties and inconsistencies reflect the processes of ethnic and racial change themselves; the 'errors' are telling us something about the flux in the concepts and identifications themselves.

In short, when examining the racial and ethnic groups found in a given society, there is a tendency to take for granted their existence. In point of fact, a given racial or ethnic group does not go back to the origins of the human species. Rather, each ethnic group was created out of dynamic processes that may have taken place over periods far longer than a given individual's lifespan. Just as various species in the plant and animal worlds are continuously changing – even though it is normally possible to point to this species or that – so too ethnic groups are under continuous flux in terms of their birth, decline, and maintenance. If people are asked for their ethnic ancestry at a given time, they are apt to give us answers that largely fit into the rubrics established and conventional at the time. Responses that do not fit these rubrics tend to be viewed as 'errors' or as failures of the enumeration instrument or the enumerator or what have you. And often that is the case. But in addition, there is a continuous flux in the categories themselves and in who defines themselves (or is defined by others) as belonging in these categories. And in this manner, there are shifts in racial and ethnic populations. Because we are dealing with populations, it is perfectly possible – particularly at some intermediate stage of change – for some persons of X ancestry to identify themselves as belonging to ethnic group X while an increasing proportion with X ancestry are now reporting themselves as Y.

Mechanisms of shift

How might the ethnic/racial origins reported in a country shift without there simply being differentials in birth, death, and international migration? No matter what causal force underlies the change (and we shall see that there are many), ultimately they must operate through a limited number of mechanisms. There are really four main ways of thinking about a respondent's ancestry: one deals with the true ancestral origins for a given respondent, i.e., what we would learn about the respondent if roots could be traced back to some specific temporal point (we can call this the 'true ancestral origin' or AO_t). Second, there are the origins that the respondent *believes* to be his or her ancestral origins at a given specified point in time. In most cases, then, AO_b is the only indicator available of AO_t. It is an imperfect indicator, but nevertheless one would hope that there is some reasonably strong association between reported and actual ancestral origins. The third and fourth measures refer to *identification*. This is either self-identification (*SI*), what a person declares as the group(s) he/she identifies with, *or* the ethnic label imposed on the person by others (*OI*). Presumably these last two facets are not randomly associated either between themselves or with the first two. It is reasonable to expect a certain association between them, albeit recognizing that the association would be less than perfect and that the linkages would be nonrecursive; for example, perceived origins would affect identification but, also, identification will affect beliefs about origins.

These four variables are actually oversimplified in the sense that there are subsets of each that could be considered in greater detail than is possible here. Even AO_t, the true ancestral origins, is more complicated than it might seem at first glance. If it were possible to trace somebody's ancestry backwards in time, there would be no 'natural' stopping point at which one could say, 'At last, here is this person's ancestry.' In theory – albeit not in practice – one could always go further back and find earlier combinations of characteristics that led to the ones just recognized. The only natural stopping points are really societal ones. In a study of the ancestral origins of the United States population, the chances are that the investigator is interested in the defined ancestral roots at the time of arrival in the New World. However, for ancestors who were here prior to the expansion of Europe in the sixteenth century, we would simply want to know what the ancestors were at that time rather than earlier, e.g., Indian tribes rather than origins at the time these people crossed into the New World much earlier. In similar fashion, *beliefs* about ancestral origins would also have certain complications which depended on the 'generational span' covered by ancestors in the information that is passed on to offspring. If it were possible for an investigator to correctly trace the actual ancestral history of each respondent as far back as relevant, there is no doubt that the information obtained in such a manner would differ in many cases from what was reported as the respondent's ancestral origins. Presumably, there is some sort of correlation between reported and true origins, but who can say how close it is?

Because the self-identification reported to others can be affected by both the audience and the social context, there are several subtypes of *SI*. Indeed, private self-identification can even be totally different from any public declaration of ethnic identification. As a matter of fact, ethnic or racial cases of 'passing' are exactly that — situations where someone's publicly declared identification is intentionally different from the person's private self-identification. In the Census, there are even more complicated variants of this because the Census does not simply ask each respondent for their self-identification, but rather in part obtains reports from one adult respondent about the ancestry (and hence presumably self-identification) of the entire household. So, if I am interviewed (in the 1979 Current Population Survey) or fill out the forms (in 1980), you learn what I say (or write) that my self-identification is. For others in the household, however, you learn what I think their self-identification is, as modified by what I choose to tell you. (To be sure people will in many cases ask others what should be written down.)

As for the identification imposed by others, *OI*, it is almost certain that parents will be a powerful force since in most cases it is from them that one obtains at least the initial sense of self-identification. However, this is not a simple cut-and-dried matter. More than one single message may be conveyed to the offspring even from within the family, particularly if parents have different identifications, Beyond this, outsiders can have certain notions of who one is that are at variance with the identification learned at home. In turn, individuals can be swept into social movements and other events during their lifetime that end up redefining their self-identification. The power of outside identifications can range enormously. The Pass Laws of South Africa and the policies of Nazi Germany represent extreme versions of this, where in effect the state will not allow certain options at all. (Thus persons of partial Jewish ancestry were suddenly identified as Jews by the State in a way that could not be avoided.) The current use of a self-enumeration procedure in the United States Census gives respondents considerably more freedom to report their own self-identification. However, this complete freedom does not mean that reported origins or identification is a free-floating matter since self-identification will still be affected by the identification placed on the individual by others and, in turn, this will affect the voluntary response in a Census or any other context.

Societal forces are more than simply *imposed* pure and simple on the population. And, of course, it is these features that are specially important to consider in the forces affecting self-identification and response in a country such as the United States. (Incidentally, until very recently, there was not complete freedom for respondents in the United States to declare whatever ancestry they wanted. Instructions to enumerators indicated very specific rules about accepting certain responses from persons of mixed non-white origins. Likewise, there used to be various state laws that defined blacks in very specific descent terms.) All of this says, then, that self-identification is a complicated variable in the sense that it is affected by a variety of societal forces. Pass Laws and completely laissez-faire policies may represent the extremes of political forces, but the actual responses in laissez-faire situations are not without their strong informal pressures. For example, the response a person of mixed white origins receives based on his or her distinctive surname, may well lead to the less visible and unidentified origin fading.

In summary, one can visualize obtaining four items of information for each respondent: Self-identification (vaguely defined since there would be contextual effects on the SI that is reported); AO_b, which refers to what the respondent believes is his/her ancestral origin; AO_t, the historically *true* origins at the time the various ancestors arrived in the New World or, if Native Americans, at the outset of the sixteenth century; and OI, the identification imposed by others. One can also visualize measuring the association between various pairings of these attributes. There is, for example: the linkage between true ancestral origins and what one believes them to be; the association between self-identification and believed origins; and the linkage between self-identification and true origins. Presumably there are positive associations between each of these pairs, but it is an open question — and one not readily answered — as to how strong they would be. In the case of self-identification and believed origins, for example, one can expect a fairly strong linkage, if only because modifications in one of these will tend to modify the other — if not within one's lifespan, then at least in the course of a few generations If SI and AO_b are highly linked such that shifts in one leads to shifts in the other, it would mean that changes in self-identification will cause the association between *believed* and *true* ancestry to drift apart and become progressively weaker. Thus the linkage between self-identification and true ancestral origins, as well as the linkage between true and believed origins, should get progressively weaker over time.

Given these distinctions, it is clear that many studies of race and ethnic relations are truncated or warped to some unknown degree. If one examines the assimilation of, say, persons of Italian ancestry, then fully lost are those either not identifying or not aware of their Italian origins. Such a subset of the population with Italian ancestry is almost certain to differ from the entire set of persons who could have accurately reported themselves of that origin. The loss or truncation is certainly affected by the research instrument; the 1980 U.S. Census and the 1979 Current Population Survey conducted by the Census both allowed for multiple responses. But this is not the case for the National Opinion Research Center studies of ethnic origin in the General Social Survey and it was not the case for earlier Census surveys.

Two forms of change

Changes will occur either within the life span of a respondent or inter-generationally. It is easy to visualize a variety of ways through which changes of the latter type can take place. If there is intermarriage and interbreeding, then the lineage of the descendants becomes increasingly complicated with each passing generation. The potential of dropping off and simplifying ethnic matters becomes great. Even endogamous mating will not necessarily avoid simplification when there are Old World geographic complications and subtleties that will be lost on each succeeding generation. For example, the descendants of Swiss-Germans will have to know that their ancestors drew a sharp distinction between Swiss-German as opposed to being German-German, and they will also have to know that being Swiss did not convey any ethnic ancestry at all. Boundary changes, incorrect and/or over-simplified knowledge of various settings, confusion, and the like will all affect intergenerational continuity even in relatively simple settings.

For the most part, knowledge of one's ancestry was not formally required in the United States, i.e., it was not required by government regulations. A sharp exception exists for blacks during almost the entire span of American history as well as for Native Americans and some other groups in certain distinctive settings. However, by and large there is no reinforcement of ethnic continuity through the pressures generated by the requirement for consistent responses. Ethnic continuity between generations through either an isolated group context and/or an extensive kin network is probably much weaker than would exist in a small village setting or in other societies. This is because the United States has experienced strikingly high levels of internal migration and there has been declining residential segregation of white ethnic groups. Again, then, the potential for intergenerational discontinuities in ethnic responses is great.

Schools and religious institutions may or may not serve to reinforce and maintain ethnic identification. Much of this depends on governmental policies. In some countries, for example, linguistic differences between the ethnic group lead to separate schools and these, in turn, mean setting off an ethnic marker at a very early age for each child. (Obviously de jure ethnic/racial school segregation can and does occur for other reasons as well.) The existence of public schools and the mixture of ethnic groups found within some of the denominations offering private schooling, e.g., Roman Catholics and Lutherans, probably did less to maintain specific ethnic identity among white groups than occurs in some other nations. Intergenerational transmission of ethnic identity will also be severely distorted by the increasingly common situation in which many children spend at least part of their life in a household in which at least one of the parents is absent through divorce, desertion, or death. Intergenerational knowledge can easily be affected in situations where: one or both parents die before their offspring reach adulthood; children are abandoned; or children are raised by relatives on one side of the family. Beyond this, there are also circumstances where promiscuity may literally lead to no knowledge of one parent's origins. Finally, there is the possibility of intentional discontinuities between parents and children in which parents attempt to hide certain 'less desirable' ethnic origins or in some way de-emphasize or shift the answer — as they know it to be — in terms of what is passed on to their offspring. To be sure, 'intentional' and 'unintentional' are polar types in a continuum and there must be many changes of this sort which do not neatly fall into one extreme or the other.

In addition, there are children with only a modest interest in their ancestral origins and who do not focus on the topic. Others become interested too late to obtain accurate information from parents who, by then, are deceased. (Such a situation presupposes a special type of society, one where a significant number of children are not that interested in the answer *and* where it is not automatically learned regardless of child's initial interest.) In similar fashion, there may be parents who have little or no interest in discussing ancestral histories with their offspring. In all of this, intergenerational shift will occur largely in one direction, i.e., from knowledge to ignorance, from detail to blur. Thus, unless exceptional effort is made, it is unlikely that knowledge about ancestral origins will be reclaimed in later generations. Such events can mean not only that members of later generations will be unable to respond, but it can also mean badly warped responses which are either totally or largely inaccurate such that a question on ancestry for *some* respondents begins to approximate a sociological form of the ink blot test.

Ethnic identification may also change *within* someone's lifespan through a variety of ways. One force is analogous to the intergenerational simplifying process, except here within someone's own lifespan a complicated ancestral history slowly changes and is simplified by forgetting or unlearning some parts of it. Even some details of a relatively simple ancestral history could be distorted and changed during a person's lifetime. In either case, there would be a deterioration in the detail with which ancestral history is reported. Certainly too there is the question of self-identification, particularly after people reach an age where they are removed from parental pressures and control. At such a point, certain changes in self-identification may be freer to come out.

The identification imposed by others on a given respondent will also influence intragenerational changes. It is my impression that regions of the country vary considerably in the degree to which residents can 'spot' or identify members of different groups. If this impression is correct, or if for other reasons someone experiences variation in the degree to which others are attuned to ethnic ancestry, then the identification imposed by others will affect the propensity for someone to identify themselves in a certain manner.

Causes

What social forces cause shifts in identification, ancestral knowledge, and in the categories themselves? By contrast, what keeps such shifts from occurring in other contexts? As a general rule, one should recognize that social organization and ethnic delineations tend to be linked. Changes in the identification of groups, by either others or themselves, will in the long run affect the organizational structure of racial and ethnic populations. On the other hand, changes in the organizational structure of racial and ethnic populations will generate new identifications (again by themselves or imposed by others) that reflect their structural position within the society. A series of forces can thus be visualized as operating to affect identification, the known ancestral origins, and the ethnic categories found in a population. Needless to say, they are not always mutually exclusive in any given context.

1. It is important to recognize that social pressures towards shift are sometimes of an idiosyncratic nature. Ryder (1955) demonstrated this rather nicely for Canada with respect to residents of German ethnic origin during World War II. The sharp downward decline in the numbers reporting themselves as German suggested a definite misreporting that reflected the unpopularity of being German. Changes of this nature might be specially likely for persons of mixed ethnic origins. It would simply be a matter of de-emphasizing one origin at the expense of another. If an historically idiosyncratic or unique feature were to operate for a relatively long time, there is a strong chance that the consequence would be a shift in self-identification and knowledge of ancestral origin that would persist even if the cause was later to disappear. This is because of the natural drift mechanism described below.

2. An ethnic ranking system means that members of some groups enjoy prestige and various advantages whereas others face handicaps or even punishments. *Ceteris paribus*, this suggests there will be a net change in the direction that will generate positive rewards and prestige, and away from those categorizations and classifications that generate disadvantages and lower status. Insofar as groups differ in their prestige and in the real advantages and disadvantages that perceived membership offers, one might expect subtle and less than subtle shifts towards 'more desirable' or less disadvantaged origins at the price of others. This could occur for those without any claims to such ancestries, and certainly for those of mixed ancestry. Thus under some circumstances, ethnic origins will be lost, identifications changed, and perhaps new nomenclature used as a device for avoiding social disadvantages. A nice example of the latter, by the way, is the use of *Czech* as an ethnic identifyer in the United States instead of *Bohemian* — the latter having certain unfavorable connotations in an earlier period. Obviously, there are many forces affecting such responses, not the least being the ability to get away with it and also the constraints on such shifts (more shortly on this).

To be sure, this is not the only response possible to such a ranking and reward system. Consequences of a far different nature involving combatting the disadvantages through legislation, protests, group organization, and the like. Acquiescence is another response, not unknown at least for the short-term. It is only possible to speculate at this point whether ancestral loss is less likely in periods of intense, organized effort by the group to alter its disadvantaged situation. For such are periods when ethnic awareness is likely to be intensified and reinforced by organized efforts. They are also periods when slight or partial shifts away from the group identification are likely to be branded as betrayals or traitorous acts. Under such circumstances, by the way, a different form of distortion can occur, to wit, the de-emphasis of other ancestries among the mixed members of groups aroused to protest and combat their disadvantaged situation. But, overall, where there is ethnic shift, it will be in the direction towards groups that provide more advantageous positions in the ethnic hierarchy.

3. The very opposite factor from that discussed above can create a certain natural drift mechanism leading to simplification and distortion. Namely, indifference to one's ethnic origin will lead to the loss of detailed or even partially accurate information on ancestry. Once this occurs, it is unlikely that the details will be recovered in later generations, although there is the possibility via grandparents or from other relatives such as aunts or uncles. Hence, for the most part, any de-emphasis or loss of interest in ethnic origins will lead to permanent losses of information and, as a consequence, possibly newer and vaguer and simpler identification schemes. In that sense, change can occur only in the direction towards distortion, and inaccuracy, and new delineations. Whether new delineations or distortions of old ones result is an open question at this point, with no clear principles operating. In South Africa, intermixture led to a new ethnic delineation, the Cape Coloured; in the United States, the offspring of black-white mixture remained as blacks. In Brazil, there is yet another outcome in which race or color is not seen as a family characteristic (in the sense that siblings with a common mother and father have the same ethnic/racial label) and is, furthermore, affected by socioeconomic position.

One feature of this drift is that it is probably more likely to occur in some directions than in others. As a general rule, one can say that voluntary drifts in identification are never towards greater disadvantages but either maintain or improve one's position within the system. The drift is bounded in that sense by shifts towards memberships and identifications which are either beneficial or at least not harmful. Hence, it is unlikely that people will give up distinctions that are beneficial by merging or joining them with categories that are beneath them in prestige and/or in the reward structure. What can happen through indifference, then, is a broader and vaguer ethnic delineation which is still not harmful even though it is no worse than the more precise ancestral delineations that previous generations would have given. As we shall see below, this is what I believe is going on with respect to the development of a new Unhyphenated white ethnic population.

4. The government and other major institutions will vary over time, and between societies, in how much formal attention is paid to ethnic/racial categories. But it is unlikely that the subject will be totally ignored in any multi-ethnic situation. As a consequence, at least some formal bureaucratic rules and definitions will be introduced and it is virtually guaranteed that such rules will, at best, be too simple to take into account the entire range of ethnic/racial complexities and the existing array of self-identifications. It is almost certain that the rules will deviate from the reality in the direction of meeting the needs of the dominant population and/or the organizations themselves (see Petersen, 1969, for an outstanding study of these factors in the delineation of ethnic groups in Hawaii). (The forces leading the dominant group to have specific interests is not a trivial consideration itself, although beyond the purview of this paper. But one need only compare the outcome of racial mixtures in the United States, South Africa, and Brazil to recognize a wide variety of such possibilities.)

Under any circumstances, governmental and other organizational forms of control will affect the delineation process. Insofar as various organizational processes formally identify ethnic lineage, it will leave less room for distortion (other than the distortions which exist in the governmental delineations themselves, such as when one-sixteenth black and fifteen-sixteenths white is defined as 'black'). Organizational forms of control are relevant to the extent that they offer advantages to some identifications and disadvantages to others. For example, insofar as tribal rolls can provide certain potential rewards in the United States at this time, there would be an incentive to remain on such rolls and be sure that one's offspring, in the case of persons of mixed origins, are aware of their Indian heritage. The number of whites (as defined by the racial self-identification question in the 1979 Current Population Survey) who reported some Indian ancestry was far greater than the number of non-whites who reported themselves as American Indian.

Governmental and other institutional delineations of racial and ethnic categories (and the criteria for inclusion) are almost certain to initially differ from all of the subtle permutations and combinations of identification and ancestry held by the populations themselves. The net effect is a massive set of distortions due to these influences combined with efforts by members of different groups to adjust to these delineations (in order to take advantages of the rewards from some categories and to escape the handicaps of others).

5. Also affecting the shifts, and their direction, will be the nature of the identification system. This can be visualized as ranging from a totally coercive system (where identification is imposed on the individual by the government or through some other institutional arrangement) to the other extreme, where it is voluntary and completely a matter of self-declaration. As noted earlier, South Africa, with its Pass Laws, and Germany during the Nazi era, represent one such extreme on the *coercive-voluntary continuum*. The laissez-faire disposition towards race in Brazil represents the other extreme. The United States is somewhere between an imposed coercive system and a purely voluntaristic one. Clearly, there have been fluctuations over time, witness the

situation for blacks and American Indians. For most white groups in the United States, it is safe to say that their ethnic/ancestral affiliations are in principle voluntary, i.e., there is no governmental or other institutional constraint on the affiliation claimed. (This, of course, does not mean there are *no* constraints per se, since there are definitional constraints imposed by both individuals and institutions that are not necessarily part of a legal system or otherwise formally declared.) Likewise, the Civil Rights legislation at present encourages some persons to maintain particular identifications at least in certain contexts in order to enjoy special programs and considerations.

6. Intergroup conflicts have consequences for labelling and identification. Certainly the dominant group's interaction with subordinate groups has a direct impact on the organization of the subordinates. The terms 'Native American' or 'American Indian' are examples of this, involving a new classification scheme ('new' in the sense of post-European conquest) which incorporates within it ethnic groups (tribes) that basically only have a oneness that is a function of the presence of the white groups and the fact that they share a common condition. In that sense, the ethnic lines and boundaries are to be viewed as floating, as a function of the interactions with other groups and, particularly, the behavior of the dominant groups towards them. In similar fashion, any sense of a common bond among the various black ethnic groups in South Africa, for example, must be a function of the behavior directed towards them by the dominant white population and, as a consequence, the common situation that they find themselves in. Another example in the United States is the newly developing Latino identification for various groups descending from Spanish-speaking ancestors.

There is also an important redevelopment possible simply because the scale and nature of the contact is different. This is particularly striking for migrant peoples who initially saw themselves as members of a given town or, at best, province or region. In the context of the United States, for example, they find themselves in contact with others from the same national homeland who, although different, still have far more in common with them than do the vast bulk of persons with whom they now co-exist. Moreover, these persons are all given a common label by the larger society, for whom these distinctions are of no interest. This was an important force among many immigrant groups to the United States who had, prior to emigration, identified with a much narrower unit.

In this regard, the ecological-demographic context will be significant; numerically smaller groups are less likely to be singled out as distinctive by the dominant group. But of course this hinges in part on the distinctiveness of the group (cultural, physical, spatial isolation, religious, etc.), the number of other groups present, and — as noted above — the importance to the dominant group of making specific distinctions. But also there will be a propensity of the dominant group to simplify the situation and description of subordinate groups. The errors and distortions made by the dominant group, in so far as they are of consequence for the life chances of the groups subjected to these actions, will in the long run affect the identifications of the groups themselves and will tend to draw them into new bonds.

7. Internal group pressures, although a necessary product of some of these other forces, merit at least brief separate mention. In the course of inter-ethnic/racial conflicts, groups often generate elaborate rituals and pressures to maintain members' identification. Self-identification becomes a central part of the socialization process and gets defined in the context of respect for parents, extended family, and friends. These thrusts towards group identification are really no different than those exerted by the larger society or nation to maintain allegiance to itself or, on the other hand, the loyalties that other groups in conflict attempt to promote, e.g., labor unions, teams, etc. Aside from the powerful pull of primary group ties, there is also a glorification of the group through such mechanisms as learning of a noble history, belief in its special and unique qualities, tales of heroes who sacrificed much for it, and the like. Such developments — at least for the short run — may well reduce inter- and intra-generational shifts.

Empirical consequences

The above analysis suggests that censuses and other survey data on racial and ethnic groups will be characterized by all sorts of volatile and erratic qualities. These, and other inconsistencies, need not be interpreted as reflecting *errors* in either enumeration procedures or in respondent behavior, although such errors cannot be ruled out. Rather such difficulties may well be reflecting the flux outlined above in the nature of race and ethnic relations in the society. It is not easy to deal with this topic as an empirical problem. The birth of new ethnic groups, and the shifts among others, do not necessarily occur overnight in a cataclysmic fashion. Although the rates of change are probably not linear, it is still the case that they are probably more gradual than sudden. It is rather unlikely that a vast segment of the population of England awoke one day to discover they were neither Saxons nor Normans nor Angles nor Jutes, but were rather English; in similar fashion the shift to Puerto Rican among persons of varying degrees of Spanish, Black, and Indian stock probably did not occur suddenly. But I believe there are data now available that support this contention that a new white ethnic group is evolving in the United States.

Although the United States has a very diverse ethnic and racial composition, only in recent years has it become possible to examine some of these hypothesized shifts and changes in at least a moderately rigorous fashion. Two important statistical developments are noteworthy here. The U.S. government asked a straight ethnic origins question in the 1980 decennial Census as well as in important sample surveys taken in recent years. Also the General Social Survey (GSS), conducted by the National Opinion Research Center, has been asking a question on ethnic origin since 1972. Its question construction and treatment of multiple entries are of interest to us in so far as they are different from that found in the Census and hence can provide additional clues as to what is going on. The N.O.R.C. surveys asked, 'From what countries or part of the world did your ancestors come?' If more than one country was named, the respondent was asked to indicate the one they felt closest to. If they couldn't decide, then they were recorded separately without any group entered. In the 1980 Census, the population was asked, 'What is this person's ancestry?' Multiple entries were accepted and recorded. (In addition the Census asked a separate question on 'Spanish/Hispanic origin or descent' and also one which seemed to elaborate on the old color or race question.)

Both the 1980 Census and the 1979 Current Population Survey accepted 'American' as an ethnic ancestry response, but it was discouraged and collected only as a response of last resort. First of all, the use of 'American' as a suffix, as in Mexican-American, Italian-American, etc. was rejected by the Census in their coding procedures. A Mexican-American response was counted as Mexican, likewise Italian-American was shortened to Italian, and so forth. Even more significantly, the 1979 CPS, which was based on interviews − as contrasted with the mail-back procedure in 1980 − explicitly instructed its interviewers as follows:

Some persons may not identify with the foreign birthplace of their ancestors or with their nationality group and may report the category 'American.' If you have explained that we are referring to the nationality group of the person or his or her ancestors before their arrival in the United States, and the person *still* says that he or she is 'American,' then print 'American.' (Italics are mine)

'American' was also discouraged in the 1980 Census with the instructions specifying that 'Ancestry (or origin or descent) may be viewed as the nationality group, the lineage, or the country in which the person or the person's parents or ancestors were born before their arrival in the United States.'

Nevertheless, out of a total United States population of 226.5 million in 1980, there were an estimated 13.3 million who gave 'American' or 'United States' as their ancestry. Just under 6 percent of the population could not name any specific ancestries − or chose not to; in the 1979 survey, the percentage was slightly higher, 6.3. (United States, 1983, Table E, page 4). To appreciate the importance of this number, consider three additional facts. First, 'American' is a major ethnic response in the nation, ranking fifth in the nation. To be sure, it trails by a massive amount the 50 million reporting English, the 49 million indicating German, the 40 million with Irish ancestry, and the 21 million who indicated black (the actual number indicating black on the direct Census 'race' question is nearly 8 million greater than the number obtained on this ethnic item). But American narrowly edges out such groups as French and Italian, and, by much greater margins, exceeds other leading ancestry responses such as Scottish, Polish, Mexican, American Indian, and Dutch (see United States, 1983, p.2).

Second, there is a strong bias against the 'American' response. The decision to exclude American as an acceptable multiple response is understandable, even though other multi-ethnic responses were accepted and recorded by the

Census Bureau in both 1979 and 1980. One assumes that many persons used 'American' along with another ancestry response only as a way of indicating that they were true-blue citizens of the United States, being neither sojourners nor of questionable loyalty. But certainly, there may have been respondents who indicated themselves as, say, Irish-Americans or some such, not for this reason but in order to convey the complexity of their mixed ancestry and/or the limits of their identification with the group specified. In this regard, the figures for various specific groups combine both persons who made such a response exclusively with those who picked the specified group in addition to one or in some cases, two other groups. In 1980, for example, there were 40 million persons recorded as having Irish ancestry, but only 25.7 percent of these reported Irish ancestry exclusively (10.3 million); whereas nearly 30 million of these included at least one other ethnic group. Now obviously many of the mixed Irish respondents would pick Irish if they were forced to select only one group; it is clear that there are more members of the Irish than the American ethnic group in the United States. Nevertheless, it is also clear that these Census procedures work towards an undercount of the population who call themselves 'American' or the equivalent.

Finally, a large number of respondents do not report any ancestry, about 23 million respondents in both 1979 and 1980; in effect, about one-tenth of the entire population. It is reasonable to assume that at least some of these would be classified as part of this new group of white Americans who are unable to specify any ethnic ancestry.

Since 1972, the General Social Survey (GSS) conducted by the National Opinion Research Center has asked respondents, 'From what countries or part of the world did your ancestors come?' Of relevance here is the fact that, from 1972 through the census year of 1980, there were 1,288 respondents who could not name *any* country at all. This amounts to 10.7 percent of those responding to the question. In addition, there were 339 who selected 'America' in response to the ancestral geography question used in the GSS. Thus about 13.5 percent of the American population could name no country or simply took the America response. (This of course ignores the very large number who named two countries but could not choose between them in terms of indicating the one that they felt closer to.) The percentage unable to name any country is larger than all but the respondents indicating German, England and Wales, black, and those unable to choose a preference between countries. Fairly substantial segments of the population, when asked about their ethnic ancestry through either an NORC or a Census type of question, cannot respond at all or respond simply as 'American.' Although the questions are different, both approaches do indicate the presence of substantial segments of the population who are unable to specify a 'conventional' ethnic response.

The Unhyphenated white component of the population is over-estimated by the calculations presented above. First, there are probably other reasons for giving these responses than either identification solely with American or total loss of one's ancestral history or the presence of such a complicated ancestral history that an over-simplified answer is the most reasonable way of responding. Second, there are blacks (i.e., persons responding on the race-type question as 'black') who in turn either pick American or otherwise do not respond to the ancestry item in either the NORC or the Census surveys.

Whites are only about 45 percent of the respondents indicating 'American' on the GSS and they are about 74 percent of the much larger number who cannot name *any* ancestral country. Between these two categories, it means that 9.2 percent of the entire population are whites who are either unable to report an ancestral nation or indicate simply that they are American. Confining ourselves to NORC survey data only for whites, one finds that the American component amounts to 10 percent of all whites in the period between 1972 and 1980. Thus the number of whites responding as either Americans or unable to name any ancestry is still an important component of the entire white population of the United States. In terms of the non-black population of the United States in 1979, then, approximately 15.4 percent either did not report ancestry or indicated 'American.' (Admittedly, this last set of Census figures include people who are neither white nor black, but the form of the Census procedure in 1979 makes it desirable to calculate in this way and the numbers are certainly minor.)

At this point, there are three issues to address. First, is there further evidence that a significant part of the white population is in what might be thought of as an ethnic flux leading towards a new American ethnic group? Second, who are these people who report themselves as American in the Census or are unable to indicate any country in the GSS survey? Finally, what indications exist about future trends with respect to the American-White group?

Evidence of flux

There are two separate indications of enormous flux in the ethnic responses among many whites. These are: comparisons in the ethnic responses obtained for the same individuals a year later; the generational makeup of 'Americans' and other new residual responses.

Inconsistency

A rare test of consistency and shift is provided by the Current Population Surveys conducted by the Bureau of the Census in March of 1971, 1972, and 1973. Not only was there a certain degree of overlap in the respondents interviewed in each year with those interviewed in the preceding, but in each case respondents were asked to report their ethnic origin. The same question was asked in each year: 'What is . . .'s origin or descent?' (This question is somewhat different from that used more recently by the Census, with the term 'ancestry' now replacing the phrase 'origin or descent' used then.) Of special interest here is the fact that the same people were matched in adjacent years. Hence, we have a rare opportunity to 'match' the ethnic origin reported for the same person a year later. (The 1972–73 matching is of less interest here since a smaller N was used in 1973 and because the enumeration procedure changed slightly. Hence, with one exception indicated below, the second pairing will be ignored. However, the results are essentially very similar to those reported here for 1971–72 comparisons.)

There is remarkably low consistency in the ethnic origins reported for persons one year later: *in only 64.7 percent of the cases was the same ethnic response obtained for the respondent one year later.* In other words, in fully one-third of the match-ups, a different response was obtained one year later. These inconsistencies probably reflect several major forces. Responses were not obtained in all cases from each individual, but rather from an adult in the household. Interviewers were instructed to obtain answers from the most knowledgeable household member and, moreover, they were also told 'to try to find a more knowledgeable respondent or to arrange to call back' (Johnson, 1974: 2) if the interviewee appeared not to know the answers. Nevertheless, it is almost certain that some part of the inconsistency is due to changes between years in the adult who ends up reporting origin for each member of the household. One can assume that temporal shifts would have been less likely if each person was asked about themselves in consecutive years.

To be sure, it is still significant if a given adult's conception of his/her origins are not correctly known by other adults in the same family unit. For if a spouse or some other adult at home is not clear about one's ethnic origins, then it is probably all the more likely that offspring will have difficulty maintaining full and exact continuity as well. Another source of inconsistency stems from the Census procedure used at that time with respect to multiple responses. For the most part, persons reporting multiple origins were placed in a residual 'Other' classification, which also included remaining single ethnic responses and the 'American' response. This itself creates no inconsistency since the same response at a later date will lead to the same category, but shifts in either direction between a given multiethnic combination and one of the specified single responses will appear to be inconsistent. Strictly speaking they are, but it would reflect merely enumeration procedures since it may merely depend on how much detail the respondent decides to give rather than a true change in consistency. (On the other hand, shift between categories will not appear to be inconsistent if both end up in the residual 'other' category.)

Given these two serious difficulties, one can understand why these surveys have hitherto not attracted widespread attention. The results do suggest that something else is going on – something that might be thought of as a true flux or vacillation in the ethnic responses that some people are giving. First of all, consider the magnitude of the inconsistency, namely an inconsistent response exists for one-third of the entire population. Beyond this, consider the fact that these inconsistencies are clearly not random within categories. The degree of fluidity varied greatly between groups: blacks, some of the Latino groups, and some of the white ethnic groups from South-Central-Eastern Europe were much more consistent. Consistency ranged from nearly

80 to more than 95 percent for Poles, Cubans, Italians, Mexicans, blacks, and Puerto Ricans. On the other hand, the consistency was much lower for white groups from Northwestern Europe, the so-called 'old' European stocks who have many ancestors going back to a large number of generations in the United States. Little more than half of the respondents giving English, Scottish, Welsh in 1971 reported a similar response a year later. Thus inconsistency varies in a systematic way: the older stock white populations from North-western Europe, containing substantial components with many generations of residence in the United States, have much lower levels of consistency than either blacks or whites from relatively more recent sources of immigration such as Italians and Poles.

Such a pattern of inconsistency is exactly what one might expect if it is assumed that flux within the white population increases by generations of residence in the United States. This would be compatible with the simple hypothesis that there is a decline in the ties and knowledge of ancestral homelands such that knowledge of − and identification with − such origins declines sharply, if all factors are held constant.

Generational comparisons

It is one matter to hypothesize that an increase in the confusion and uncertainty about ancestral origins (as well as perhaps indifference) is a pathway to the development of a new ethnic conception; it is another matter to see if the evidence supports such a claim. The evidence is fairly convincing on this matter, however.

The NORC survey permits a distinction in terms of four generations, applying the procedure described by Alba and Chamlin (1983). Some 57 percent of the entire U.S. population is at least fourth generation, i.e., the United States is the country of birth for themselves, both of their parents, and all four of their grandparents. Among 'Unhyphenated whites' (those unable to name any ancestral country or choosing 'American'), 97 percent were of at least fourth-generation ancestry. Thus Unhyphenated whites make up fully 16 percent of all Americans with at least four generations' residence in the country, and therefore about 20 percent of the non-black population with at least four generations' residence in the United States. By contrast, Unhyphenated whites are one percent or less of the third, second, and first generations. (This sharp difference by generation − with such small percentages for earlier generations − suggests that the data are quite meaningful. One would be suspicious if many of the immigrants or their offspring were unable to state the countries or part of the world from which their ancestors came and/or if the American response was given after only such a short generational stay in the United States.)

An added hypothesis about ethnic origins is suggested by the distinctive regional distribution of these Unhyphenated whites. Compared with all whites, Unhyphenated whites are specially likely to be found in the South, particularly in the South Atlantic states (38 percent of all Unhyphenated whites are found in the South Atlantic states, and 67 percent are in the entire South). By contrast, only about 30 percent of the entire white population surveyed by NORC lives in the South. The distribution of Unhyphenated whites, in varying degrees throughout the rest of the nation, is less than other whites. This difference from the rest of the country could reflect several different forces:

1. The historically large black population of the South could have led to a relative de-emphasis of ethnic distinctions.
2. The white ethnic composition of the South is proportionately more of various Northwestern European origins and perhaps they are specially likely to shift, net of generations in the country.
3. The relative absence of significant new European immigration meant that there was less 'renewal' of ethnic ties for older groups and less regeneration of ethnic issues for them in the sense of reminding the older groups of white subdivisions.
4. On the other hand, regional differences could simply reflect the fact that proportionately more of the whites found in that region are of 4+ generations residence. It would certainly be the case that there was relatively moderate migration to the South for quite some time. Moreover, it might well be the case that the average length of generations within the 4+ category is greater among those in the South.

With the available data, it is not really possible to evaluate most of these interpretations. But a few elementary comparisons are at least possible. Among all whites in the United States, about 53 percent have at least four generations of residence in the country. By contrast, 80 percent of whites in the South have 4+ generations of residence in the country. This would lead one to expect disproportionately more Unhyphenated whites to be in the South. But the concentration is even greater; two-thirds of Unhyphenated whites are found in the South whereas half of all 4+ generation whites are located in this part of the country (67 vs. 46 percent). However, the meaning of this result is not entirely clear because the chances are very strong that the generational distribution *within* the 4+ category is different in the South than elsewhere. Very likely the average number of generations is higher in the Southern 4+ category than in the remainder of the country. Hence, if shift to Unhyphenated white is a function of length of generation, there would still be an uncontrolled factor favoring the South and it is not possible to determine if there is Southern effect per se.

Characteristics

Neither the Census nor the GSS data allow for determination of the true ancestral origins (AO_t) of those reporting themselves as Unhyphenated white. Indeed, as matters are now constructed, all one can obtain is either some belief about such origins (AO_b) or some declaration of self-identification or a mixture of the two. This means that one of the more interesting questions cannot be answered at this time, to wit, the ancestral origins of those who become Unhyphenated whites. Nevertheless, some of this population's social characteristics can be compared with the entire white population. The data shown below are drawn from various GSS data sets obtained between 1972 and 1980. (Since the American-white group is a small percentage of the latter, adjustments for the part-whole problem are not made, so in that sense the gaps between Unhyphenated whites and the *remainder* of the white population are slightly underestimated.)

Not only is the new white ethnic population disproportionately located in the South, but they are specially concentrated in rural areas. In the United States as a whole, 33 percent of all Unhyphenated whites are located in what NORC refers to as 'Open Country.' By contrast, 17 percent of all whites are located in the Open Country. This is more than a reflection of regional differences and the former's concentration in the South. Some 27 percent of all whites living in the South are found in Open Country; by comparison 42 percent of Unhyphenated whites living in the South are in these rural areas. It is not easy to decide whether these are areas with relatively little in the way of ethnic heterogeneity and hence shift is thereby encouraged. But all of this is speculative at this point.

The vast majority of Unhyphenated whites were raised as Protestant (87 percent) compared with all whites in the country (64 percent). Although Roman Catholics are clearly less likely to report themselves in this category (8 percent compared with 29 percent of the total white population), it is significant that the category is not exclusively Protestant. If the theoretical exposition presented earlier is valid, one may speculate that the Roman Catholic component will increase in the years ahead, particularly with the generational changes that will occur. Among those giving either of the American-white responses, less than 0.5 percent reported themselves as having been raised as Jews.

As a general rule, the Unhyphenated white population tends to be of lower SES than the entire white population in the United States. American-whites have considerably lower levels of educational attainment. For example, 15 percent of all whites had four or more years of college compared with 4 percent of Unhyphenated whites; by contrast, 19 percent of the latter had no more than seven years of schooling, compared with 7 percent of all whites. (The Index of Net Difference is .34, a rather large value meaning that in pairings between all whites and American-whites, situations in which the latter have lower education is 34 percentage points more common than the opposite difference.) Also noteworthy are some important occupational differences, with the proportion of Unhyphenated whites in professional-technical occupations amounting to less than half that found for all whites. There is a massive difference in the opposite direction with respect to concentration in the relatively unskilled operatives—transport category.

The overall occupational prestige score for all whites is 40.7 and 38.9, respectively, for men and women. For purposes of calibration, it is about 31 for black men and women. The score for Unhyphenated white men, 36.0, falls just about midway between all white men and black men; the mean prestige score for Unhyphenated white women is 33.6, is considerably closer to the level for black women than all white women. In the ten-word vocabulary test used by NORC, the average number of correct responses for all whites is 6.17, compared with 4.54 for Unhyphenated whites. (This is the lowest score obtained for any of the larger populations specified as part of a general study of the topic, being very slightly lower than the level obtained for blacks.) The general cross-tabulation between educational attainment and vocabulary for the entire population was used to determine the expected number for Unhyphenated whites that takes into account their lower educational levels and the obvious influence of education on vocabulary. Using this variant of standardization, one would have expected 5.22 correct words for Unhyphenated whites; thus their actual level is even lower than would be expected after taking into their lower levels of formal education.

In terms of conventional political labels, there are only modest differences between whites and this new ethnic population. About the same percentages are Democrats (subclassified by 'strong' or 'not very strong'), independents of one sort or another, or Republicans (likewise subdivided). At most, the differences between all whites and Unhyphenated whites in any of these categories is no more than three percentage points. In similar fashion, there are only modest differences between them in their self-conception along liberal—conservative lines. The biggest gap is again rather modest, with 40 percent of all whites and 44 percent of Unhyphenated whites describing themselves as 'moderate.' There are some bigger differences with respect to specific political issues, but for the most part the new Unhyphenated white group is not distinctive in conventional political terms.

On the normative issues that were considered, somewhat larger gaps turned up, but for the most part they are hardly of the magnitude to suggest a strikingly unique subset of whites. There are some differences with respect to values for children. Given a list of characteristics, subjects were asked to select the most desired characteristic for a child. The three most common ones picked by all whites in the country were: honesty (39 percent of those able to choose one characteristic); sound judgement (17); obeys parents (13 percent). By contrast, these characteristics were picked by 41, 12, and 21 percent of Unhyphenated whites as the most desirable. Admittedly, the new ethnic population tends to favor obedience more than do whites generally (a difference of eight percentage points) and are less concerned about sound judgment, but the gaps are not terribly great. In point of fact, about 40 percent of both groups pick honesty as the most important characteristic. Of course, this type of measure is not necessarily a good substitute for observing actual behavior. More of a gap turns up on some specific political issues, suggesting that Unhyphenated whites are more 'conservative' than the total white population. The former is more likely to think that too much is being spent to improve conditions of blacks (41 vs. 29 percent for all whites) and are less likely to object to the level of military spending (19 vs. 28 percent thinking too much is spent). A particularly large difference exists with respect to the civil liberties question regarding whether a Communist should be allowed to make a speech; two-thirds of Unhyphenated whites thought they should *not* whereas close to 60 percent of all whites thought just the opposite (throughout, persons with no response or indicating 'don't know,' etc., are excluded from the computations). On the other hand, the gap is very small (four percentage points) between Unhyphenated whites and all whites with respect to favoring the death penalty. In short, the results are mixed with respect to the attitudinal-normative qualities of the new white group – on some dimensions they are very close to all whites and on other respects there are moderate to fairly large differences.

A final note

In recent years, considerable attention has been paid to two related theses about white ethnic groups in the United States:

1. The rediscovery and re-emphasis of ethnic identification among white groups in recent years in the United States. Presumably, the assertions of black pride and black awareness served as a catalyst for this new emphasis among white ethnic groups.
2. The presumed failure of the ethnic melting pot to work as advertised and believed for many years.

It may well be the case that the melting pot is beginning to work in a different way than has been discussed in the literature. In addition to different groups acting increasingly alike, it may well be that a *new* population is in process of forming. Whether this is the case or not requires considerably more evidence than it was possible to present here. For one, the strongest test will occur in the 1990 Census, when it will be possible to make longitudinal comparisons over time and deal with the question of whether there is an increase in the 'Unhyphenated white' type of response for the same age- and generational-specific cohort as they age (cross-sectionally, at the present time, the proportions giving such responses seem to be concentrated in the older age groups, but with data for one period it is impossible to separate the age, cohort, and period effects).

A second issue pertains to meaning of the responses. Given the relatively low SES positions held by the Unhyphenated white population, as measured with NORC data, there is always the possibility that people giving these responses are selective on various characteristics and are not truly representative of a new ethnic thrust. In this regard, the two subsets of the population defined as Unhyphenated white with NORC data – those reporting themselves as American as opposed to those unable to name a group – do differ on some dimensions. For example, the specifically American subset do appear to be *relatively* higher in SES, less likely to reside in the South, and more Catholic when compared with the other subset. But they are still different from all whites. Obviously, more will be done on this matter. Under any circumstance, it would be helpful to understand why the population giving these responses are relatively concentrated in lower SES positions. Further clues may well develop when the Census data on American whites are examined. The concentration in the South, in my estimation, is less of a puzzle since it is more a matter of choosing and evaluating several plausible explanations for that fact. However, an evaluation of these different causal forces may well help provide important clues as to the factors generating this new ethnic population in America.

Note

* A revised version of the paper presented at the SUNY-Albany Conference on Ethnicity and Race in the Last Quarter of the 20th Century, April, 1984. This is part of a larger Social Science Research Council Census Monograph project supported by the Russell Sage Foundation, which will be co-authored by Lawrence Santi. His assistance, as well as that of Mark Scarbecz and Mary C. Waters is gratefully acknowledged. I am indebted to Guy E. Swanson, who suggested the term 'Unhyphenated whites.'

References

ALBA, RICHARD D., and MITCHELL B. CHAMLIN 1983 'A preliminary examination of ethnic identification among whites.' *American Sociological Review* 48: 240–7.
JOHNSON, CHARLES E., Jr. 1974 *Consistency of Reporting of Ethnic Origin in the Current Population Survey*. Technical Paper No. 31, Current Population Survey. Washington, D.C.: U.S. Government Printing Office.
PETERSEN, WILLIAM 1969 'The classification of subnations in Hawaii: an essay in the sociology of knowledge.' *American Sociological Review* 34: 863–77.
RYDER, NORMAN B. 1955 'The interpretation of origin statistics.' *Canadian Journal of Economics and Political Science* 21: 466–79.
U.S. BUREAU OF THE CENSUS 1983 *Ancestry of the Population by State: 1980*, Supplementary Report, PC80–S1–10. Washington, D.C.: U.S. Government Printing Office.
YANCEY, WILLIAM L., EUGENE P. ERICKSEN, and RICHARD N. JULIANI 1976 'Emergent Ethnicity: A Review and Reformulation.' *American Sociological Review* 41: 391–403.

Name index

Subject index

acculturation: Hispanics, 64; Indians, 31, 32, 35, 37–8; and the war, 143
agency towns, 38
Alcatraz Island, 43
'American' as ancestry response, 171–2, 173
ancestry: census responses, 170–3; concepts of, 161; groups, 68, 70; interest in, 164–5, 167; *see also* ethnicity
apatheid, *see* segregation
Asians: assimilation, 75, 89–90; background, 77–8, 81; discrimination, 79; earnings, 75, 76, 83, 84, 89; education, 81–2, 83, 84, 89; ethnic enterprise, 85–8; occupations, 82–4, 88
assimilation, 94, 112, 134; Chinese, 90; Cubans, 66; and ethnicity, 134–6; Hispanics, 52, 75; ideology, 52; indexes of, 75, 135; Indians, 30, 31, 32, 37; Italians, 139, 140–1, 152; Japanese, 90; studies of, 76–7; time taken, 75; types, 135–6; and the war 143
association, patterns of, 102
A.T. & T. consent decree (1973), 12
Athapaskan Indians, 44

benefits, state 23
blacks: association patterns, 102; civil rights, 4–6; earnings, 10–14, 24; educational attainment, 6–8, 24; elite, 24; family income, 20–2, 24; future ethnicity, 113; homogeneity, 107, 110; Judaism, 127–8; occupational prestige, 8–9, 24; poverty, 22–3, 24; public schools, 18–20; residential segregation, 17–18, 96; unemployment, 15–17, 24
boundary shift, 135–6, 144
Brandywine Indians, 39
Brass Ankle Indians, 39

California, Asians in, 77, 78–9, 81
Canada, Indians in, 29, 30, 31, 41
capitalist expansion, and race, 52
caste system, American, 75
Catholics: association patterns, 99, 102; future ethnicity, 112–13; homogeneity, 109
census, inconsistencies, 170–3, 173–5

Chata Indians, 33, 34
Cherokee Indians, 32
Chicanos, 55–6, 71; *see also* Mexicans
Chinese: arrival, 77, 84, 88; assimilation, 90; earnings, 75, 83, 84, 85, 88, 89; education, 81–2, 83, 84–5, 89; occupations, 82–4; small businesses, 85–8
Chinese Exclusion Act (1882), 77
Chipewyan Indians, 32
Chippewa Indians, 36
Choctaw Indians, 33, 34
Christianity and Judaism, 126–7
citizenship, acquisition of, 80, 88, 118, 143
Civil Rights Act (1964), 5
Civil Rights Act (1965), 5
Civil Rights Act (1968), 5, 17
civil rights movement, 4–6
class, and ethnic divisions, 49–50, 52, 64, 69–71, 90, 105
Cuban Refugee Program, 59
Cubans, 50, 53, 58–60; assimilation, 66; class background, 59–60; education, 60–4; enclave economy, 59–60, 66; English-speaking, 64, 68; ethnic identity, 68, 71, 72; household income, 64; occupational status, 59, 64–7, 68

Dawes Severalty Act (1887), 31
Democracy, and blacks, 4–6
Dene Nation, 44
discrimination: earnings, 14; factors affecting, 79; in housing, 17

earnings: Asians, 75, 76, 83, 84, 89; blacks, 10–14, 24; family income, blacks, 20–2; Filipinos, 75, 83, 85, 88, 89, 90
education: Asians, 81–2, 83, 89; blacks, 6–8, 24; Cubans, 60–4; expansion, 142; Filipinos, 82, 83, 85, 89–90; Hispanics, 60–4; Italians, 138, 140, 144–6; segregated schools, 18–20
employment, *see* occupations; unemployment
enclavement, 32, 43, 66, 76, 85–8
equality, 4
ethnic economy, 76–7, 85–8
ethnic groups: antecedents and con-

184